LEGENDARY LOCALS

OF

HUDSON

NEW HAMPSHIRE

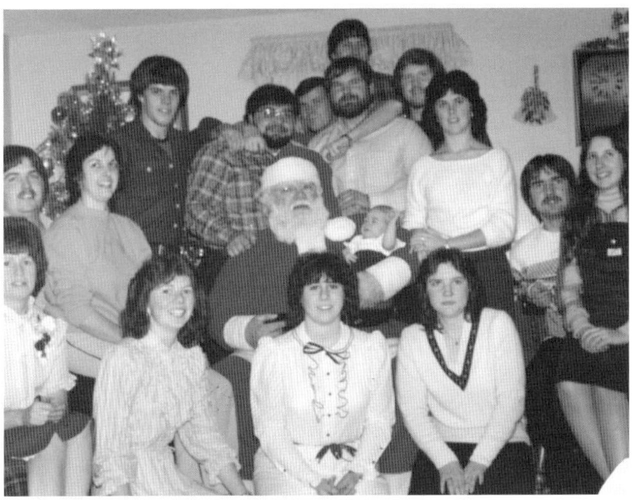

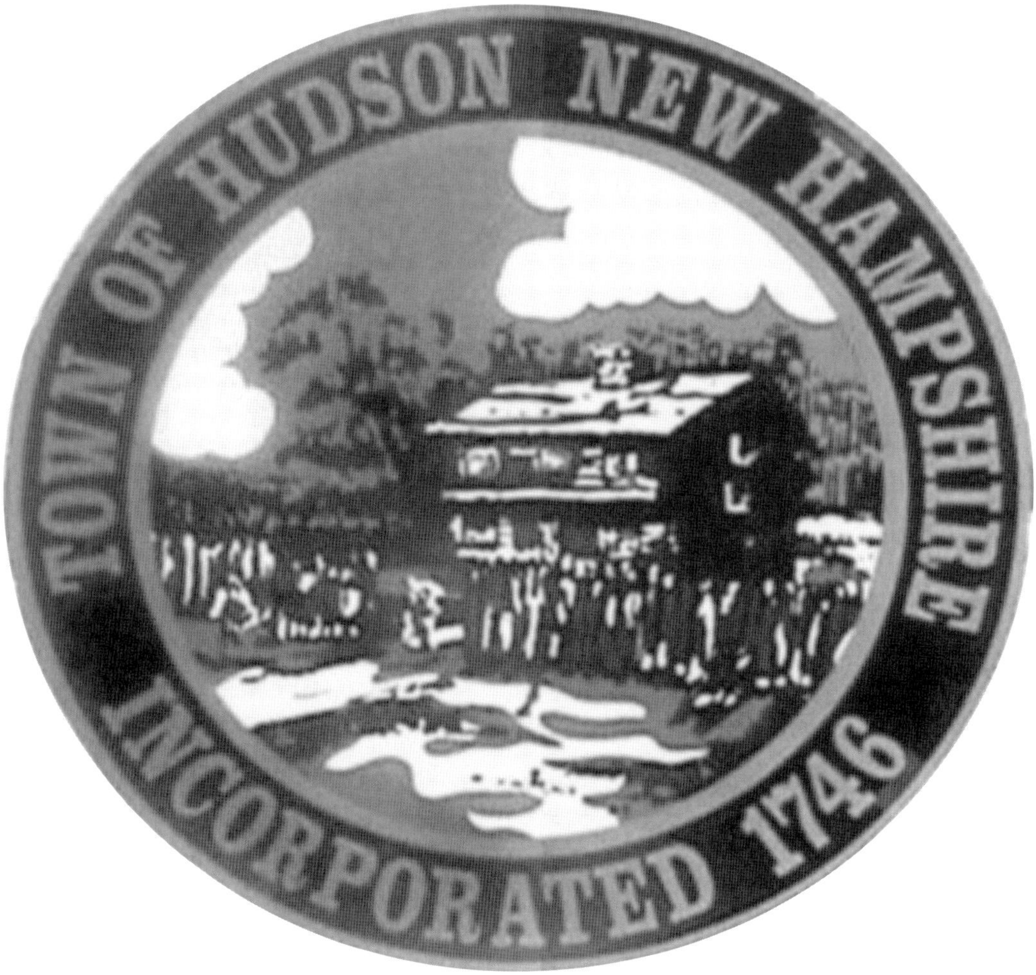

Hudson Town Seal

Henry Fraser of Reed Street made the Hudson town seal for a design contest in the 1950s. It depicts the Hills Garrison, taken from a painting from Kimball Webster's *History of Hudson, New Hampshire, 1673 to 1913*. (Courtesy the Town of Hudson.)

Page 1: Santa and His Friends, 1983

Shirley Nadeau (see page 109) has always loved entertaining, especially at Christmas. Many of the people in this photograph still live in Hudson. Santa Claus (Paul "Moose" Anger) is seen at the center of the group (See page 123). Pictured from left to right are (first row) Shirley Nadeau, Lori Nadeau, Lisa Sirois, and Charlene Huntington; (second row) Paul "Moose" Anger, holding Dustin Small; (third row) Eddie Small, Valerie Small, Emery Nadeau Jr., Joe Anger, Richard Houle, Shawn Jasper (see page 109), Bob Boucher, Gordon Huntington, Elizabeth Nadeau, Brian Southwick, and Karen Southwick. (Courtesy Shirley Nadeau.)

LEGENDARY LOCALS

OF

HUDSON

NEW HAMPSHIRE

SHAWN N. JASPER AND LAURIE A. JASPER

LEGENDARY LOCALS

ISBN 978-1-4671-0183-7

Legendary Locals is an imprint of Arcadia Publishing
Charleston, South Carolina

Printed in the United States of America

Library of Congress Control Number: 2014942218

For all general information, please contact Arcadia Publishing:
Telephone 843-853-2070
Fax 843-853-0044
E-mail sales@arcadiapublishing.com
For customer service and orders:
Toll-Free 1-888-313-2665

Visit us on the Internet at www.arcadiapublishing.com

Dedication
We dedicate this book with love to our daughter, Sarah Jean Jasper. You will always be our greatest collaboration.

On the Front Cover: Clockwise from top left:
Building committee (Courtesy the Jasper family; see page 95), Leonard and Claire Smith (Courtesy Ann Brooke Smith; see page 67), police chief Andrew Polak (Courtesy Hudson Historical Society; see page 41), Robert Jasper (Courtesy Jasper family; see page 81), Stanley Searles at the statehouse (Courtesy Vicky Searles Vaccaro; see page 107), Zachary Tompkins (Courtesy *Hudson-Litchfield News*; see page 124), Gathering of ladies (Courtesy the Jasper family; see page 80), Grant Jasper (Courtesy the Jasper family; see page 79), and Mallory Gray (Courtesy the Gray family; see page 121).

On the Back Cover: From left to right:
Pink Madison, Benson's Wild Animal Farm elephant handler (Courtesy Hudson Historical Society; see page 117), deputy chief Harry Emerson and fire and police chief Harry Connell (Courtesy Hudson Historical Society; see page 34).

CONTENTS

ACKNOWLEDGMENTS

The authors thank all the people who shared photographs and information within these pages. We wish to give special acknowledgement to Ruth M. Parker, the Hudson Historical Society (hereafter noted as HHS), Rodgers Memorial Library, the Hudson Fire Department and Capt. David Morin, and the *Hudson-Litchfield News*.

Hudson is most fortunate to have been the home of Kimball Webster, whose extensive research spanning over 30 years resulted in the publication of *Webster's History of Hudson, New Hampshire, 1673 to 1913*. His careful attention to detail has long been a great source for the authors, and we are most grateful for this and many other contributions to Hudson.

As we took on this project, neither one of us fully understood what a monumental task this would be. As the deadline approached and we did more research and attempted to contact individuals and searched for information, it became painfully obvious to us that there was no possible way for us to include everyone who should be part of this book. We wish to assure everyone that no person was purposely excluded, and we recognize that a second volume will be necessary to include even a fraction of the people and families who have made Hudson the great community that it is. It is our hope to start collecting information for that volume shortly after we have recovered from this undertaking. Your input as to who should be included in the next volume will be welcomed.

Unless otherwise noted, images are from the authors' collection.

INTRODUCTION

Hudson, New Hampshire, is located in Hillsborough County in the southern part of the state, approximately one hour north of Boston, Massachusetts, along the east bank of the Merrimack River. With a population of approximately 25,000 residents, Hudson is one of the largest towns in New Hampshire and covers about 29 square miles. Bordered by Litchfield and Londonderry, New Hampshire, to the north, Windham and Pelham, New Hampshire, to the east, 77, Massachusetts, to the south, and Nashua, New Hampshire, to the west, Hudson is a convenient distance to New Hampshire's mountains, lakes, and beaches along the Atlantic Ocean. One does not need to leave Hudson to find similar opportunities, such as swimming at Robinson Pond Recreation Area or walking, hiking, and picnicking at Benson Park.

The first grant of land in the area that is now called Hudson was made in 1661 to Joseph Hills, of Malden, Massachusetts, and was a total of 500 acres. It is believed that three of his grandsons, Nathaniel, Henry, and James, were the first settlers, sometime around 1710. They built the Hills Garrison on the land in that time period. A garrison was a house that was built to withstand hostile attacks by the Native Americans. According to Webster's *History of Hudson*, famed scalp hunter Capt. John Lovewell of Nashua, New Hampshire, stayed at the Hills Garrison before setting off to battle.

Hudson was a part of Dunstable, Massachusetts, from 1673 to 1733. From 1733 to 1741, as more people settled near the Merrimack River in the area, an area was set apart and called Nottingham, Massachusetts. During this time, the first settled minister, Rev. Nathaniel Merrill, arrived in Nottingham. It was part of the District of Nottingham from 1741 to 1746. The area became a part of New Hampshire in 1746, and since there was already a town in New Hampshire called Nottingham, the land was called Nottingham West until 1830, when the town name was changed to Hudson. For the purpose of this book, we will refer to the town as Hudson unless otherwise noted.

As mentioned in Images of America: *Hudson, New Hampshire*, published by Arcadia in 1999, Hudson does not have a centrally located downtown area typical to small towns. Before 1913, Hudson's main area was Hudson Center, now the area of Route 111 by Central and Greeley Streets. Then the Bridge Area, near Ferry Street, became the more central location as transportation improved and connected the town more easily with neighboring Nashua, New Hampshire, just across the Merrimack River.

Hudson was predominantly farmland, but through the efforts of businessmen such as Gerald Nash, business and industry was brought into the town and the local area, boosting the economy and creating many jobs, especially in the 1950s and 1960s.

Hudson has always met the needs of the student population, from the one-room schoolhouses that were once the norm to the larger, four-room Webster School and the present-day school system. Currently, Hudson schools include Alvirne High School; Hudson Memorial School for grades six through eight; Nottingham West and Hills Garrison, which each hold grades two through five; and Library Street School for kindergarten and nearby Dr. H.O. Smith School for first grade, which together create an early-learning campus. Until 1950, students from Hudson attended high school in Nashua. Thanks to the generosity of Dr. Alfred K. Hills, Alvirne High School was built. The name Alvirne was coined by Dr. Hills, as it combines his name, "Al," and his nickname for his second wife, Ida Virginia, which was "Virne" or "Virnie." He named the summer home they built in 1890 Alvirne Hills House. It was fitting that the name be used for the high school.

In reviewing town and school reports and newspaper articles from the past, it is safe to say that the residents of Hudson are very careful with their tax dollars. At times, this has caused disagreements as to what might be considered needs versus wants. For over 30 years, for example, the town tried and failed in many attempts to either expand Hills Memorial Library or build a new library. Thanks to the generosity of Alvin and Philip Rodgers, who donated $4 million to the town for this purpose, the George H. and Ella M. Rodgers Memorial Library, named in honor of their parents, was built in 2009.

Hudson has always been home to many who give back to their town, volunteering on town boards, in the schools, and at sports activities. This is most evident at Benson Park, the former location of Benson's Wild Animal Farm. John T. Benson put Hudson on the map when he purchased the property in 1922 as a place to quarantine and train animals for zoos and circuses. He eventually opened the park to the public, and the "Strangest Farm on Earth" was born. Arthur Provencher, the business's third and final owner, took over in 1979 and put a lot of money and hard work into the park, but it closed in 1987. The New Hampshire Department of Transportation bought the property for $4 million for wetlands mitigation, but the place was left in disrepair. In the 1990s, the Town of Hudson began putting money aside to purchase the land, and talks continued for years. The original Benson Park Committee was formed in 2001 to work with the state to come up with a plan for the property that would be mutually agreed upon. After many years, on January 23, 2009, Hudson officially purchased the land from the state in a ceremony hosted by Gov. John Lynch at the statehouse.

Once a sad, neglected shell of its former self, Benson Park today is a shining example of teamwork, volunteerism, and vision. This passive recreation park boasts walking and hiking trails, picnic areas, a playground, and even a dog park. It is also home to Hudson's 9/11 Memorial, which was dedicated on the 10th anniversary of the attack on our nation, a beautiful tribute and remembrance that includes a beam from one of New York's Twin Towers. The proud members of Hudson's Highway Department take great care of the town of Hudson through flooding, hurricanes, blizzards, and heat waves, and they take a special pride in the upkeep of Benson Park. In addition, the park has many hardworking volunteers who are there, some every day, keeping the park in pristine conditions. Monthly Benson Park Clean Up Days find dozens of enthusiastic people working together.

As one member of the community aptly said, "The H in Hudson stands for heart." Members of the Hudson community, past and present, make this town a wonderful place to call home.

CHAPTER ONE

Hills Family

Hudson would be a much different community today if it were not for the Hills family. The farms stretching from Alvirne Drive to 64 Old Derry Road were all settled by members of the Hills family. The Hills played a large role in the founding and growth of the town; they fought in war and served the town during peace. However, it was Dr. Alfred K. Hills, a member of the fourth generation of the family, who had the greatest impact on the town. His contributions were made during his lifetime, and his legacy will continue as long as Hudson exists. It is hard to think of Hudson without the Hills Memorial Library, Library Park, the Alvirne Memorial Chapel, the Hills House (home of the historical society), Alvirne High School, and finally the trust fund, which continues to grow, that helps support the school. Today only one Hills farm remains in the Hills family, located on Barretts Hill Road.

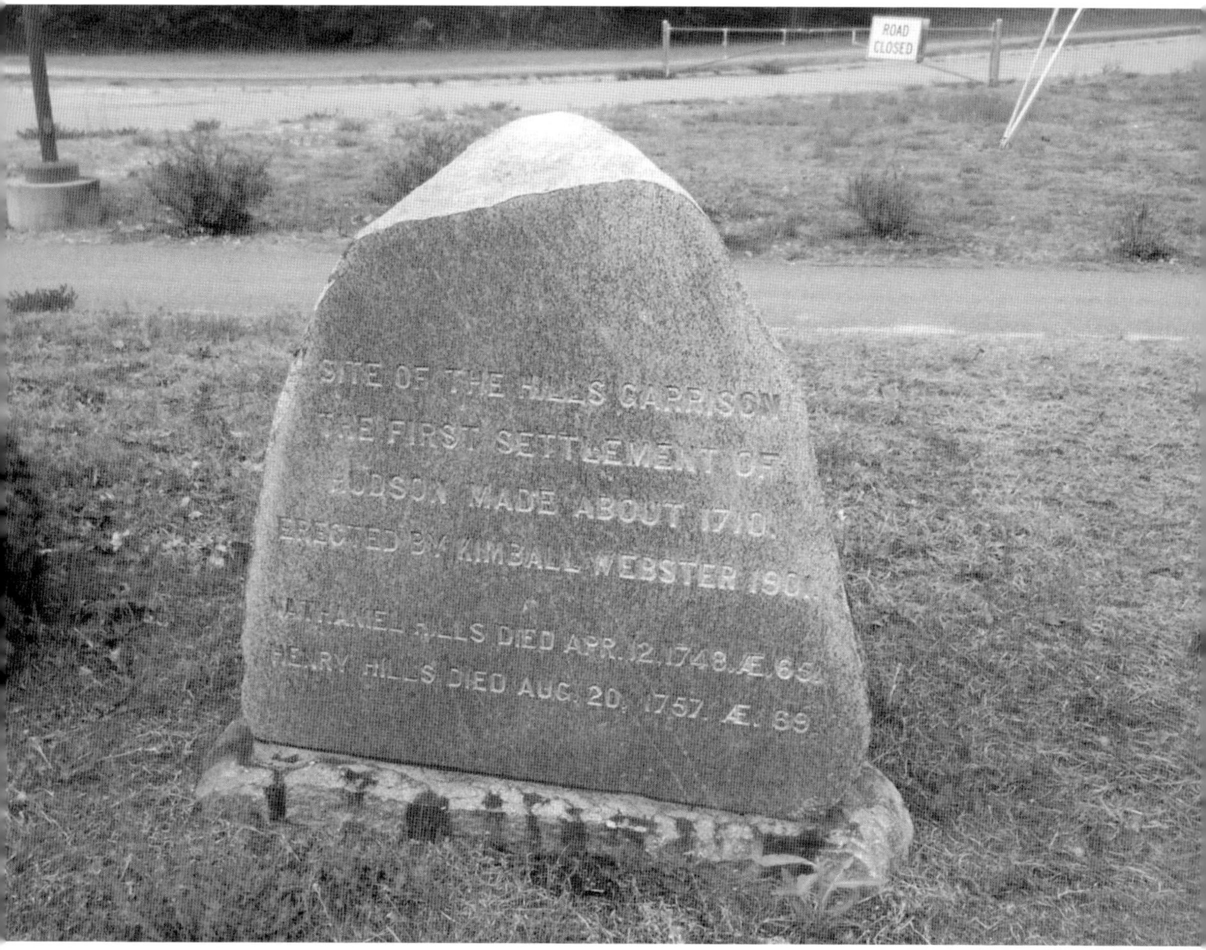

Garrison Marker

The first settlers of Hudson included the Hills family. Joseph Hills received a land grant for 500 acres in 1661. His son Samuel had three sons, Henry, Nathaniel, and James Hills. Henry, Nathaniel, and James erected a garrison together sometime after 1710. The Hills Garrison School was built on Hills land. The marker had been originally placed on land off of Webster Street before it was moved for safekeeping. (Courtesy Laurie Jasper.)

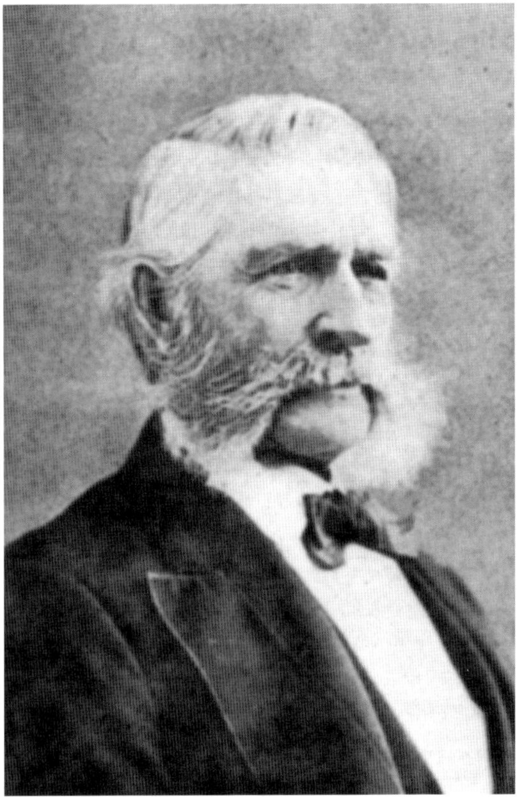

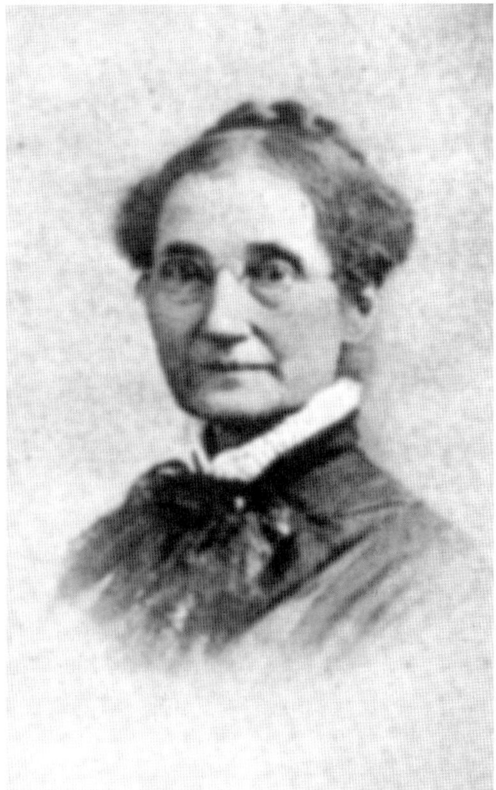

Alden and Nancy Hills
Alden Hills was born in Hudson in 1807. His wife, Nancy Currier Kimball Hills, was born in Groton, New Hampshire, in 1814. They were the parents of Dr. Alfred Kimball Hills. Alden was a farmer and lived on the family homestead all his life. His father, Elijah, was a son of James, one of the original settlers of the town. Elijah was an ensign in the Revolutionary War. Alden Hills served as a selectman from 1863 through 1864. While he was living, the farmhouse burned down, and he built the current house at the Alvirne School Farm. He died in 1891 at the age of 83. In 1910, Nancy Hills died in Somerville, Massachusetts, where she had been staying with her daughter for the winter. She died just a week before her 95th birthday. Nancy Kimball Hills was the first person to have a funeral in the newly constructed Alvirne Memorial Chapel. They are buried in Hills Farms Cemetery with a prominent monument. (Courtesy HHS.)

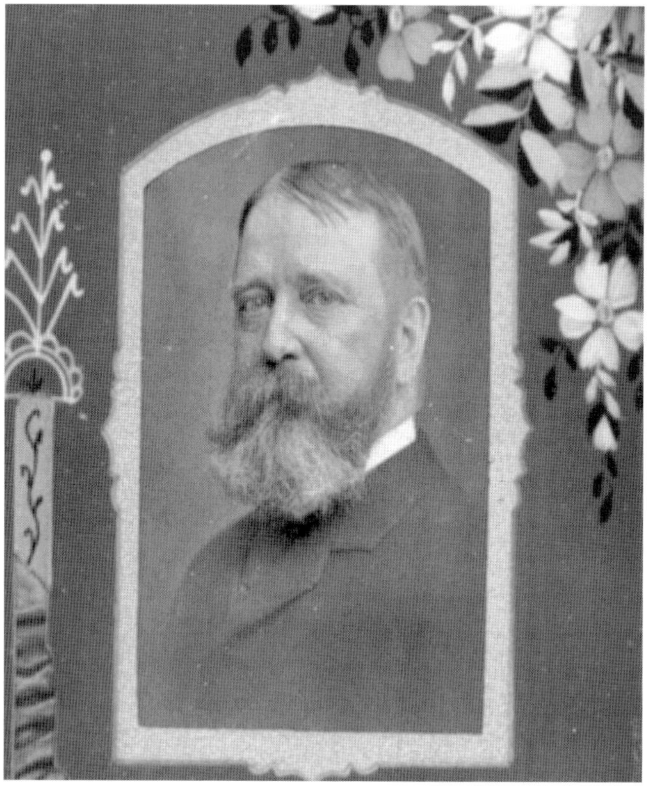

Dr. Alfred K. Hills

Dr. Alfred Kimball Hills was born in Hudson in 1840 and descended from the original settlers of Hudson. A son of Alden and Nancy Currier Kimball Hills, he married his first wife, Martha Simmons, on June 6, 1865, when he was 25 and she was 40. It was his first marriage but her second. Until recently, not much was known about Hills's first wife. However, through research, it is now known that Martha's maiden name was Vinton; she was born in Rhode Island and married John Simmons Jr. on January 18, 1843. They had a son, John Simmons III, born October 11, 1844, in Boston, Massachusetts, who died August 30, 1854, at age nine. In 1846, John Simmons Jr. died in Cuba of tuberculosis. Simmons's father was John Simmons Sr., a prominent clothier and businessman in Boston who died in 1870 and left a portion of his estate to found Simmons College in Massachusetts.

After Hills's first marriage, he graduated from Harvard University in 1868, Harvard Medical School in 1869, and Hahnemann Medical School in 1870. He then began his medical practice in New York and was a noted surgeon. Martha Hills died in 1885.

Dr. Hills married his second wife, Ida Virginia Creutzborg Hills, on June 11, 1887. In 1890, Hills purchased over 180 acres of land in Hudson from his father and built Alvirne Hills House on Derry Road as a summer home for himself and Ida Virginia. It has even been written that it was a Christmas gift to his wife. The name Alvirne is derived from part of his first name and part of the nickname he had for her, which was "Virne" or "Virnie."

They had two daughters, both of whom died as infants: Gladys Marguerite in 1891 and Mary Virginia in 1895. Ida Virginia Hills died suddenly in 1908 at the age of 51. She was interred, along with her children, in the Alvirne Chapel, which was built shortly after her death. The Hills Memorial Library was built in her memory with funds from her husband and her mother, Mary Creutzborg, and dedicated on June 11, 1909, the anniversary of Alfred and Ida Virginia's wedding.

Dr. Hills married Jessie Norwell Hills in 1910. He died in 1920 and bequeathed a large sum of money to the town to build what is now known as Alvirne High School. (Courtesy HHS.)

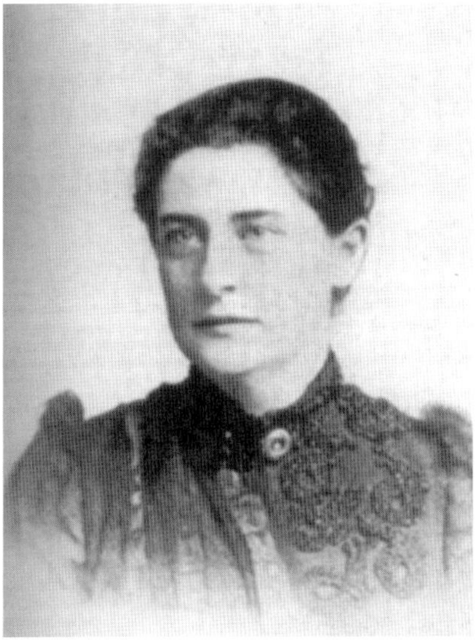

Ida Virginia Hills
Ida Virginia Hills married Dr. Alfred Kimball Hills on June 11, 1887. They had two children, but neither survived beyond infancy. Ida Virginia Hills died suddenly in 1908. Alvirne Chapel was built in 1909, and she was interred there. Her two children were then also interred in the chapel as well. She was a lovely woman who loved books and reading. In fact, a year after Alvirne Hills House was built in 1890, the addition of the library was built onto the home (which is now known as the meeting room). Ida Virginia worked with the architects to achieve her ideals for the room. When she died, Dr. Hills hired the same architects to design Hills Memorial Library using many of her details. Hills Memorial Library was dedicated to Ida Virginia Hills's memory on June 11, 1909, the anniversary of their wedding date. (Courtesy HHS.)

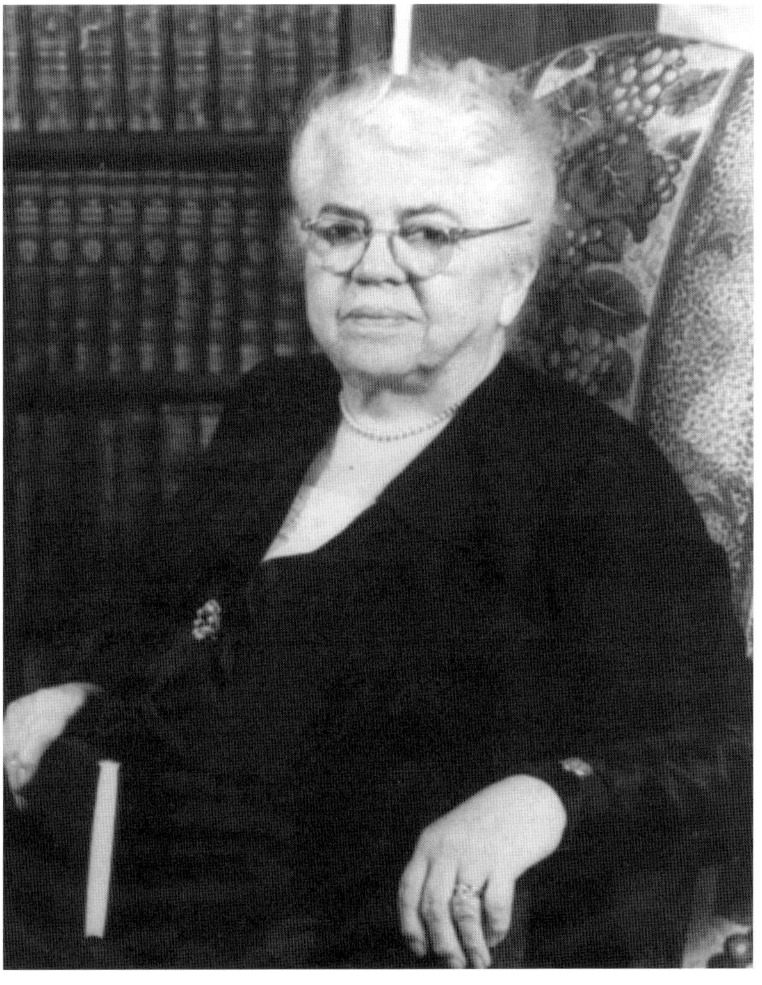

Jessie Norwell Hills
Jessie Norwell Hills was the third wife of Dr. Alfred K. Hills, and they married in 1910. She survived Dr. Hills by 43 years and died in 1963. Since Dr. Hills had no surviving children, there were no direct heirs to the estate, although there were many relatives. Jessie Hills was one of the first members of the Alvirne Board of Trustees. She allowed classes to be held in her home (Alvirne) in order to fulfill the stipulations of Dr. Hills's will that a school be started. Otherwise, the town would have lost the money to build the high school. Prior to the construction of Alvirne High School, Hudson students attended high school in Nashua. (Courtesy HHS.)

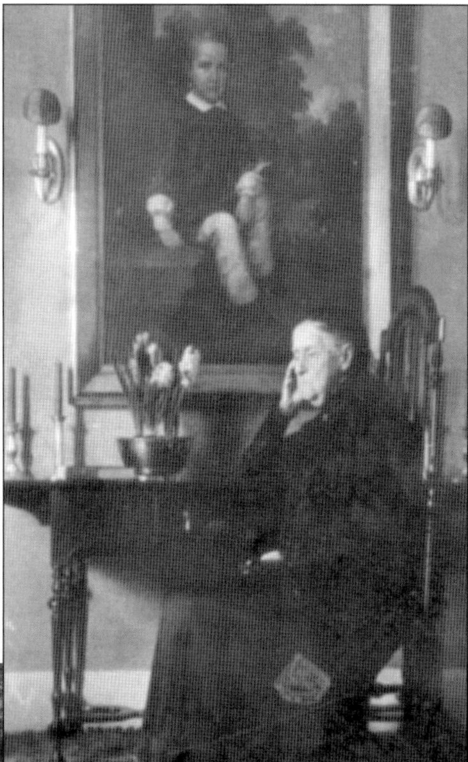

Mary Field Creutzborg

Mary Field Creutzborg was the mother of Ida Virginia Hills. Born in Philadelphia, Pennsylvania, on April 18, 1826, she died at the age of 102 in Nashua, New Hampshire. When her son-in-law Dr. Alfred K. Hills died in 1920, Mary lived with Alfred's third wife, Jessie Norwell Hills, until her death, even celebrating her 100th birthday at Alvirne Hills House. Mary Creutzborg also contributed greatly to this town, joining with her son-in-law to build Hills Memorial Library in her daughter's memory. She also donated the money to the town to purchase the plot of land diagonally across from Hills Memorial Library for a public park. Those who know their Hudson history call this pretty spot of land Library Park. The photographs show Mary Creutzborg, age 97, at Alvirne Hills House, seated in front of an oil painting of her oldest child, Lewis Clark Creutzborg, who died in 1853 at the age of 5, and the trolley stop at Library Park. (Both, courtesy HHS.)

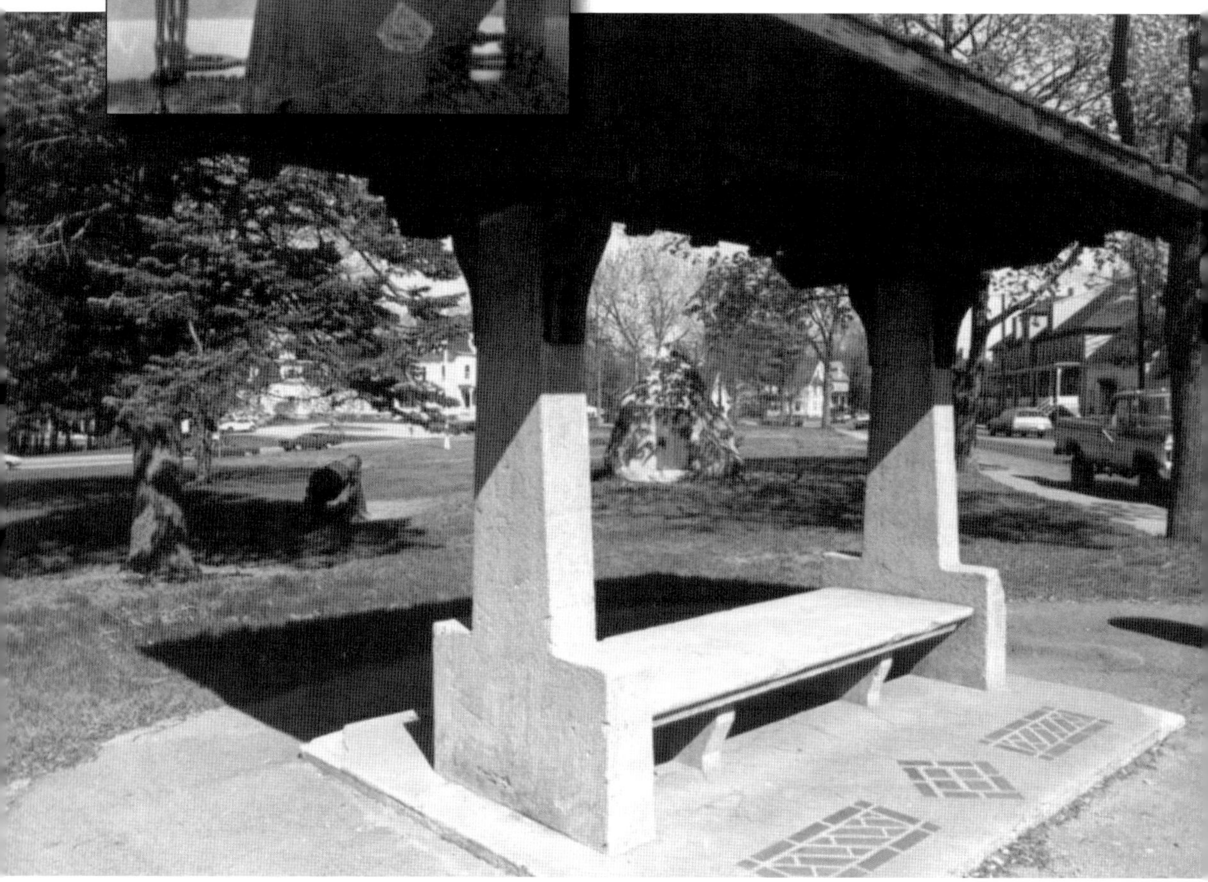

CHAPTER TWO

Founding Families

Hudson, New Hampshire, is located in the southern portion of New Hampshire, approximately one hour north of Boston, Massachusetts, and it is the ninth largest town in the state. Litchfield and Londonderry border it to the north, Windham and Pelham to the east, Nashua the west, and Tyngsborough, Massachusetts, to the south. The town was known as Nottingham, Massachusetts, from 1733 to 1741, the District of Nottingham from 1741 to 1746, called Nottingham West, New Hampshire, from 1746 to 1830, and finally named Hudson in 1830. According to *Webster's History of Hudson, New Hampshire, 1673 to 1913*, the first land grant in what is now Hudson was 500 acres to Joseph Hills of Malden, Massachusetts, in 1662. Joseph's descendants built the first settlement of Hudson, the Hills Garrison, on a portion of that land in 1710. The name Hills continues to be well known in Hudson, as described in the previous chapter. Kimball Webster's detailed history of Hudson continues to be the authority on Hudson's past, as Webster had a deep sense of history and community and a keen attention to detail. Other pioneer families who contributed greatly to Hudson's history include the Colburns, the Greeleys, the Davises, and the Cummings.

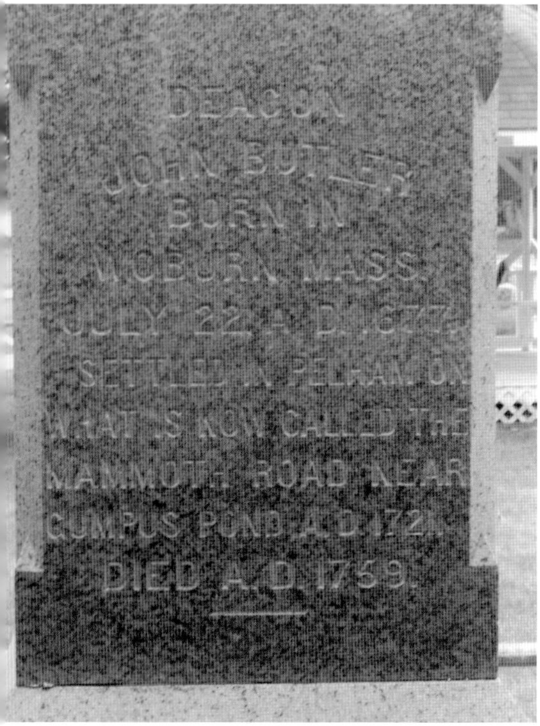

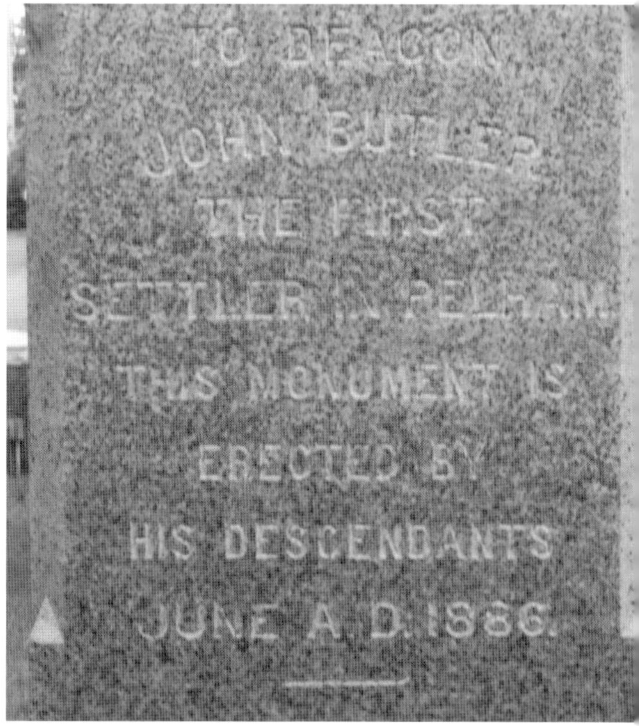

John Butler

John Butler came to town from Woburn, Massachusetts. He purchased land in 1722 from Jonathan Tyng, of Tyngsborough, Massachusetts, and then built a log garrison house. He was on the first board of selectmen when Nottingham was divided out of Dunstable in 1733. He was elected to be on a committee to build the first meetinghouse in 1734. Kimball Webster wrote that Butler was one of the most prominent and useful men in Nottingham. He was moderator of the town meetings in 1735 and 1741, and in 1746, the part of town in which he lived became part of the new town of Pelham, New Hampshire. He is considered the first settler in that town and was on the first board of selectmen there. A monument dedicated to his memory stands in the middle of town in Pelham. He died in 1759, leaving many descendants, including Shawn Jasper.

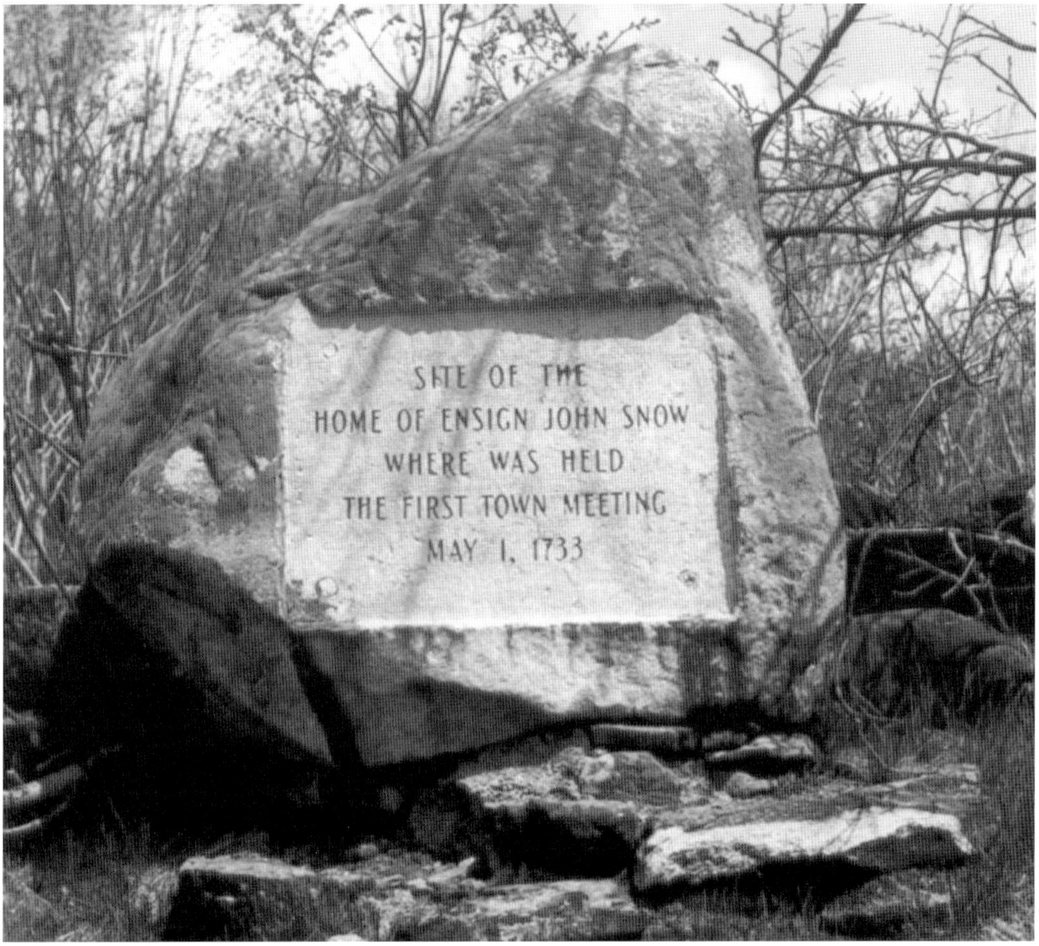

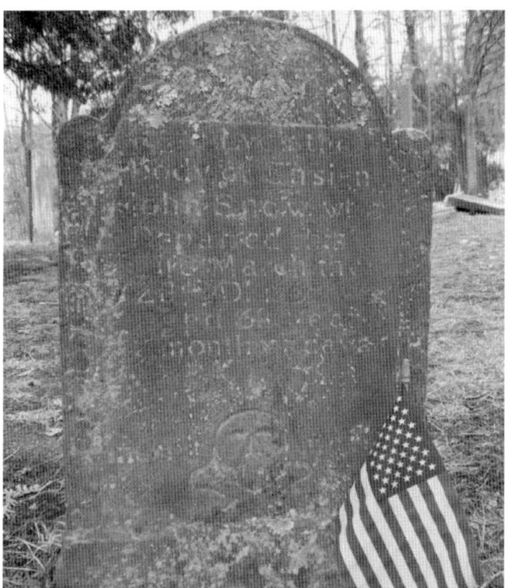

Ens. John Snow

Ens. John Snow was one of 18 original settlers of what is now known as Hudson. The first general town meeting of Nottingham was held at his home, as well as subsequent meetings until the first meeting hall was built. There is a monument to the spot on Musquash Road. He was elected the first town treasurer. The monument and his gravestone are shown here. (Above, courtesy HHS; left, courtesy Paula Mae Deprey.)

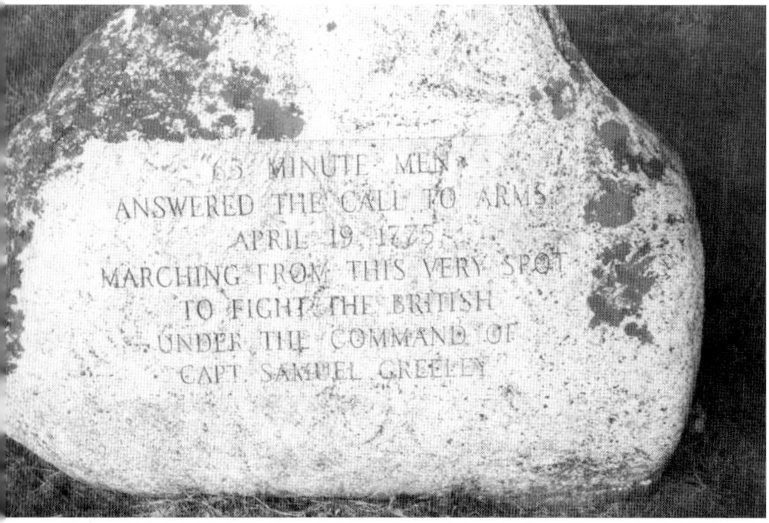

Capt. Samuel Greeley
Capt. Samuel Greeley organized the Minutemen on the common at Hudson Center on April 19, 1775, and marched to the Battle of Lexington and Concord, Massachusetts against the Redcoats. He was born in Haverhill, Massachusetts, on May 10, 1721. His son Joseph was 18 and also joined the Minutemen. Joseph was wounded during the battle but recovered from his wounds.

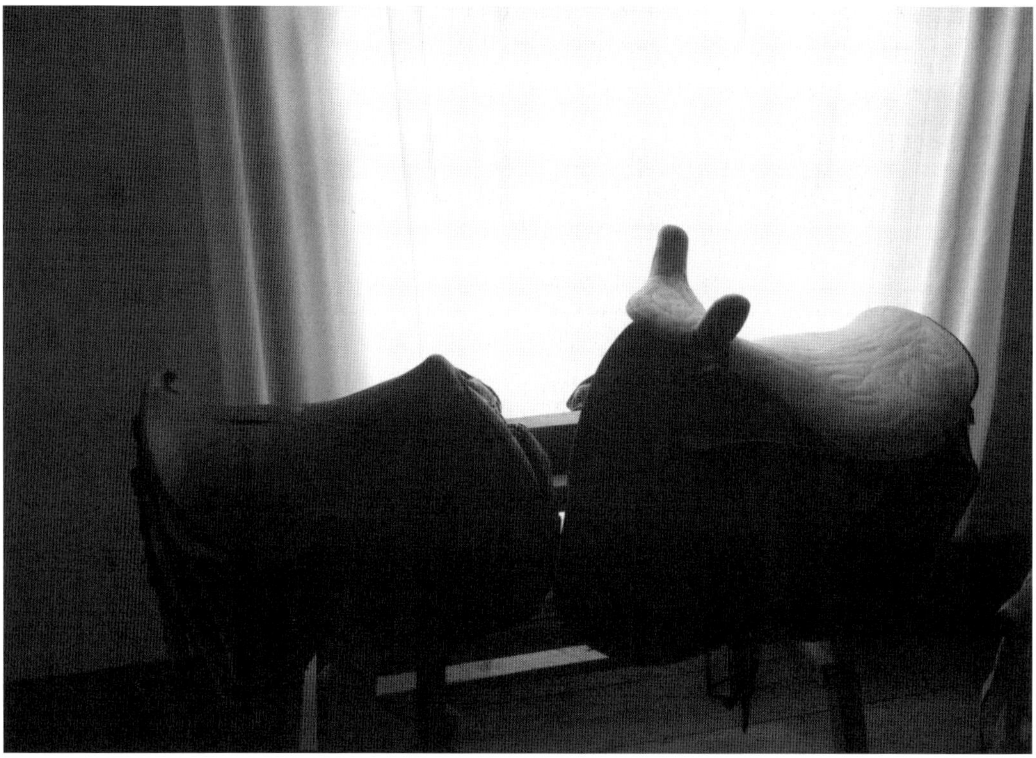

Asa Davis
Asa Davis was a Minuteman. Born in 1737 in Amesbury, Massachusetts, he lived in Nottingham West, New Hampshire, (as Hudson was called then) when, on April 19, 1775, he received word at his house on Bush Hill from a messenger traveling by horse that the British were planning an attack at Lexington and Concord, Massachusetts, approximately 40 miles away. He joined the Minutemen already gathered at Hudson Center Common (Kimball Hill and Central Street). There is a monument to the gathering at the site. He was a selectman for many years. The saddle Asa used to ride to Lexington and Concord, as well as his wife's saddle from the same time period, are in the Hudson Historical Society's collection.

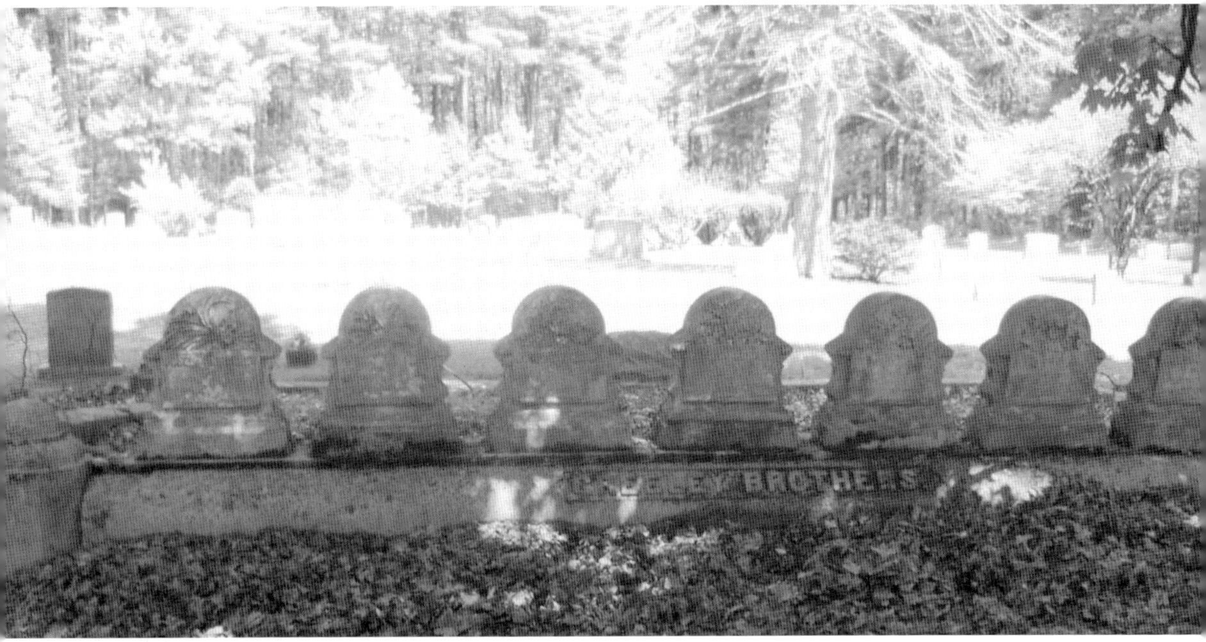

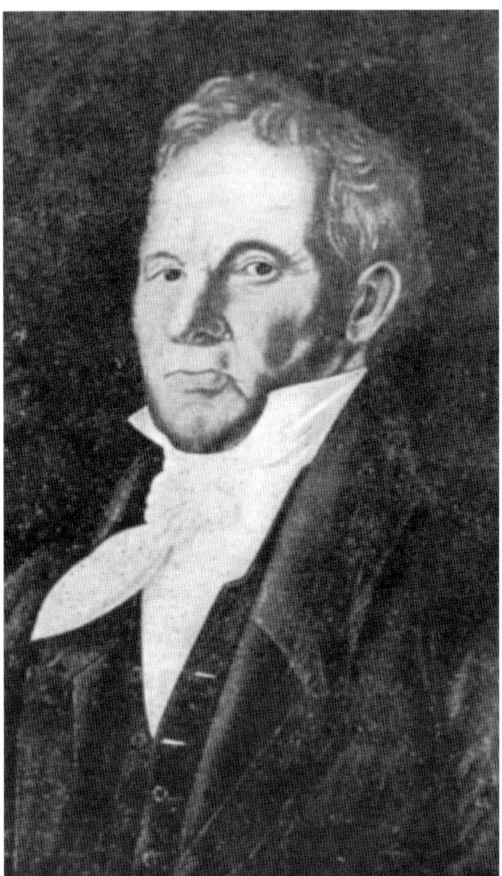

The Greeley Brothers

The Greeley family moved to Nottingham West in 1740; they came from Haverhill, Massachusetts, as did many of the founding families of town. Deacon Moses Greeley was of the fourth generation of his family to live here. He settled on the farm that is now known as the Nadeau Farm, on Old Derry Road. He built the house in the late 1790s or early 1800s, having previously had another house on the property. Moses and his brother Joseph Jr. served on the board of selectmen together in 1813–1814. Moses died in 1848 at age 84. His farm passed into the possession of his son Jackson E. Greeley, who prospered as a farmer and extensively remodeled the house. He died at age 78 in 1894. The farm was sold by his heirs to Joseph Lambert, and it remained in his family for over 100 years. Stephen Greeley, Jackson's brother, purchased the Henry Hills Jr. Farm and remodeled the house; today it no longer looks like the post-and-beam Colonial house that it is but a Greek Revival style. Stephen was very active in local and state politics, serving as town moderator in 1879–1880, selectman for several terms from 1848 to 1868, and state representative in 1864. He died at age 81 in 1892. The Greeley brothers' grave markers, shown here, are prominent at Hills Farms Cemetery and are a tribute to the brothers and their wives. (Above, courtesy L. Jasper; left, courtesy HHS.)

James Merrill

The Merrill family played a role in town affairs for nearly 250 years. James Merrill was a great-grandson of Rev. Nathaniel Merrill. He was born in Nottingham West, now Hudson, in May 1824. He represented Hudson in the legislature and was on the board of selectmen. He was also town clerk, town treasurer, and a charter member of Grange No. 11 as its first secretary. James Merrill died in 1901. (Courtesy HHS.)

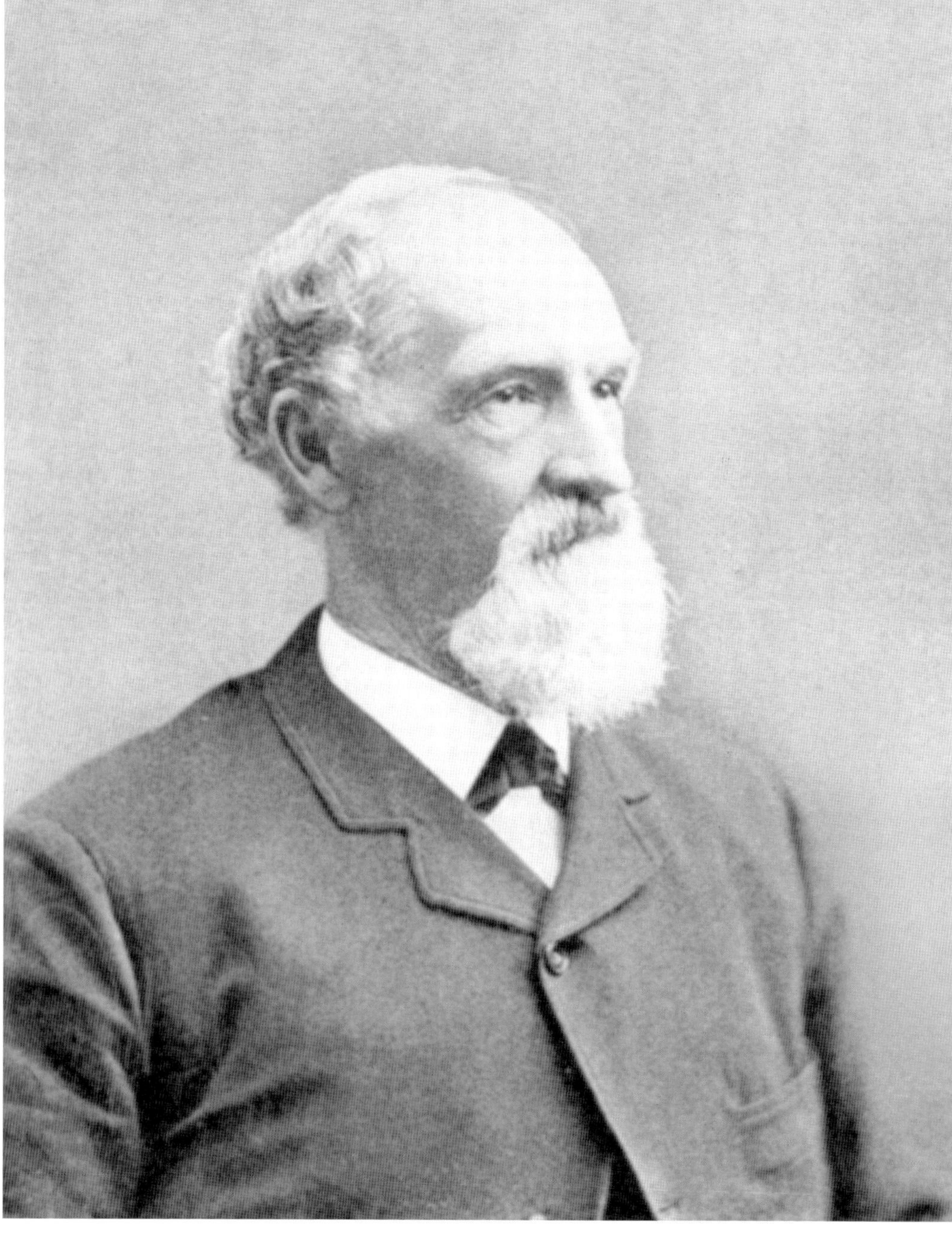

Nathaniel Merrill

This marker, located at Ford Cemetery, states that Nathaniel Merrill was born on March 1, 1713, was ordained in Nottingham West on November 30, 1737, and died in 1786 at the age of 83. It also reads that Betsey, his wife, died in April 1795 at 80. Nathaniel Merrill's son John served in the Revolution, as did several other relatives who had settled in town. Seven members of the Merrill family served the town as selectmen between 1751 and 1902, including Isaac and James. Otis and Austin served in the Civil War. Natalie Merrill taught school in Hudson for many years during the mid-1900s, and she also played an important role in the early years of the Hudson Historical Society, donating many items from the family to the society.

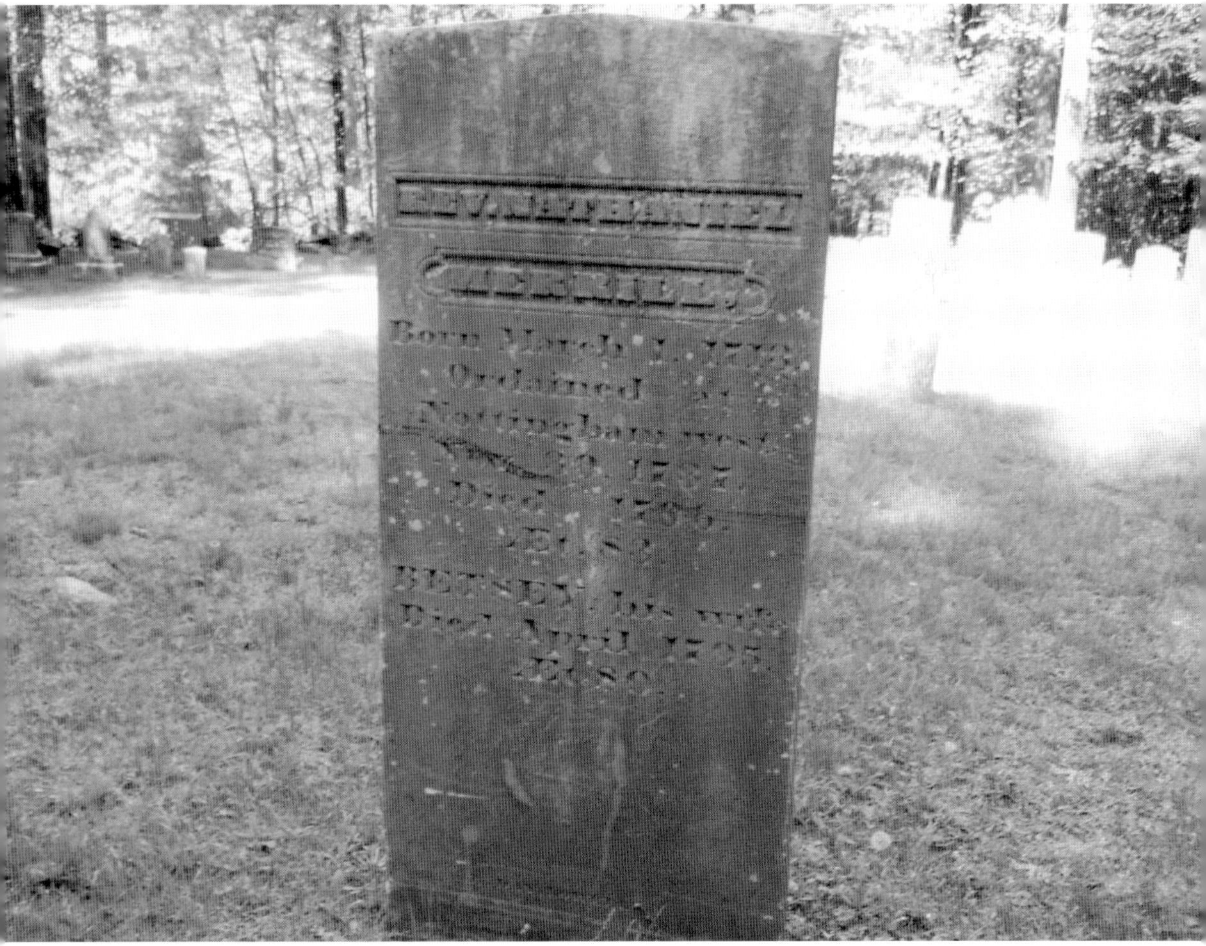

First Minister

Nathaniel Merrill was the first minister to settle in the town in 1737, and the monument on Musquash Road signifies this. The Rodgers Memorial Library has the book *Baptisms and Marriages Solemnized, 1737–1795*, by Rev. Nathaniel Merrill in Nottingham, Massachusetts, which became the District of Nottingham, New Hampshire (1741), Nottingham West, New Hampshire (1746), and Hudson, New Hampshire (1830).

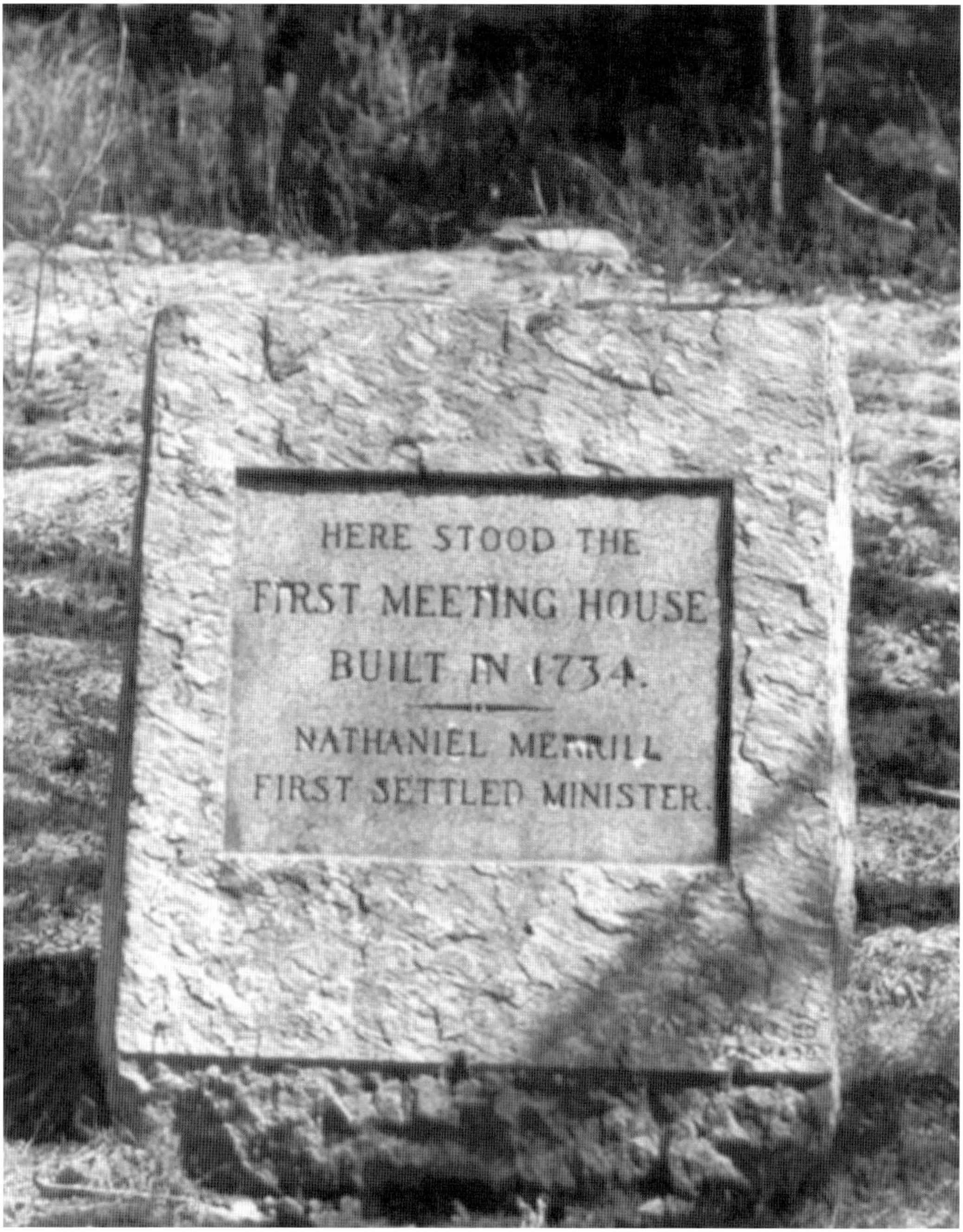

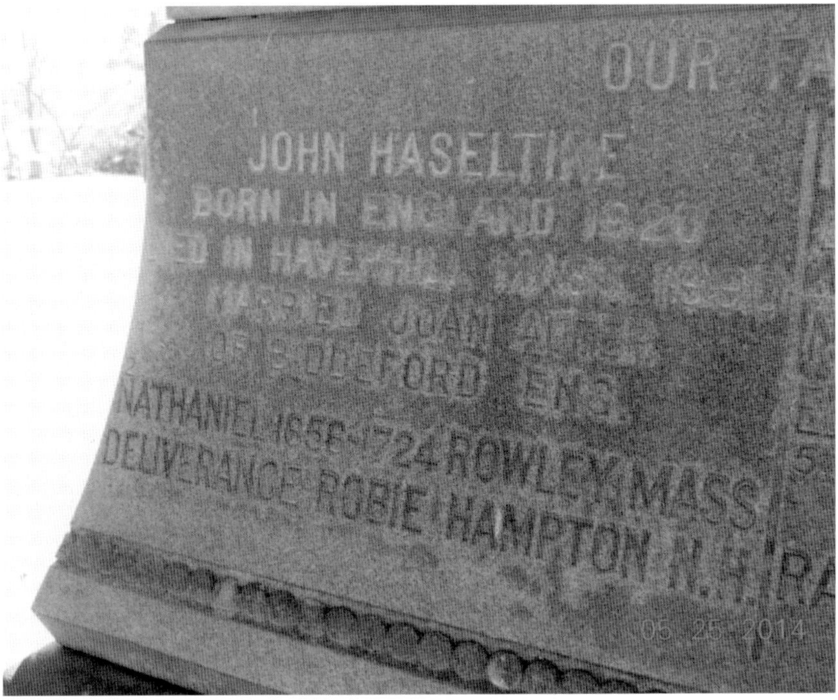

Haselton/Hazeltine

Nathaniel Haseltine (the family name is spelled several different ways in various accounts) served in the Revolutionary War, as did his kinsman Capt. John Hazelton, who had also served in the French and Indian War. The family farmed in the area of what is now Bush Hill Road. The Haselton Barn on Bush Hill Road, by Flying Rock Road, is now part of the town-owned Benson Park. The farmhouse across from the barn is still owned by relatives of the Haselton family.

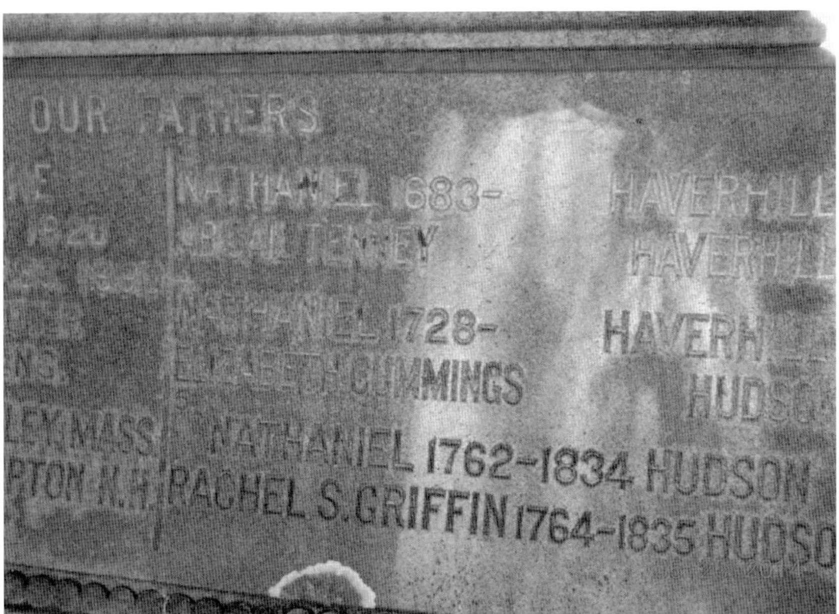

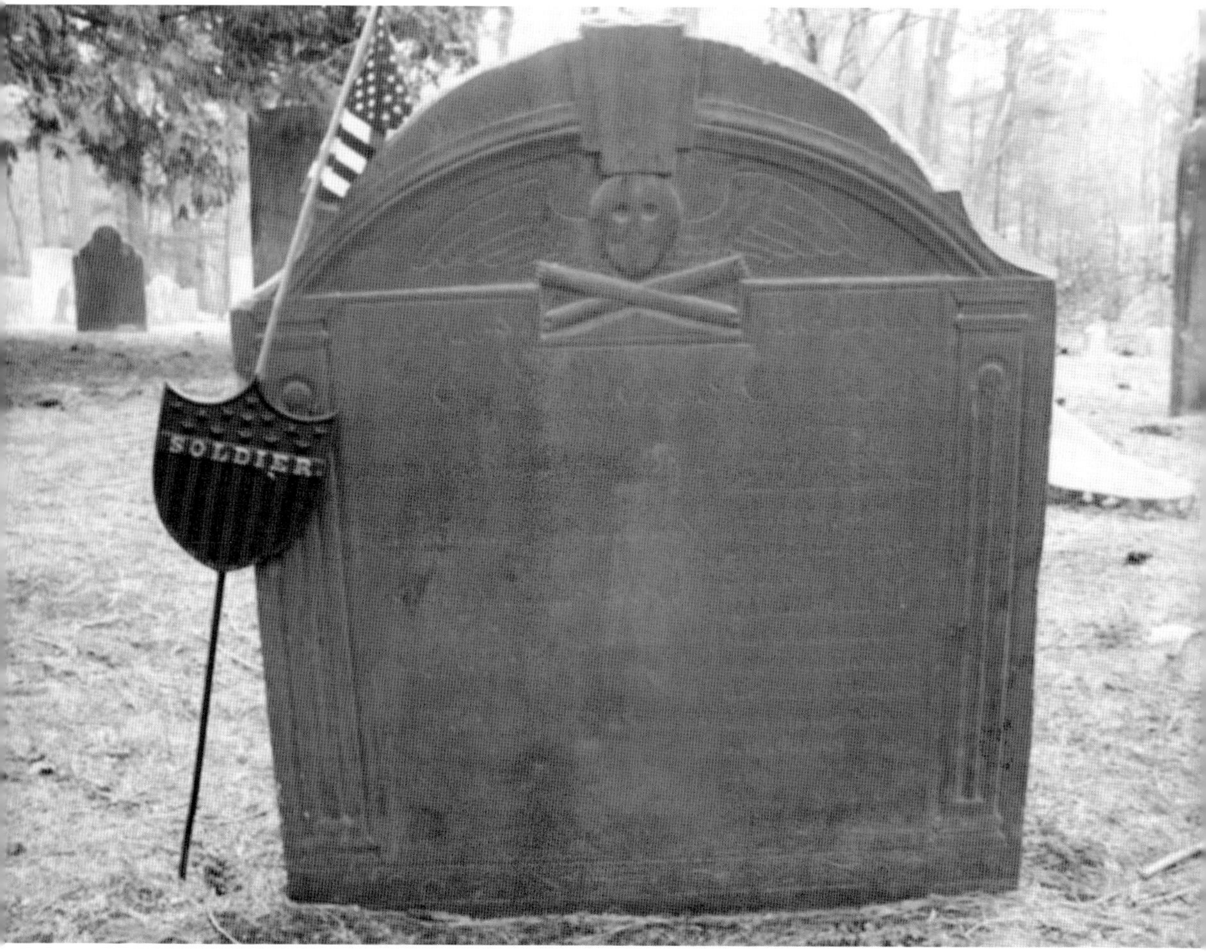

The Colburn Family

Capt. Thomas Colburn was a prominent citizen. He was one of the selectmen in 1735 and chairman from 1740 to 1748 and in 1754. He was town moderator for nine years and a delegate to the Massachusetts General Court in 1741. His first wife, Hannah, died on March 26, 1756, at age 53. There are no records of children with his first wife. He married his second wife, Mary, and they had three children. According to town records and the inscription on his gravestone in Ford Cemetery, Capt. Thomas Colburn lost his life in what Hudson school children still refer to as "the crazy death." The town records state: "Captain Thomas Colburn died August 30, 1765, in the 64th year of his age. Thomas Colburn, Jr., son of Capt. Thomas and Mary Colburn, died August 30, 1765, in the 4th year of his age. Both killed by lightning." (Courtesy Paula Mae Deprey.)

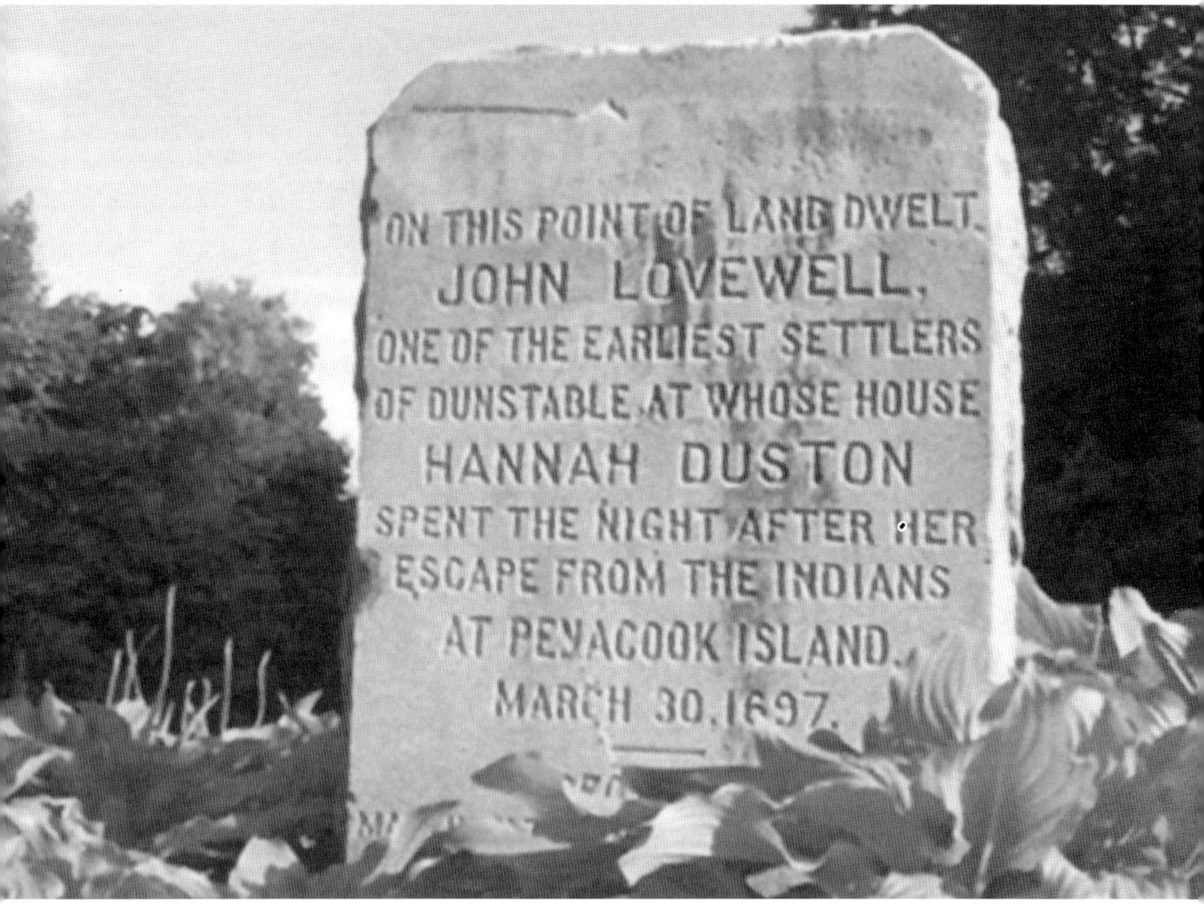

John Lovewell

Originally Hudson was part of Dunstable, Massachusetts. Obviously, it was a very large township, stretching from present-day Dunstable, including all or parts of Nashua, Hollis, Hudson, Pelham, Litchfield, and Merrimack. Although Capt. John Lovewell lived in the part of town that is now Nashua, his actions were significant for Hudson's side of the Merrimack River. There was a 50-year period of hostility with the native population. In 1723, William Lund was taken captive. John Lovewell raised a company of men and pursued the Indians to the area of Fryeburg, Maine. Ultimately, Lovewell headed three expeditions, the final one being fatal for him and many of his men. In the end, the reputation of the men from Dunstable and their tireless pursuit of those who would attack them seems to have prevented any further attacks on the townspeople, even while there were hostilities in other parts of the region.

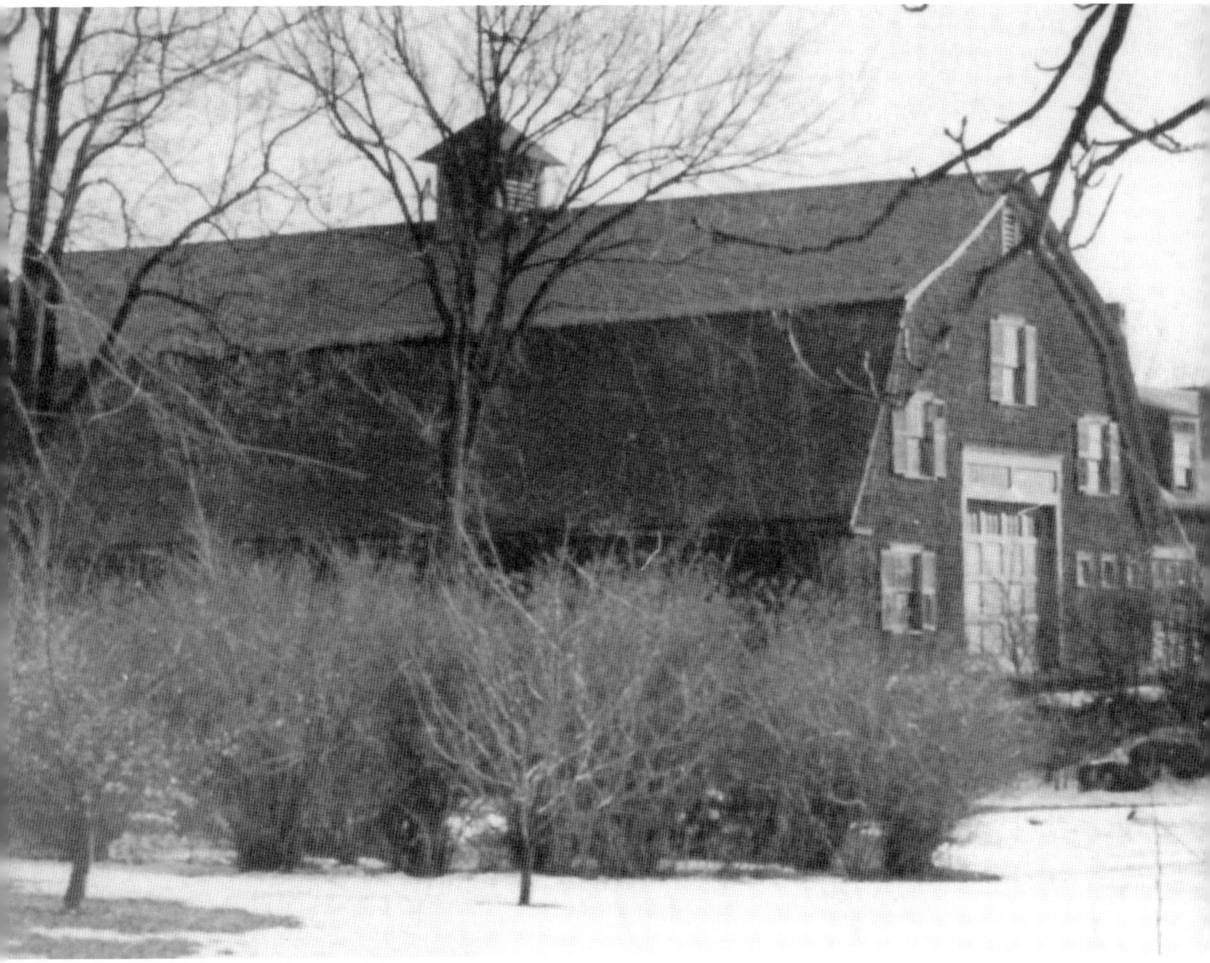

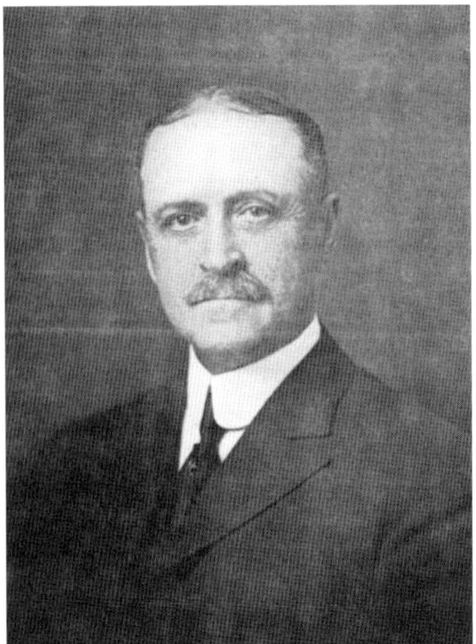

The Marsh Family

Two members of the Marsh family served in the Revolution, Thomas and Capt. Samuel Marsh. Two members of the Marsh family also served as selectmen, John Marsh in 1750 and Samuel Marsh for 11 years between 1762 and 1797. John was a delegate to the New Hampshire General Court in 1747. Samuel served as a state representative from 1784 to 1786; Hiram in 1855 and 1860; Otis in 1872. John and Otis Marsh served in the Civil War. Walter H. Marsh was born in 1852, the fifth generation of the Marsh family to live in Hudson. He worked for the Buttrick Publishing House of New York City as its New England manager and general agent. In 1900, he became the owner of the Marsh homestead on Marsh Road, which had been settled by Thomas Marsh, his great-grandfather. The Marsh homestead now serves as the clubhouse for the Whip-Poor-Will Golf Course. Walter died in Hudson at age 87 in 1940. Pictured here are the farm and Walter H. Marsh.

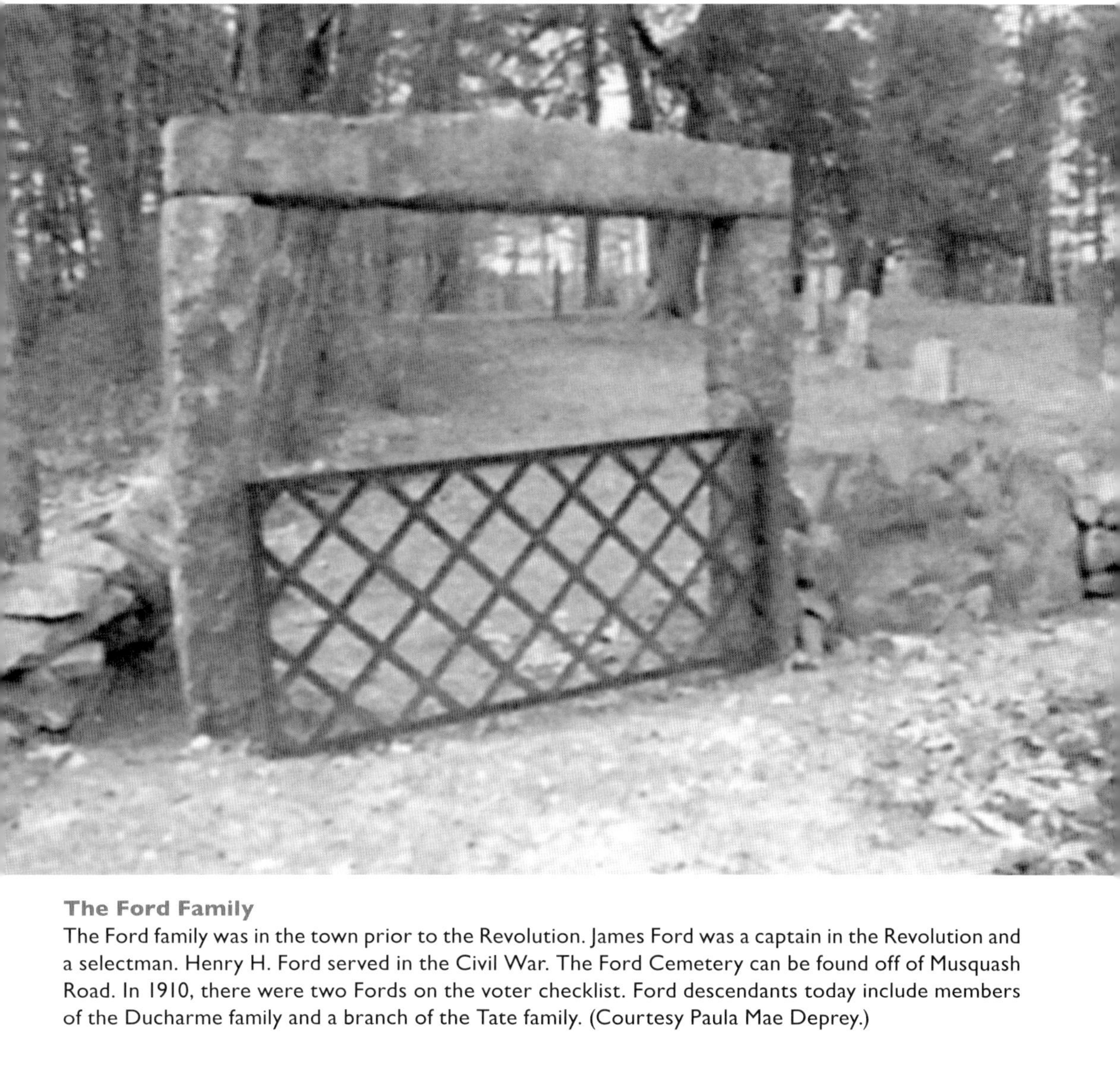

The Ford Family
The Ford family was in the town prior to the Revolution. James Ford was a captain in the Revolution and a selectman. Henry H. Ford served in the Civil War. The Ford Cemetery can be found off of Musquash Road. In 1910, there were two Fords on the voter checklist. Ford descendants today include members of the Ducharme family and a branch of the Tate family. (Courtesy Paula Mae Deprey.)

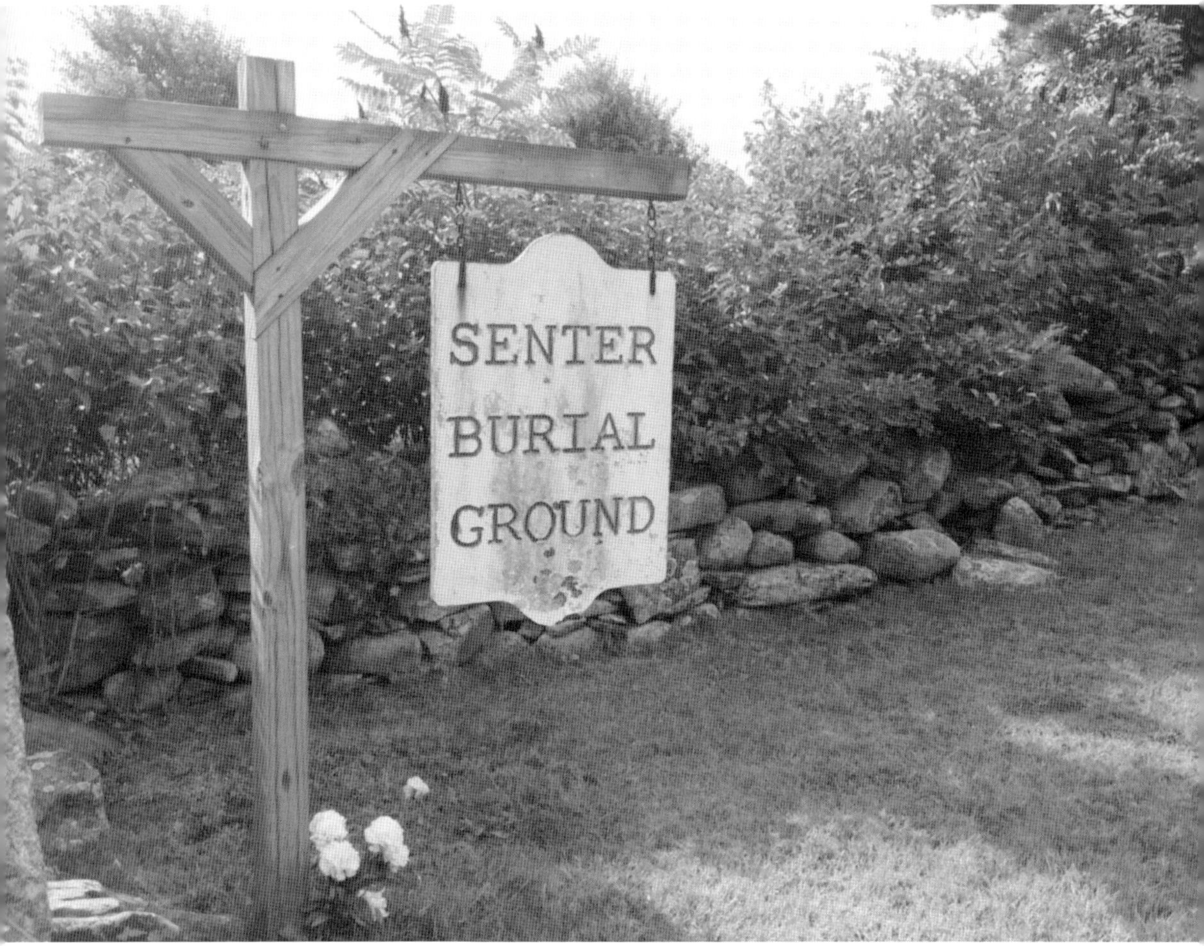

The Senter Family

The Senter family was here prior to the Revolution and owned a large farm in the area of what is now Old Derry Road and Robinson Road; the Senter Burial Ground is located on what was part of the original farm. Lt. Joseph Senter was a member of the militia as early as 1764, and Thomas Senter served as a selectman in 1798. Almon, George, and Thomas Senter served in the Civil War. Senter Farm Road off of Old Derry Road is named for this family, and descendant John Senter was responsible for placing the stone with his family name at the burial ground.

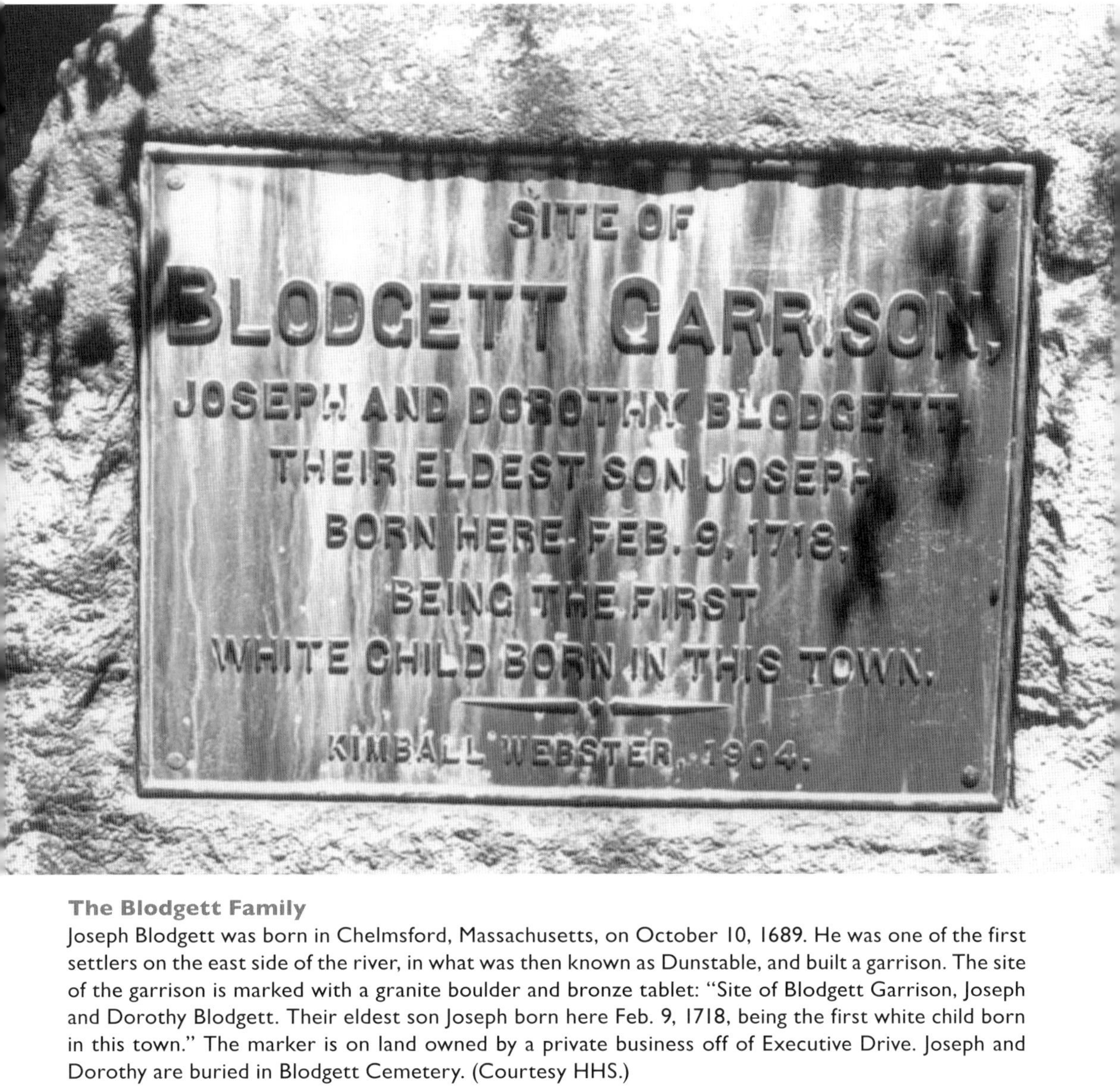

The Blodgett Family
Joseph Blodgett was born in Chelmsford, Massachusetts, on October 10, 1689. He was one of the first settlers on the east side of the river, in what was then known as Dunstable, and built a garrison. The site of the garrison is marked with a granite boulder and bronze tablet: "Site of Blodgett Garrison, Joseph and Dorothy Blodgett. Their eldest son Joseph born here Feb. 9, 1718, being the first white child born in this town." The marker is on land owned by a private business off of Executive Drive. Joseph and Dorothy are buried in Blodgett Cemetery. (Courtesy HHS.)

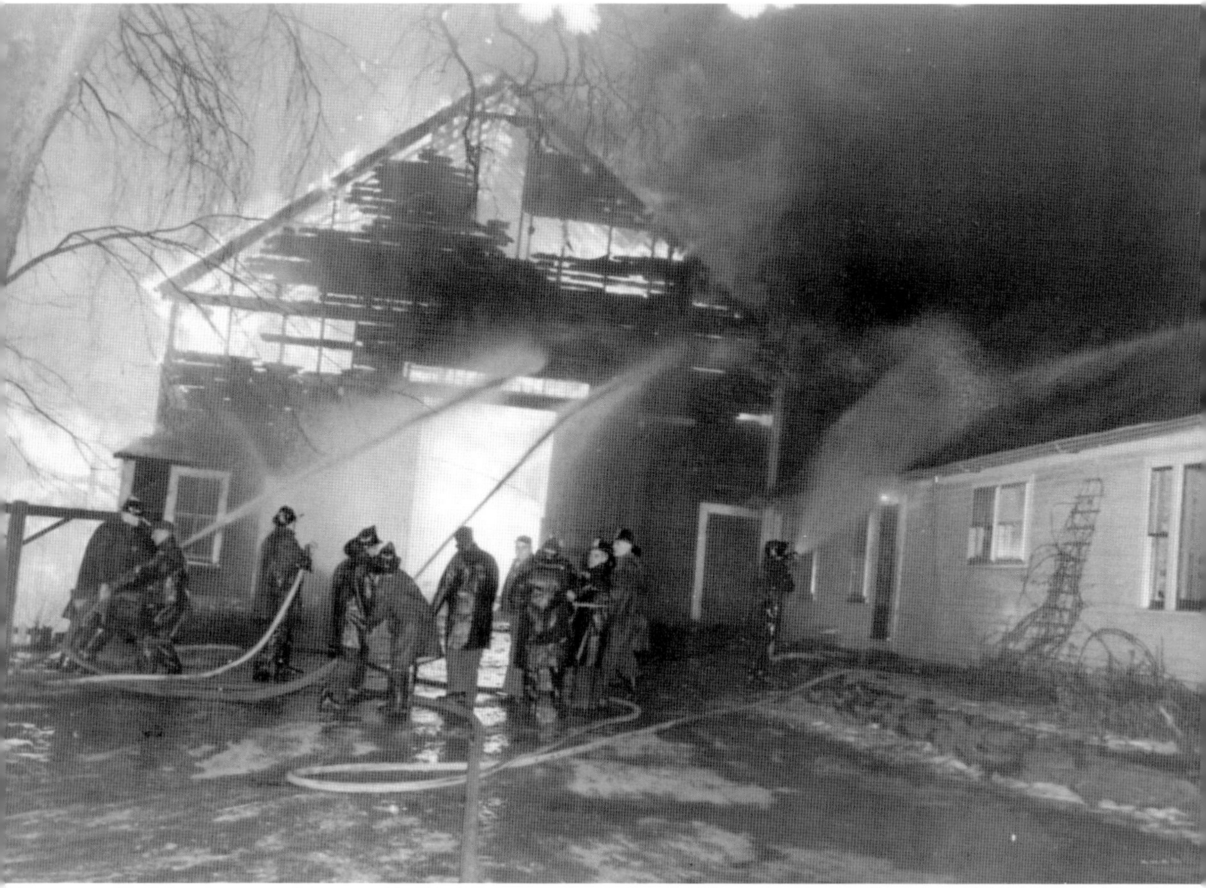

The Winn Family (ABOVE AND OPPOSITE PAGE)
Joseph Winn was one of three surveyors for the town chosen at the first meeting in 1733. Joseph's son Joseph Jr., along with a grandson, fought in the French and Indian War. Joseph Jr. and his son Joseph both fought in the Revolutionary War as well. Two members of the Winn family served as selectmen between 1749 and 1902. In 1909, there were six men named Winn on the voter checklist. The Winn Farm on Lowell Road was last owned by Frank Winn, a member of the sixth generation of the family to live in Hudson; the farm was on the site of what is now Tokyo Joe's Karate Studio. Pictured above is the Winn barn fire in 1948; above opposite are Effie and Frank Winn; and below opposite is the Winn Farm. (All, courtesy Winn relatives.)

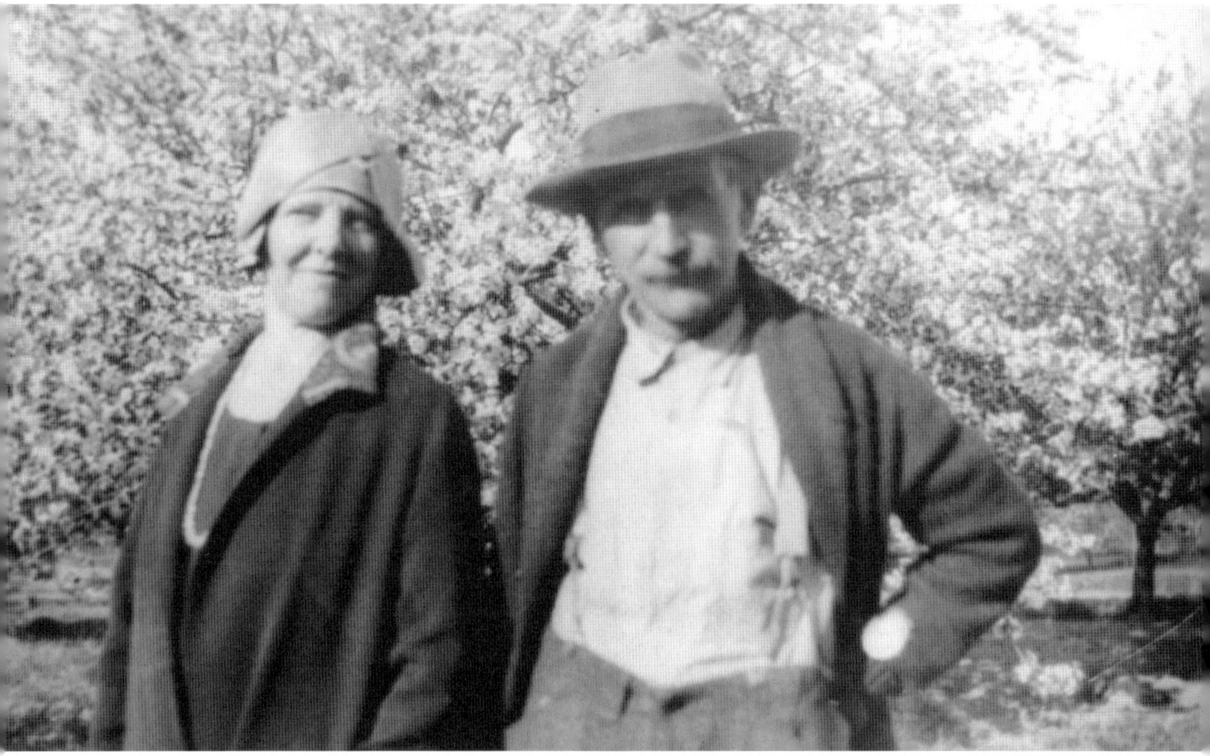

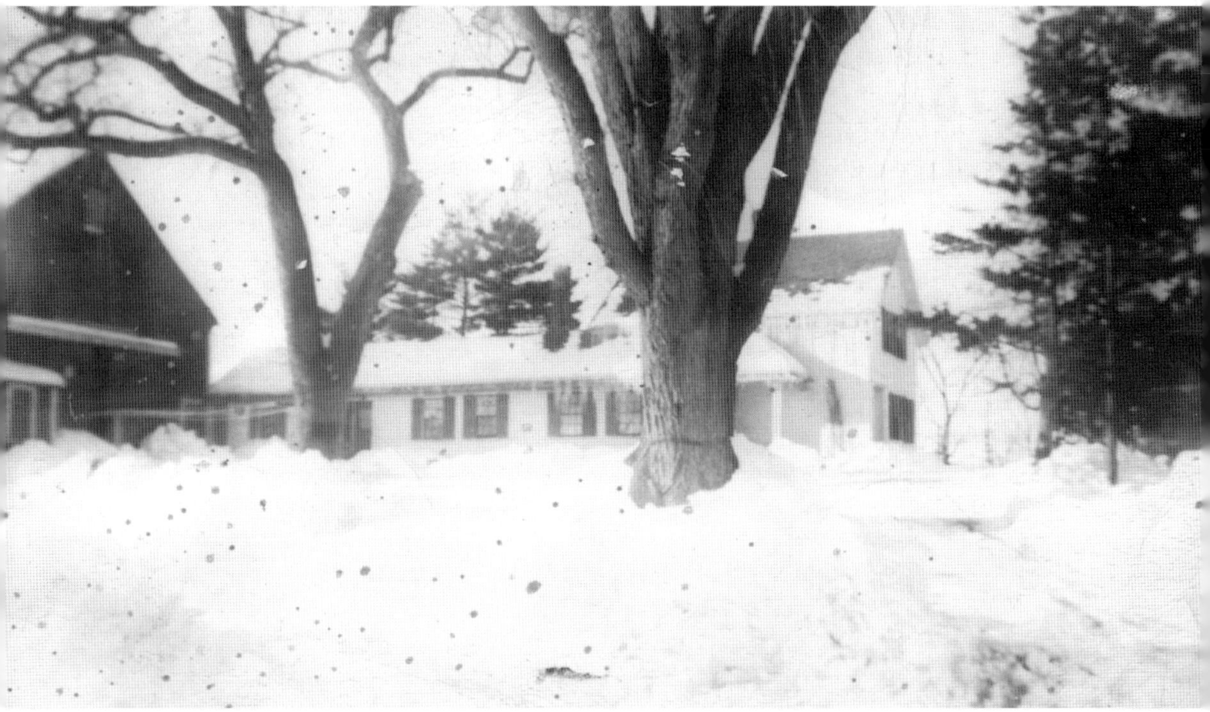

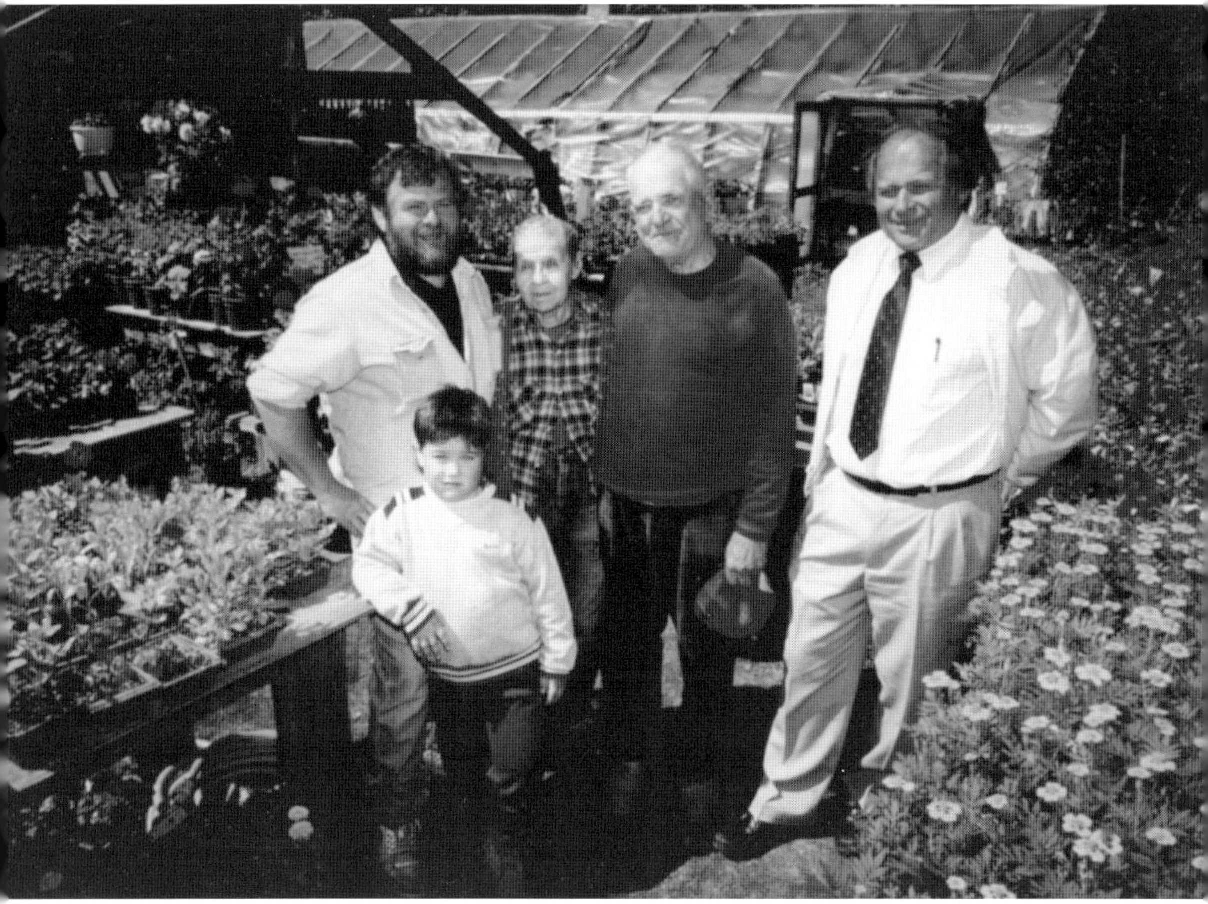

The Smith Family

Thomas "Tom" Smith's family began farming in Hudson before the Revolutionary War. His ancestor Samuel Smith fought in the Revolution. Dustin Smith, Tom's great-grandfather, was a sharpshooter during the Civil War, and his farm on what is now Clement Road remains in the Harold Smith branch of the family. Tom's father and grandfather worked in the Jackson Mills in Nashua, even after they relocated from the center of town back to Kimball Hill, the area in which the family originally settled. Elmer, Tom's grandfather was a part-time Hudson police officer who helped train Andy Polak, the town's future police chief. Tom's father, Henry, and his mother, Mary (Kayros), took up dairy farming and raised a family of four children, Nancy, Dustin, Tim, and Tom. By the 1960s, they realized that vegetable farming was more profitable than dairy cows, and it smelled better, too. Tom continues to run the farm with the help of his wife, Tina (Vassilakos), and Tim's wife, Charli, and his son Dylan. The town was primarily a farming community until the early 1960s, and H.E. Smith and Sons, on Kimball Hill Road, stands as the last full-time farm in Hudson. (Courtesy Thomas Smith.)

CHAPTER THREE

Service in Uniform

From its founding as part of Dunstable, Massachusetts, in 1673, Hudson has always had men who were willing to risk their lives for members of the community in war or as members of the police and fire departments. Hudson has had many such men throughout the 341 years since the land was first settled by Europeans, and as such it is impossible to do their service justice with so few words and images. In the days of the founders, being a member of the militia was required of every able-bodied man. When Hudson was a wilderness, it was typical that every few homes would be garrisons with strong stockade fences to protect the area families and the livestock in times of Indian trouble. In later years, the trouble came from not only the Indians but from the French with whom they had allied. By the time of the Revolution, the troubles with the Indians had ceased, but the militia had continued, preparing the men for the battles to come. Hudson men saw service in the War of 1812 and have continued to serve in every war and conflict since. Before the days of police departments, towns elected constables to keep the peace; thankfully this was a town that had little in the way of crime. It was not until towns had villages that fire brigades were formed; up until that point, if a house caught fire and the occupants could not put it out in the first few minutes, there was nothing that could be done.

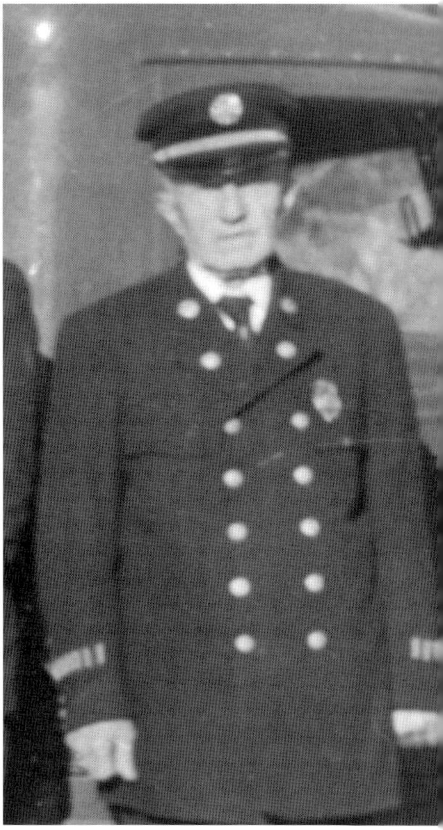

Harry Connell

Harry J. Connell was born in Hudson in 1880; his father was Philip J. Connell, who served as a selectman from 1891 to 1892 and as state representative in 1902. In 1913, Harry and his brothers Phillip and Robert made up three-fifths of the part-time police department. Harry Connell was the first permanent police officer for the town of Hudson. He was appointed in 1921, and his salary was $1,232 from a $1,520 budget. The 1922 town report shows that Harry was also a fire warden; this was in the years before Hudson had a fire department. In 1924, he was the chief of police and the cochief fire warden, and the next year, he would be the chief warden. It was not until the early 1940s that the Hudson Town Report refers to a fire department. In 1945, he retired as chief of police. In 1946, he became a state representative and a member of the planning board, and he still held the position of fire chief. Connell died in 1947, and the town report was dedicated to him that year. The image at right shows Harry Connell in uniform, and below is Chief Connell (right) and his deputy chief Harry Emerson (left) enjoying some quiet time. Deputy Emerson became the new chief upon the death of Harry Connell. (Right, courtesy Hudson Fire Department; below, courtesy HHS.)

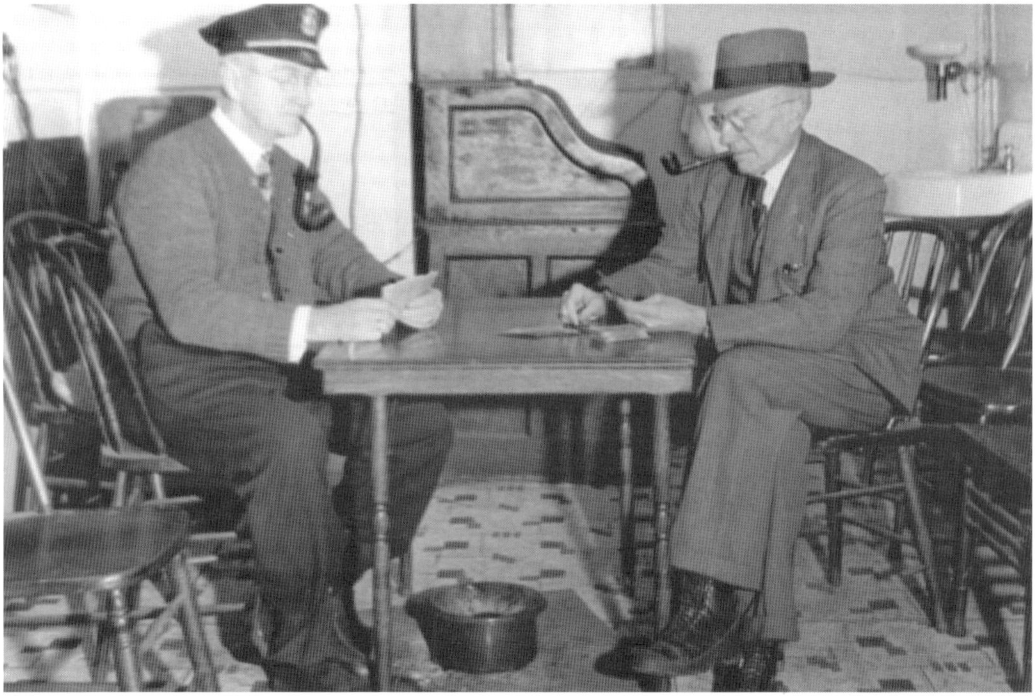

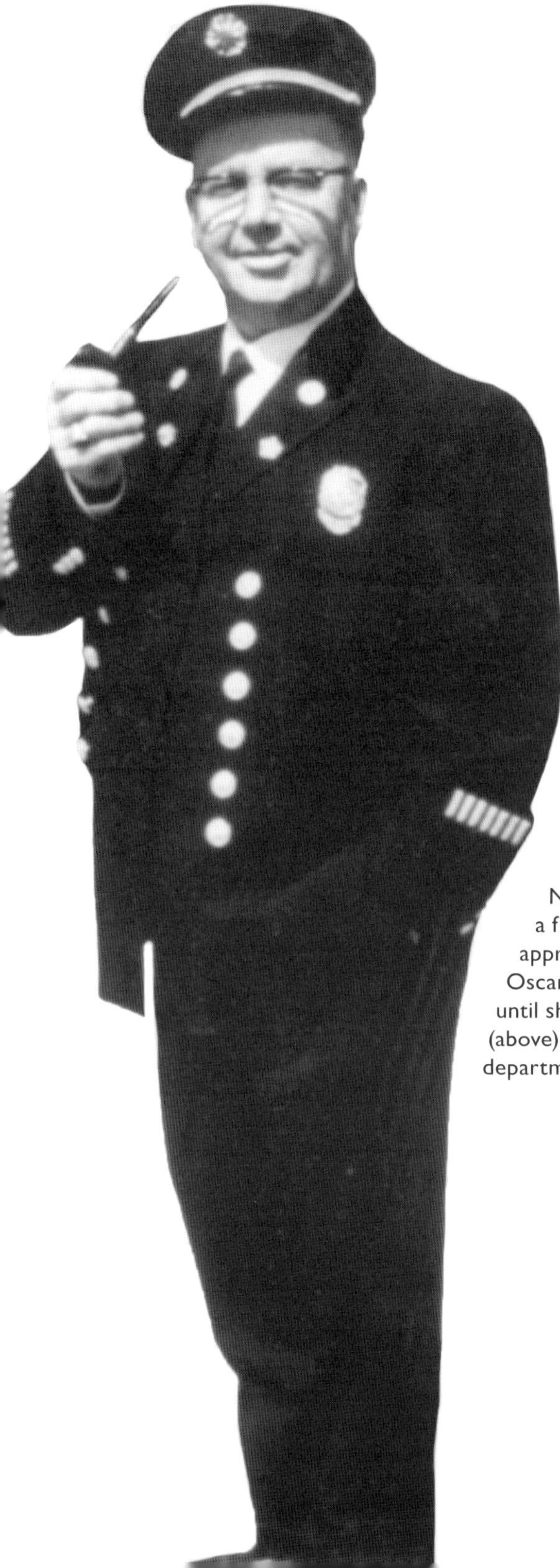

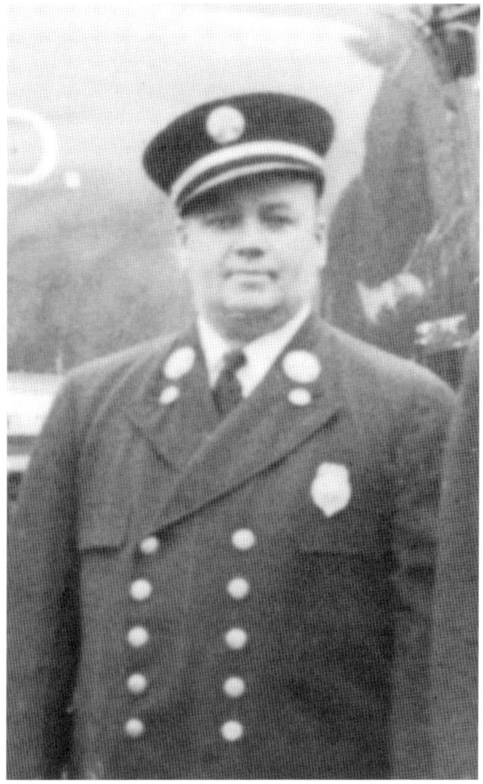

Robert Campbell and Oscar Campbell
Bradford Campbell was born in Bedford, New Hampshire, in 1844, but he was living in Hudson by the time of the Civil War and served in the 13th New Hampshire Regiment. His son Orman was a fireman, and Orman's son Oscar (left) began his apprenticeship in 1932 fighting grass and brush fires. Oscar became fire chief in 1954 and held that position until shortly before his death in 1973. Robert Campbell (above), Oscar's son, was a longtime deputy chief of the department. (Both, courtesy Hudson Fire Department.)

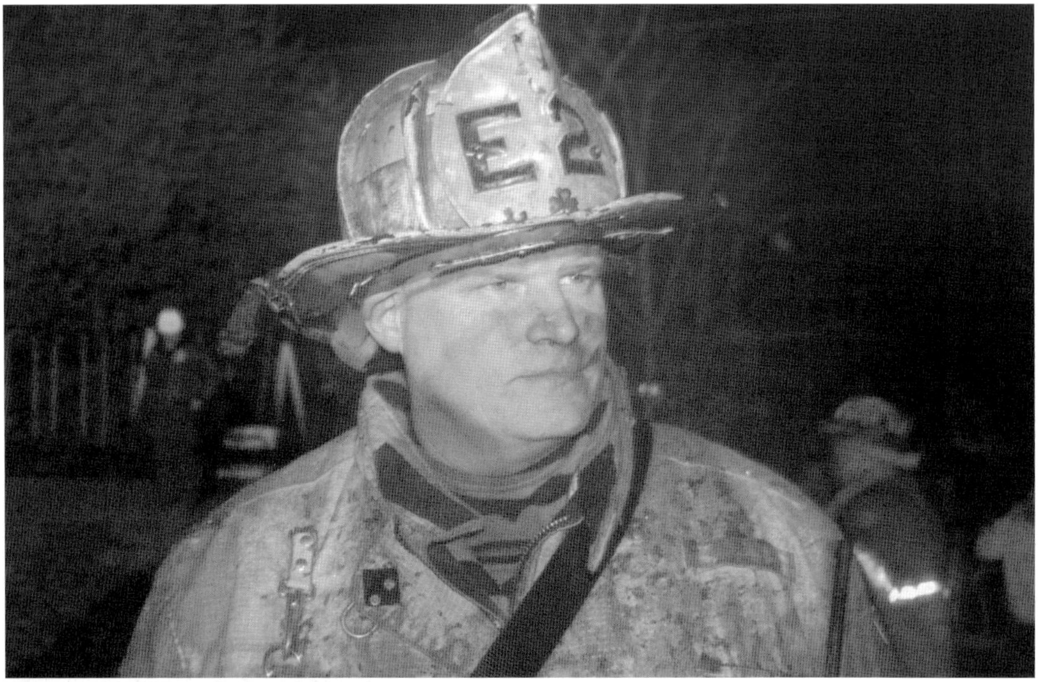

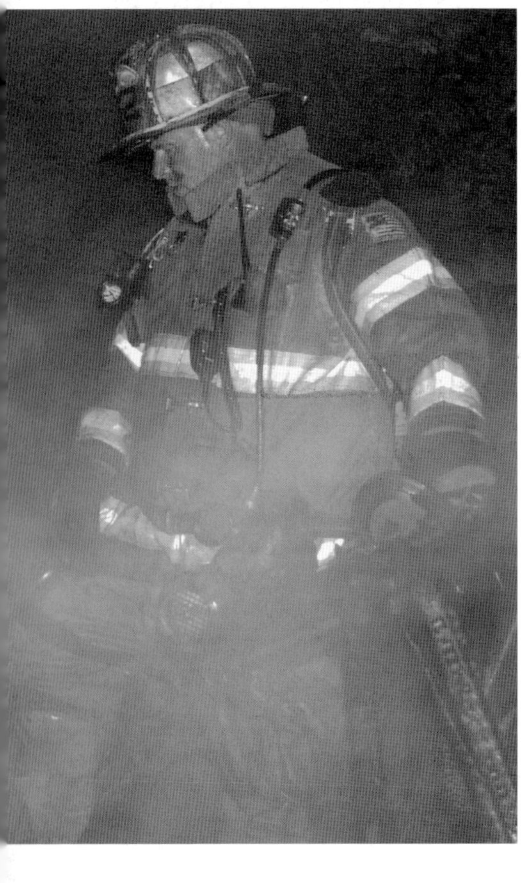

David Morin

David "Dave" Morin is a captain on the Hudson Fire Department and has been a member of the department for over 30 years, first joining the department in 1981 as a call firefighter. He became a full-time member of the department in 1984, achieving the rank of lieutenant in 1997 and captain in 2007. He is a dedicated, caring firefighter, as well as the department's historian and newsletter editor-in-chief. He has been involved in various town events and activities through the years and was instrumental in the construction of the Firefighters' Memorial at Hammond Park on Central Street, chairing that committee. In fact, one of the sketches in the granite is of Morin and his daughter, Taylor. Dave Morin was also chairman of the 9/11 Memorial at Benson Park. Among Dave's accomplishments are heading the annual Muscular Dystrophy Boot Drive, CPR community instructor, St. Vincent de Paul volunteer, member of the honor guard, president of the Hudson Firefighters Relief Association, and many other activities. Awards include the Purple Cross in 1996 and 1998, 1997 VFW, Hudson Grange and State Grange Firefighter of the Year, Chief's Award in 2000, 2009, and 2011, Distinguished Service Award, and 2012 Greater Hudson Chamber of Commerce Citizen of the Year. If Dave Morin is on the team, everything is under control and done well. Dave and his wife, Sue, have two grown children: son Corey, who is also a firefighter, and daughter Taylor. (Both, courtesy Hudson Fire Department.)

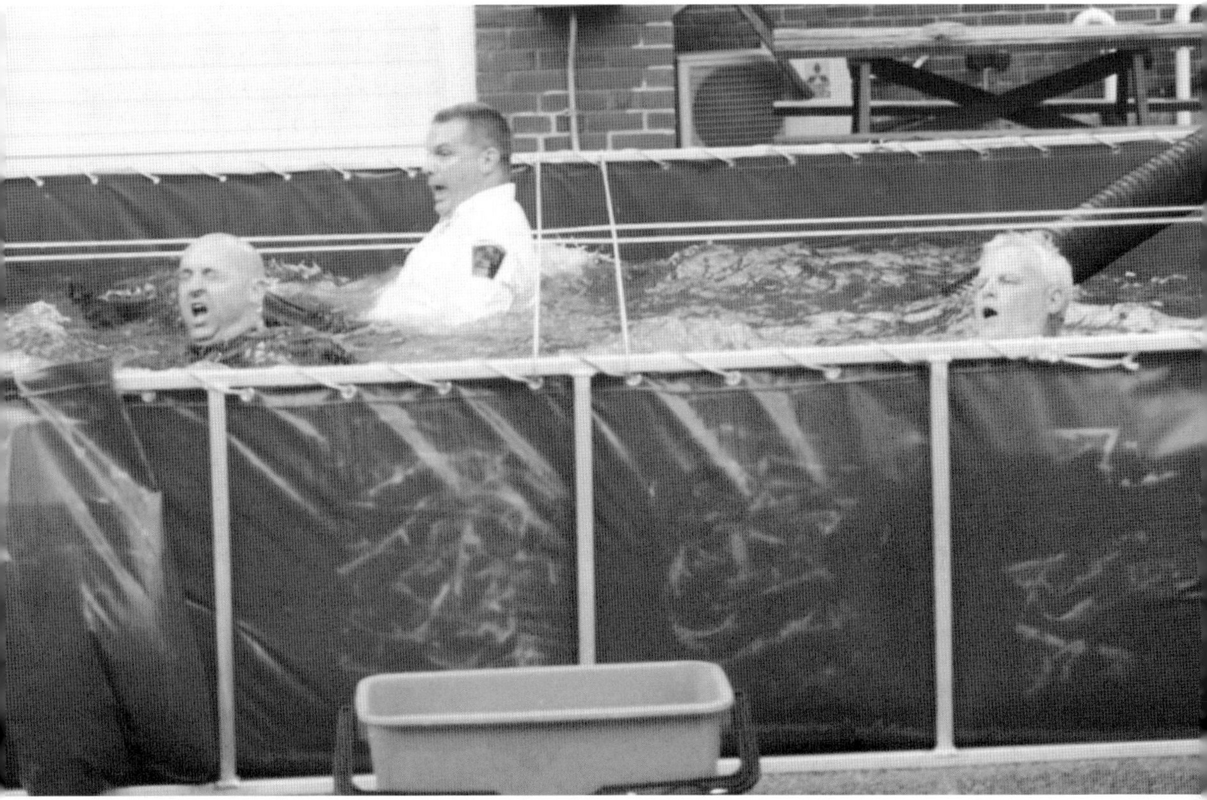

Robert "Rob" Buxton and the Ice Bucket Challenge

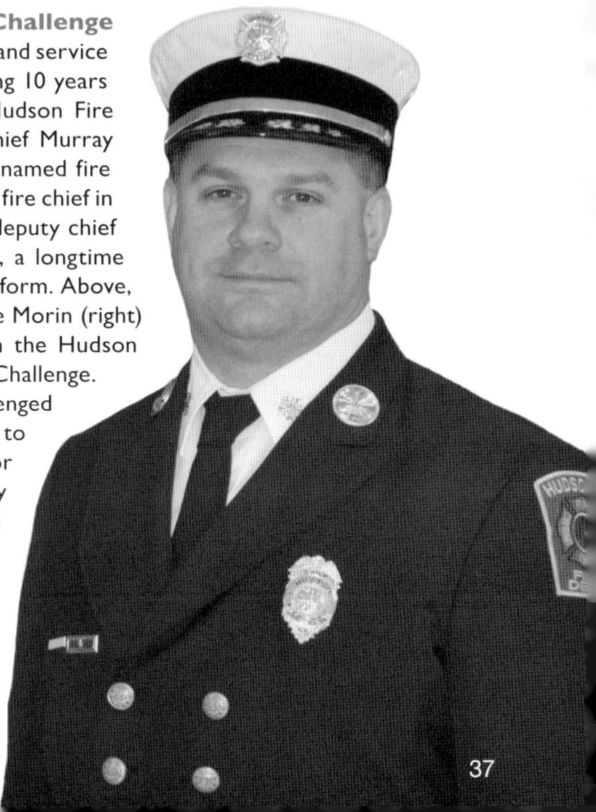

Robert Buxton comes from a long line of firefighters, and service is in his blood. A 22-year veteran firefighter, including 10 years in Nashua, Rob became deputy fire chief of the Hudson Fire Department under Chief Shawn Murray. When Chief Murray retired to work in Massachusetts, Rob Buxton was named fire chief in 2013. He is a son of Michael Buxton, who was fire chief in Nashua; is a grandson of Robert Buxton, who was deputy chief in Hudson; and is a great-grandson of Paul Buxton, a longtime firefighter in Hudson. Rob is shown in his Class A uniform. Above, Chief Rob Buxton (center) is shown with Capt. Dave Morin (right) and firefighter David Cormier (left) participating in the Hudson Fire Department's version of the ALS Ice Bucket Challenge. During the summer of 2014, people were challenged to dump buckets of ice water over themselves to promote awareness and raise money to find a cure for amyotrophic lateral sclerosis (ALS). (Above, courtesy *Hudson-Litchfield News*; right, courtesy Hudson Fire Department.)

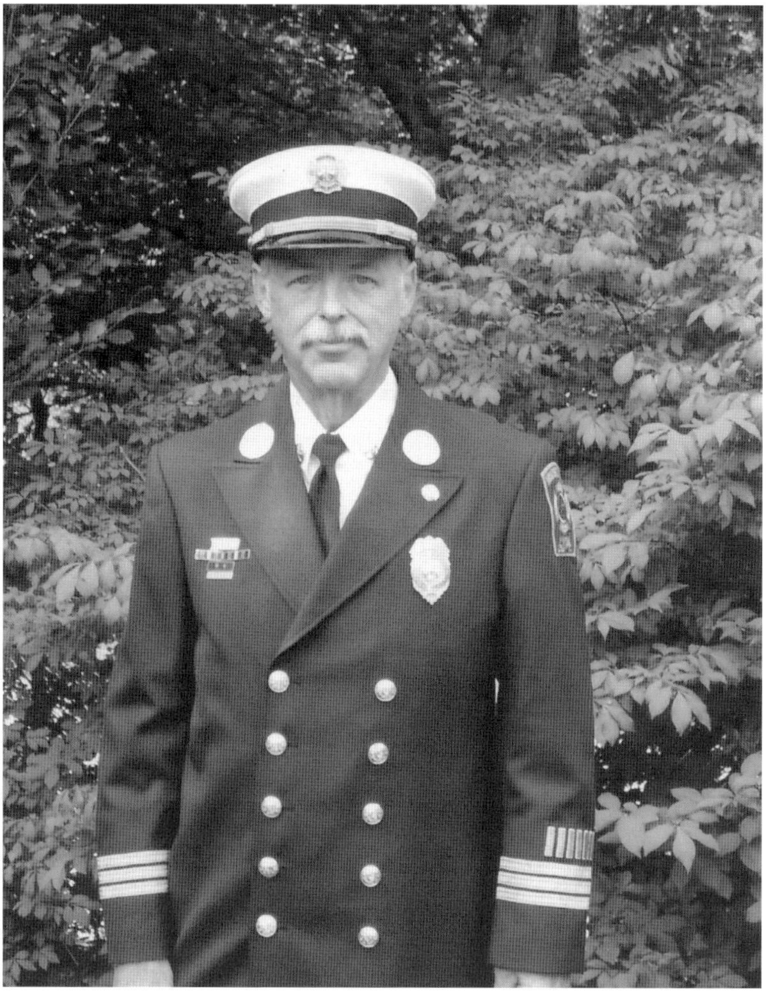

Gary Rodgers

Gary Rodgers joined the Hudson Fire Department as a junior firefighter in 1972 under Chief Oscar Campbell. He graduated from Alvirne High School in 1976 and became an auxiliary, then a call firefighter, and was hired as a full-time firefighter in October 1978 under the CETA (Comprehensive Employment and Training Act) program. Once that program ended, the town hired Gary in 1979. He married his wife, Robin, in 1981. Through the years, Gary rose up the ranks, being promoted to lieutenant in 1986, captain in 1989, and acting fire chief in 1996. Gary became deputy chief in 1997 and retired on April 1, 2007. Gary was always known as one of the very best fire ground officers, remaining calm and in control of a situation, whether it was a structure fire or motor vehicle accident. Gary has also been an active member of the community. He was named Hudson Citizen of the Year in 2000 and was elected district governor of New Hampshire Lions Clubs International in 2002. He served on numerous boards as a member and as chairman, including the Hudson Historical Society and its Hudson Old Home Days Committee, the Hudson School Board, and the Hudson Firefighter Relief Association, of which he is a lifetime member. He chaired the Hudson Fire Department Centennial, is a member of the Hudson Chamber of Commerce, and is a lifetime member of the New Hampshire Association of Fire Chiefs. Gary and Robin have two grown, married children. Their son Jeffrey is married to Kathleen. Their daughter Kate is married to Bob Dufour and they have two daughters, Lyla Elizabeth and Adria. Gary is a son of Alvin and Betty Rodgers. (Courtesy the Rodgers family.)

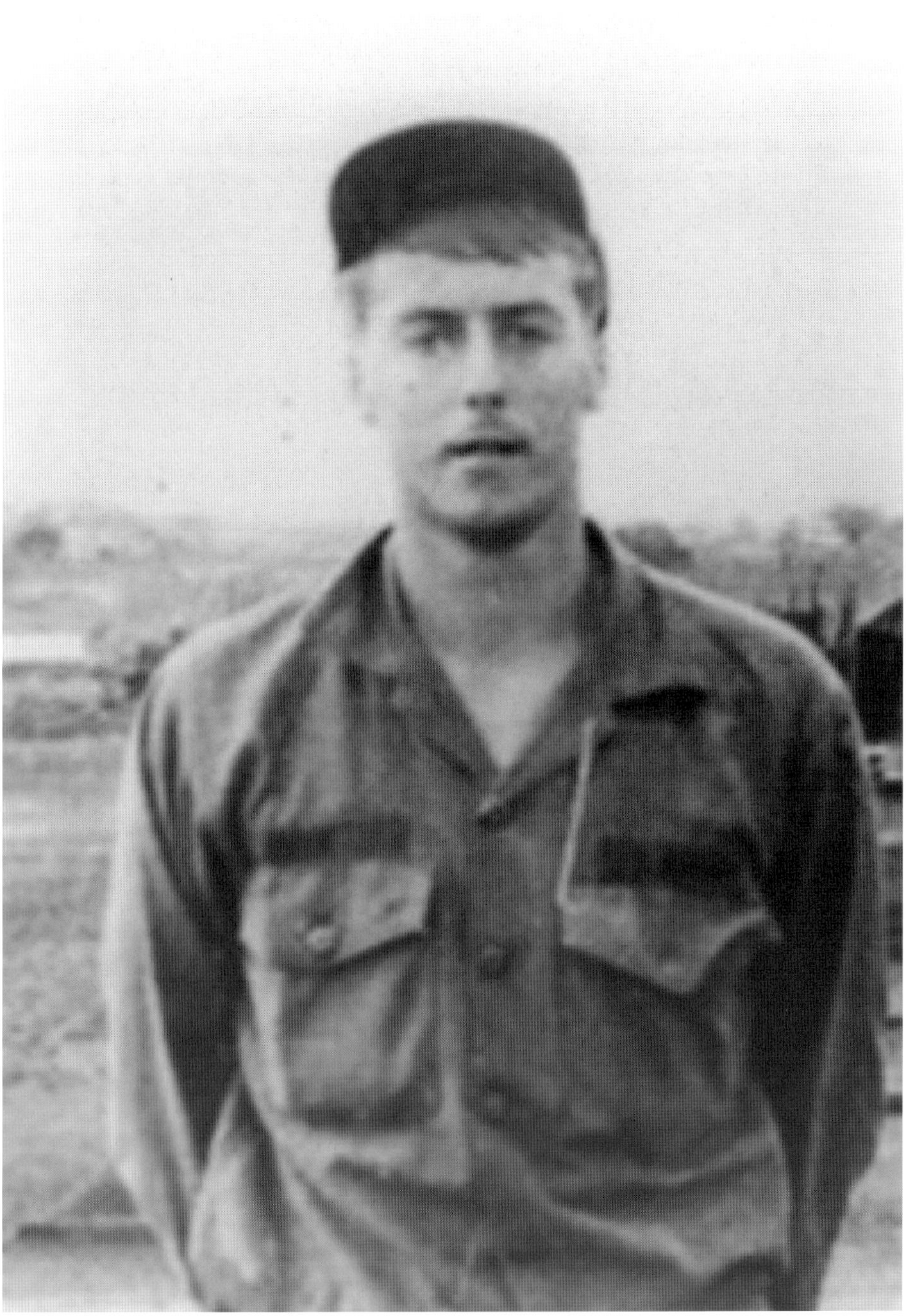

Leonard Nute
Leonard King Nute was a 1965 graduate of Alvirne High School. Specialist Four Nute was killed in action on May 25, 1967, in the Vietnam War, the first Hudson serviceman to give his life during that conflict. He was posthumously awarded the Bronze Star and the Purple Heart for meritorious service. The Republic of Vietnam also honored his bravery and service with the Military Merit Medal and the Gallantry Cross. Hudson dedicated the Memorial School gymnasium in his memory on October 29, 1967. (Courtesy Virtual Vietnam Veterans Wall of Faces.)

Frank Nutting

It was under the leadership of Chief Frank Nutting that the Hudson Fire Department became a modern full-time department with an ambulance service. Frank served as a member of the department from 1941 to 1984, becoming the first full-time chief in Hudson upon the retirement of Chief Oscar Campbell in 1972. He resigned his seat on the board of selectmen, which he had held continuously since 1950, to take the position. Under Chief Nutting's leadership, the first full-time firefighters and the ambulance service were soon added. An often-told story within the department was that on the night of the Alvirne Fire in 1974, Frank was in Wells, Maine. It was decided that he needed to be notified, and he signed on the scene 45 minutes later, a rather incredible feat. In order to site the two outlying stations, he used a map and compass to insure that the maximum number of homes were within a three-mile radius of a station; this was to insure a lower fire insurance rate for almost everyone in town. He was always looking to save money for the taxpayers, while at the same time providing the best services. In one notable example, when the Burns Hill Fire Station was built, he used the ladder truck to put the roof trusses in place. Both the Burns Hill and Robinson Road stations were built using as much volunteer labor (primarily members of the department) as possible, just as the Central Station had been built in 1950. A few years before his retirement, the selectmen felt that compared to other employees, he was underpaid. Nutting refused a raise, stating that he did not need any more money. After 42 years with the department, he retired as chief and walked away. It was a difficult thing to do, but he never wanted to be seen as second-guessing the new chief by showing up at the scene of a fire. Upon his retirement, the front cover of the 1984 report featured a drawing of Nutting and Central Fire Station. In 2010, Chief Nutting died at age 95 in Wells, Maine, and the Hudson Town Report was dedicated to him. (Courtesy Hudson Fire Department.)

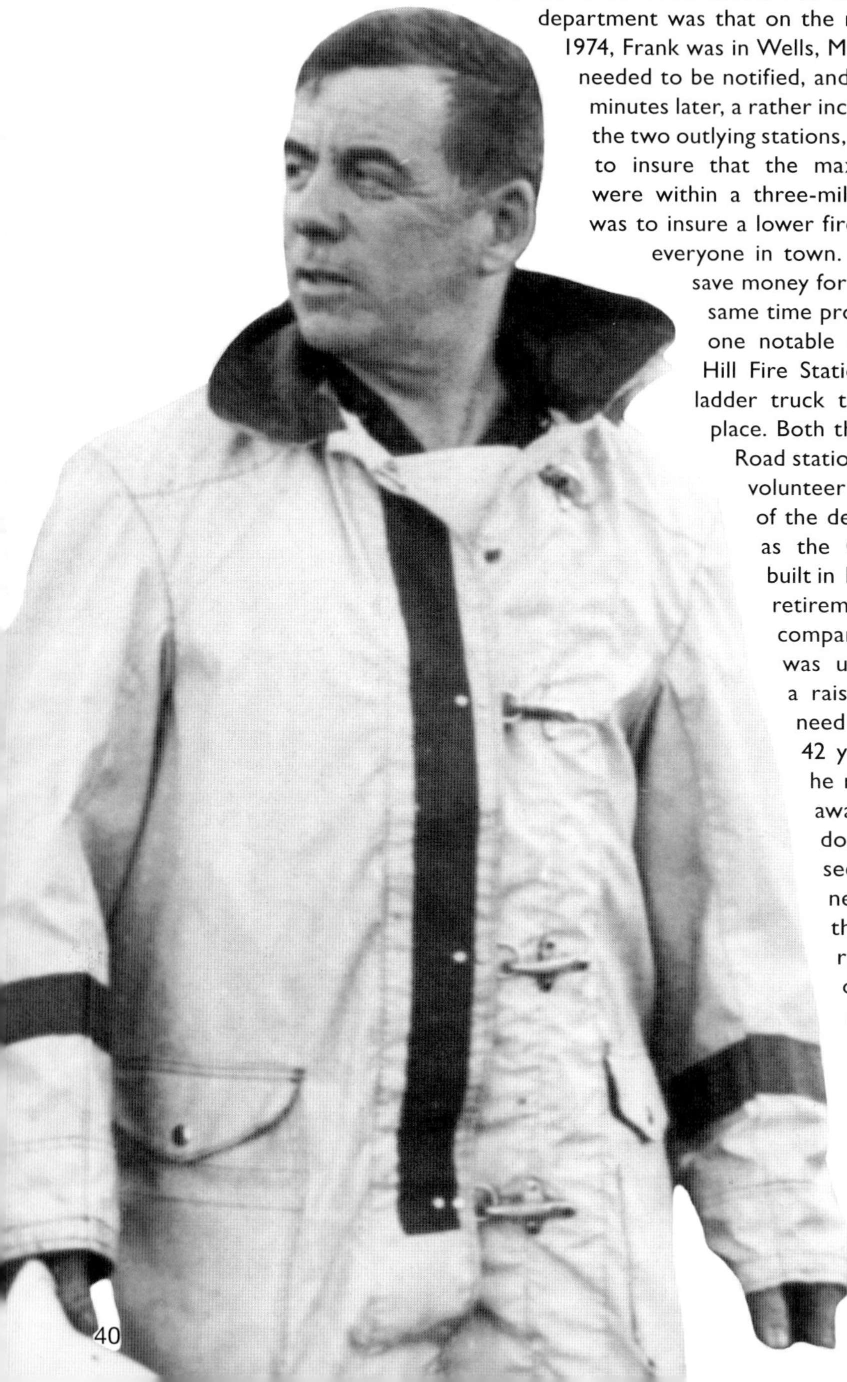

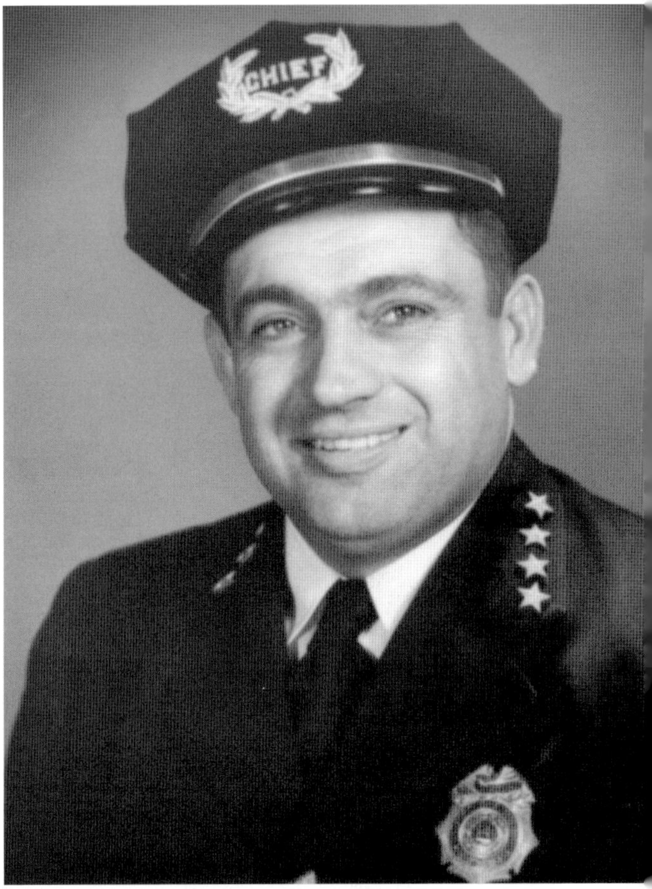

Andrew Polak

Andrew Polak was police chief for Hudson for 26 years, retiring in 1972 after 34 years in the department. He started as a police officer in 1938 and was appointed chief after Harry Connell retired. His wife, Stella, worked out of their home as dispatcher for the department. In his life, he was also a semi-professional wrestler, a state legislator, and Hillsborough County deputy sheriff. In 2000, Andrew Polak donated his police uniform to the Hudson Historical Society and shared many stories from his days on the department. Here, the chief is show in uniform; the photograph below is of him and his wife, Stella, at the Hudson Historical Society in 2000. Andrew Polak died on April 3, 2006, at 94 years old. (Both, courtesy HHS.)

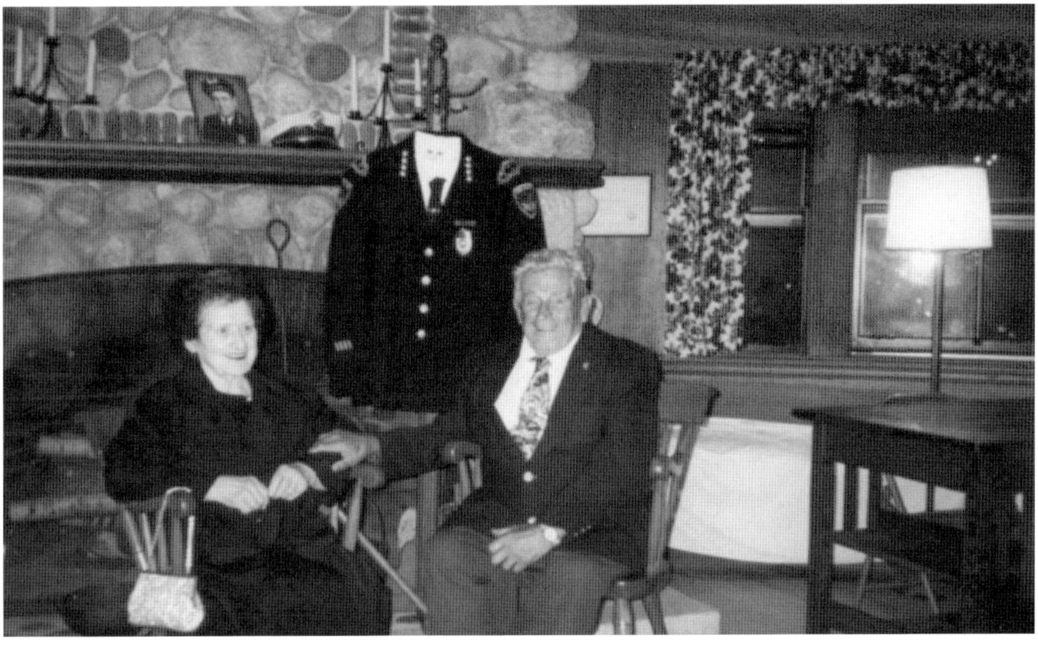

Richard "Dick" Gendron

Gendron started with the Hudson Police Department as a part-time officer in 1978. He was hired full time in September 1979, attended the New Hampshire Police Academy in 1980, and worked as a patrol officer until March 1985, when he was promoted to sergeant. Promoted to lieutenant in September 1985 and then to captain in 1987, he was responsible for the operations division, both patrol and detectives. The Hudson Town Council promoted Dick to acting police chief in 1990. Although he was offered the position of chief, he was reluctant to accept because he had 12 years of experience on the Hudson force, and the political climate was not good at the time. Dick accepted the position in December 1993 with the understanding that the Hudson Board of Selectmen would work with him to reorganize the department, change the philosophy of the agencies, review salaries, and construct a much-needed new police facility.

In 1995, the police department moved into a brand new 14,000-square-foot facility on Constitution Drive. Prior to that, the department's headquarters had been in the basement of town hall. Nearly 20 years later, the police station on Constitution Drive still looks brand new both inside and out, a tribute to the hardworking men and women of the department. The new facility reflected a new era. With the support of the board of selectmen, the department initiated major changes in the way it policed and implemented the principles of community policing. Under Chief Gendron's leadership, the department created school resource officers, citizen police academies, police baseball cards, participation in Old Home Days, mountain bike patrols, and a neighborhood crime watch.

In 1999, Chief Gendron attended the National FBI Academy in Quantico, Virginia, for 13 weeks. In 2003, the Hudson Police Department became only the seventh police agency in the state of New Hampshire to be awarded by the Commission on Accreditation for Law Enforcement Agencies (CALEA). In 2009, after 31 years with the department, Chief Gendron retired. Dick and his wife, Lynn (Colburn), who have been married since 1976, now live in central Florida. They have two adult children: Jonathan and Amie. They also have one granddaughter. Chief Gendron is shown here with fire chief Shawn Murray, who was hired as assistant chief in May 2001 and became chief in December 2003. He retired in 2013. (Courtesy Hudson Fire Department.)

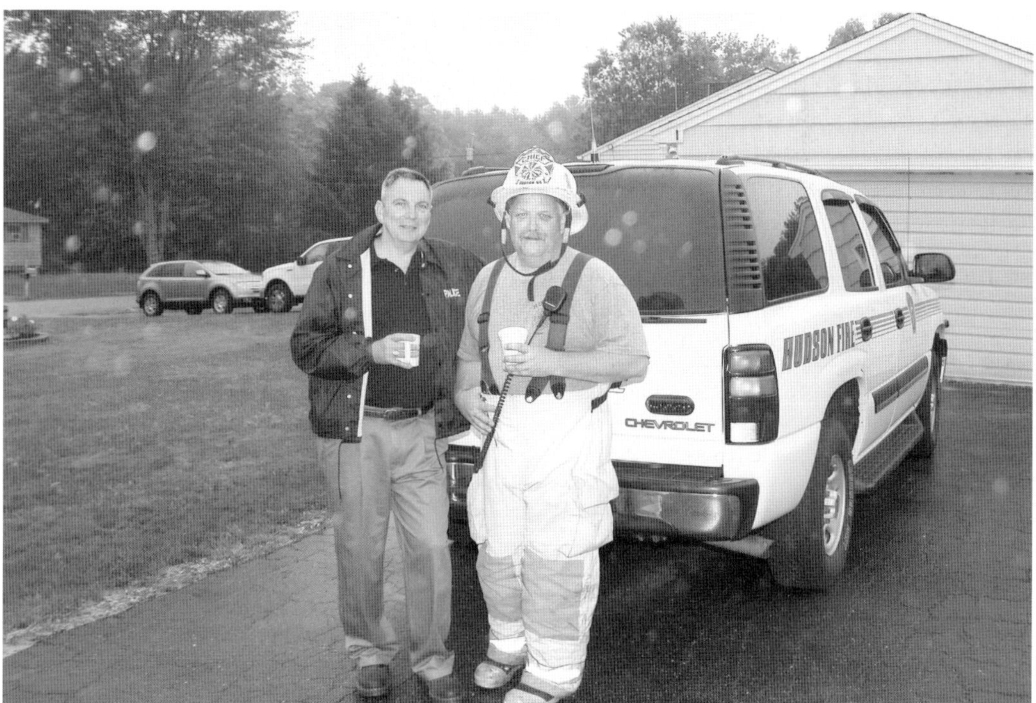

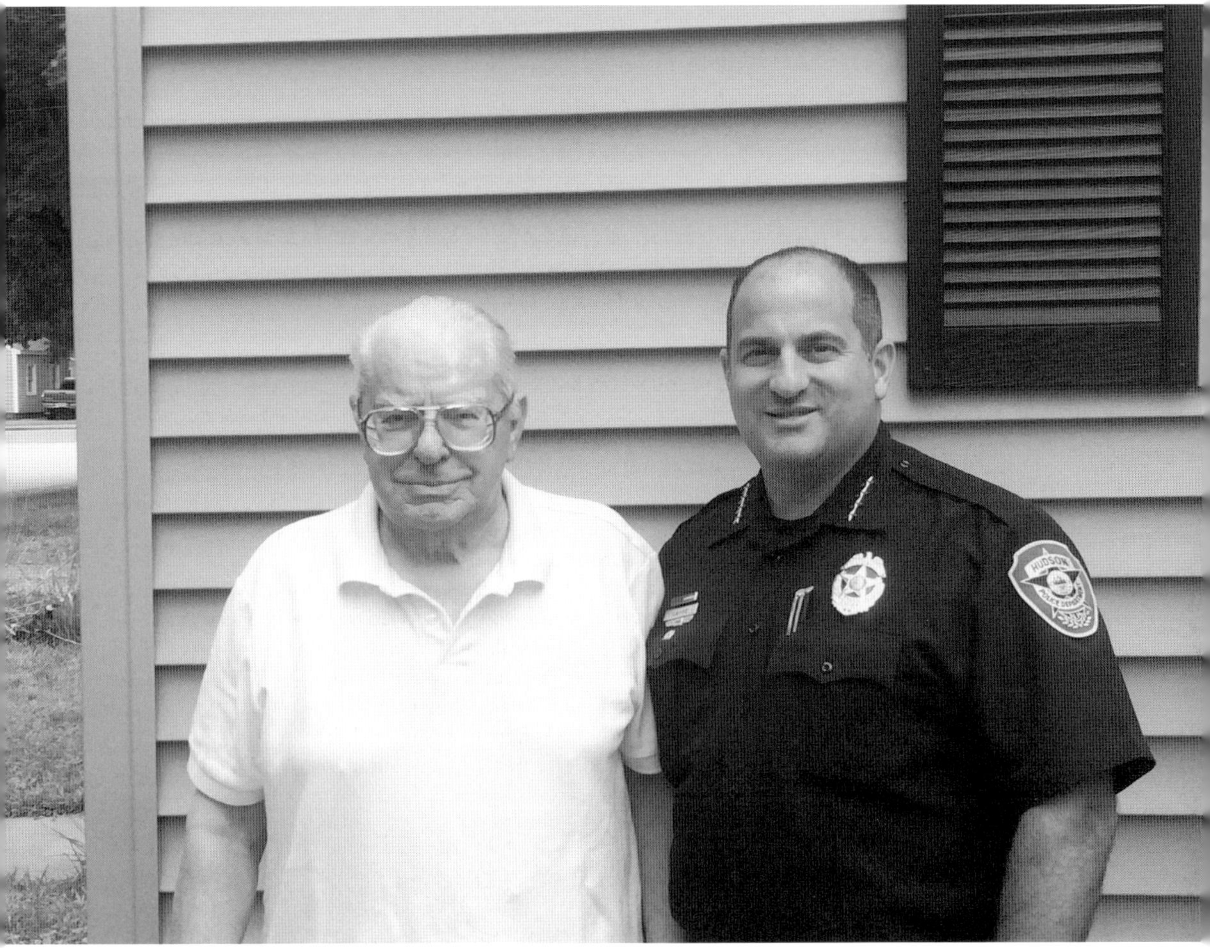

Jason Lavoie
Police chief Jason Lavoie's family has been part of the community for 60 years. His father, John Lavoie Sr., worked at times for Jasper Poultry Farms and for David Campbell, who was a vegetable farmer and chief of police in Litchfield. His brother John Lavoie Jr. was a member of the town council for a period of time. John's wife, Beth, is a graduate of Alvirne, as are John and Jason, and she is a longtime teacher at Alvirne. Jason's grandfather Lucius Salter worked at Benson's in the early 1940s with the horses as well as feeding the lions and tigers. John Sr., John Jr., and Jason have all coached youth sports for a combined total of about 50 seasons. Jason is a graduate of Plymouth State College and was hired by acting chief Richard Gendron in 1991; he was hired to succeed Chief Gendron upon his retirement in 2009. The Lavoie family is very proud of their record of community service and even prouder to call Hudson their home. (Courtesy the Lavoie family.)

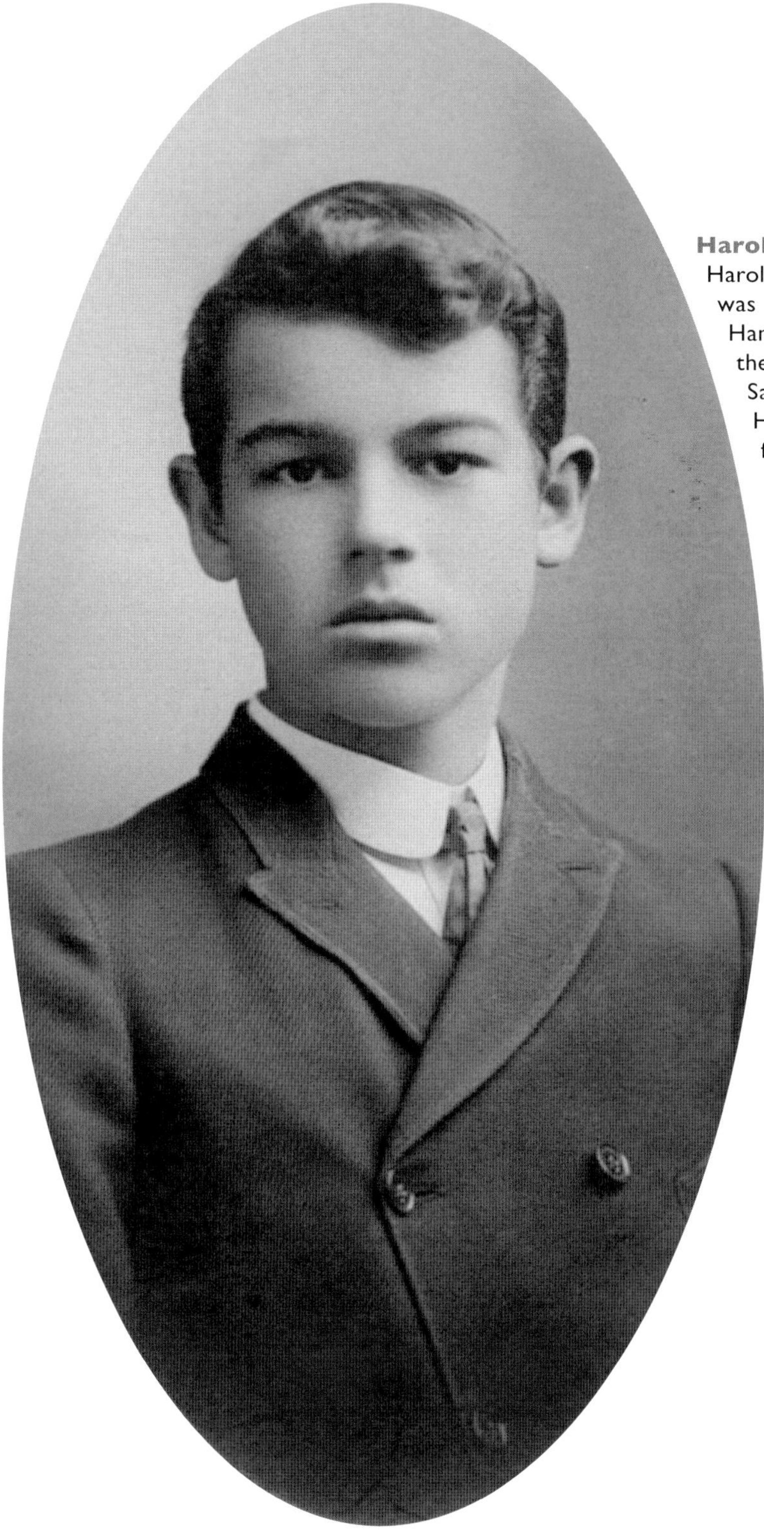

Harold Spaulding
Harold Merrill Spaulding was born in Hudson, New Hampshire, in 1889. He was the son of Charles Laton and Sarah (Merrill) Spaulding. He worked as a locomotive fireman for the New England Gas and Coke Company in Everett, Massachusetts, and in 1917, he registered for the draft during World War I. He died in 1920 at the age of 31 in France. Three maple trees were planted near Library Park by women of the Grand Army of the Republic in memory of three servicemen from Hudson who died as a result of World War I: Privates Harold Merrill Spaulding, Leland H. Woods, and Carlton L. Petry. (Courtesy HHS.)

CHAPTER FOUR

Education

There are few things more important in life than education, and Hudson has been blessed with more than a few people who have dedicated their working lives and beyond to the town's children. In the early days of the town, the records are silent, and it was not until 1766 that the town first mentioned raising money for education. In those early years, the town was broken into four districts, and it is very likely that then and even prior to that children were taught in their homes. It was not until 1806 that the first of the 10 schoolhouses were built around town. Kimball Webster could find no record of school attendance prior to 1847, but the population of the town was virtually unchanged since the building of the schoolhouses. In 1847, winter sessions were attended by 346 students. At that time, all of the teachers were men from prominent families in town. Each school district operated independently, and the money raised for the schoolhouse came from the families in each district. It was not until 1885 that the town became one school district. Kimball Webster and Dr. D.O. Smith were two of the first three school board members in town. It was at that time that schoolhouses were closed or consolidated due to enrollments as small as seven students; the number of schools was then seven. The school year was increased from 21.7 weeks to 30. It was not until 1896 that the Smith School (at Hudson Center) and the Kimball Webster School were built. Over the next 40 years, all of the one-room schoolhouses closed, Webster School received an addition as well as a portable classroom, and the Smith School burned and was replaced with the Hudson Center School (located on Kimball Hill Road, on the east side, nearly across from the Senior Center). In 1939, Hudson received money through the Depression-era Work Projects Administration (WPA) and was able to build a junior high school. It is known today as the Dr. H.O. Smith Elementary School. Alvirne High School opened in 1950; prior to this, high school students went to Nashua. The 1950s saw a rapid school-age population growth, and children were taught in the library, the fire station, and the modern-day American Legion Building, while the district struggled to meet the needs and financial ability of the town. Buildings and additions were added rapidly after that until the year 2000, when the last projects to expand capacity took place.

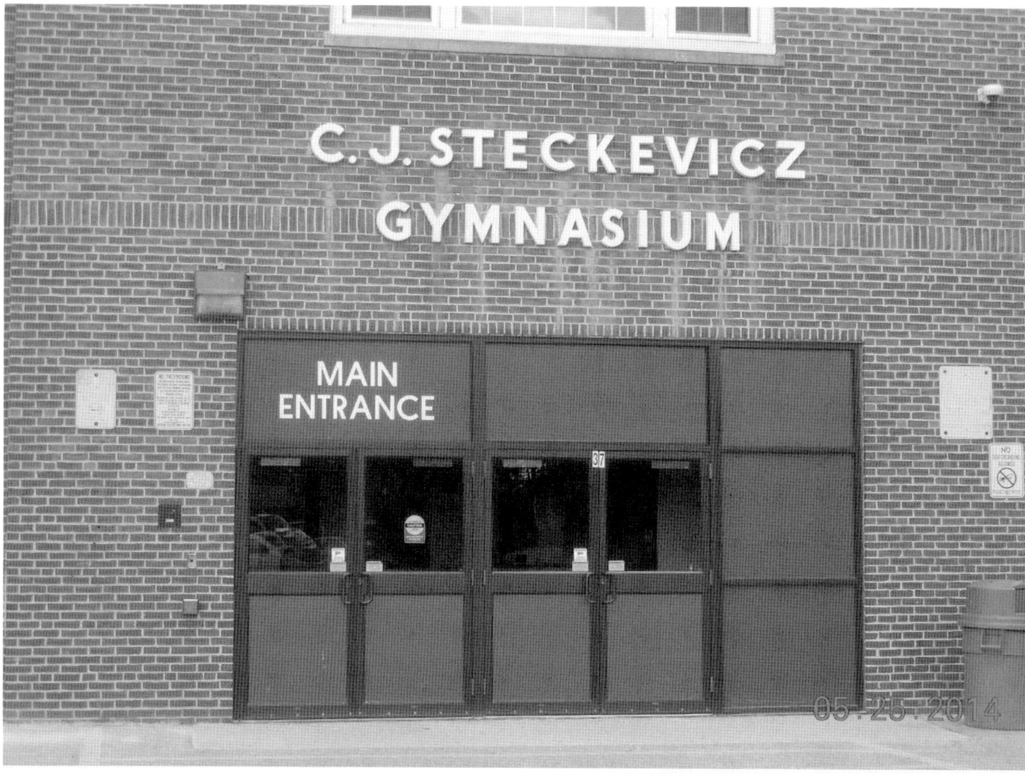

Chester "Chet" J. Steckevicz

Chester "Chet" Steckevicz was the principal of Alvirne High School from 1957 until 1972. He died suddenly on June 10, 1972, at the age of 49, shortly before Alvirne's graduation. Classes were cancelled at Alvirne High School on June 13, the day of his funeral, out of respect for the well-liked and universally admired principal. Chet served in the Army in World War II. The summer of 1972 began the Steckevicz-Alvirne Quarter Plan at the school, a year-round concept designed to give a wider choice of studies and short-term quarters. At the rededication of Alvirne High School in December 1975, after the devastating fire of 1974, the gymnasium was named in honor of Chester Steckevicz. (Above, courtesy L. Jasper; right, courtesy HHS.)

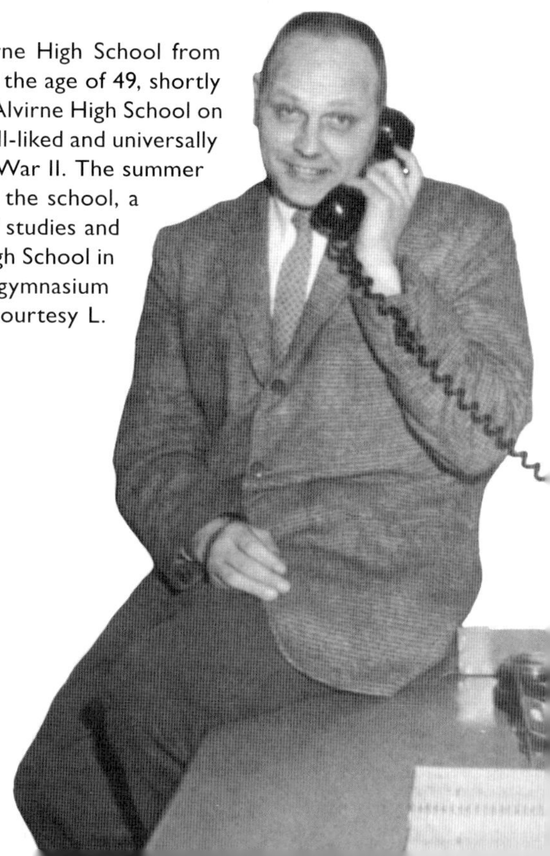

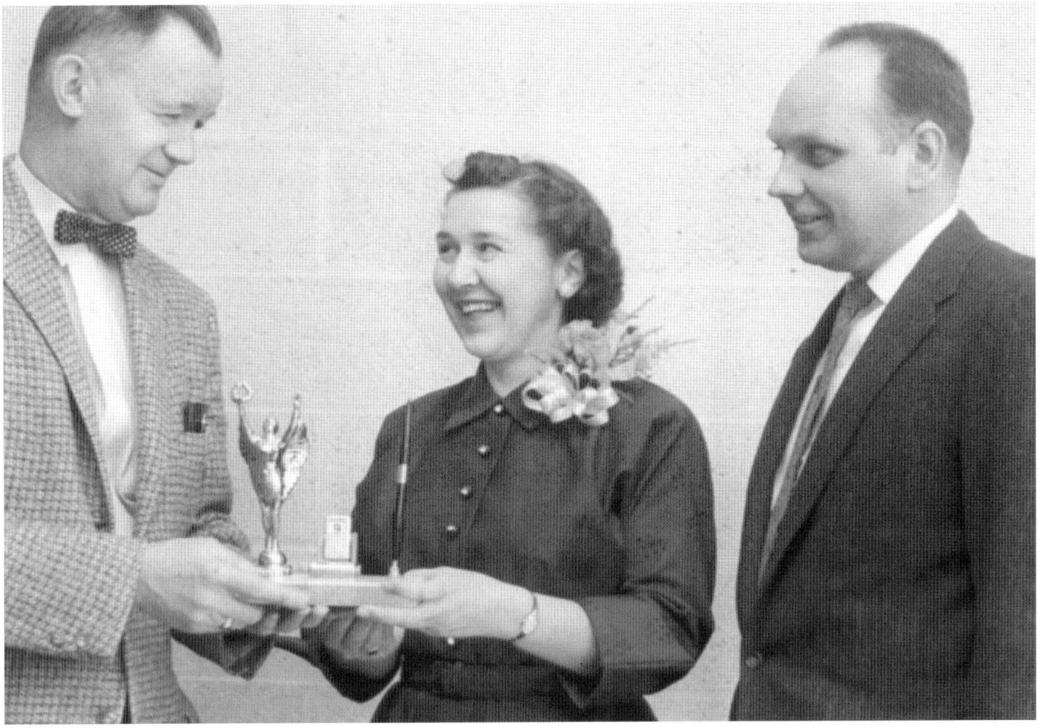

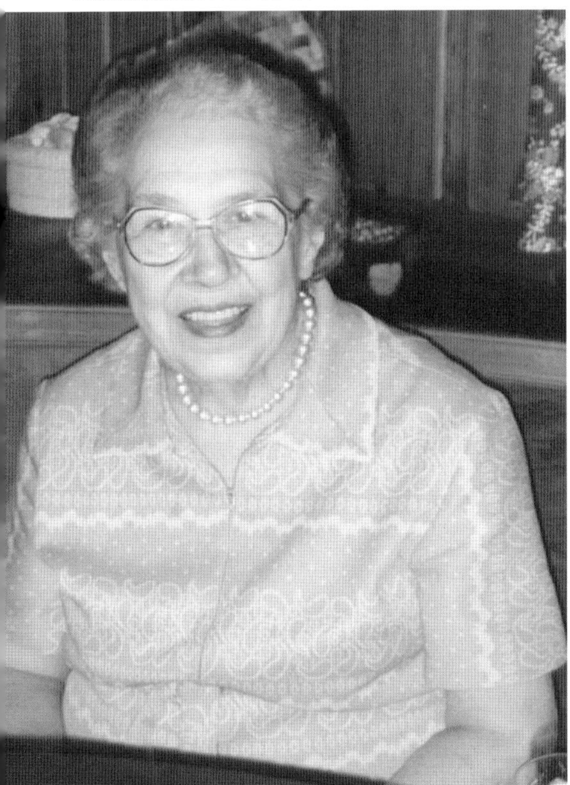

Barbara Fuller

Barbara Fuller was a beloved teacher in Hudson for over 40 years. In addition to teaching, she was also a longtime guidance counselor at Alvirne and faculty advisor for several student groups. Barbara was also an active member of the community; as a member of the Hudson Fortnightly Club, she helped bring Hudson history up to date. She was also involved in the 4-H Club and Girls' Camp for many years and active in the Hudson Community Church. In 1958, she was selected Teacher of the Year by the Hudson Fortnightly Club and received her award from superintendent Louis Ramsey and Alvirne principal Chester Steckevicz, who was also a former pupil. She was surprised with the added accolade of being named New Hampshire Teacher of the Year by the New Hampshire Federation of Women's Clubs. Barbara retired in 1974 after 24 years at Alvirne High School and was the guest speaker at that year's graduation. She was senior class advisor, cofounder of Alvirne's National Honor Society, and yearbook advisor. After her retirement, she was an Alvirne trustee. She died in 2003. Barbara is seen above receiving the award from Louis Ramsey (left) and Chester Steckevicz and at left in her retirement. (Both, courtesy HHS.)

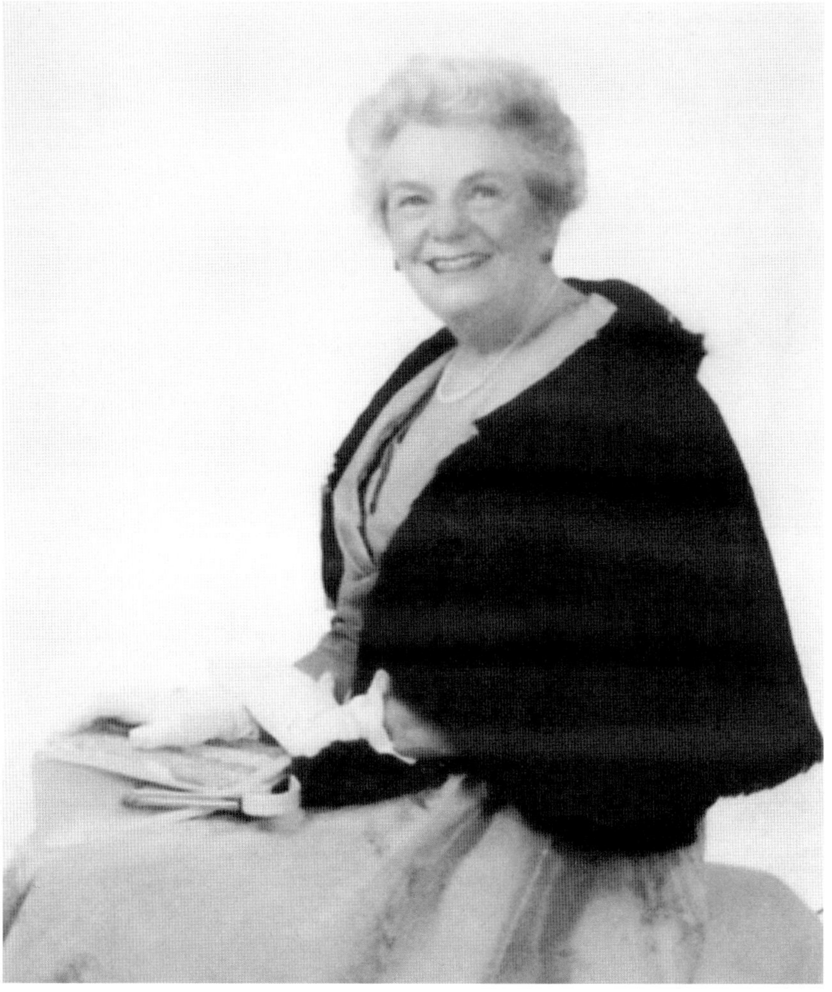

Maude French

Maude French grew up in Henniker, New Hampshire, and it was there that she married Harold French of Hudson (See page 84 for more on the French family). Their home was a former one-room schoolhouse (which has since burned down) on the Derry Road, which stood just south of Phillips Drive. The stove from that schoolhouse is now in the No. 9 schoolhouse on the Old Derry Road. It was there that they raised their children, Gordon, Richard, and Patricia. Maude was an active 4-H leader, and in 1936, her club took the honors of being the best 4-H Club in America. She served the town as a longtime library trustee, but she will best be remembered as the first teacher at Alvirne High School. On June 7, 1948, just hours before the deadline that would have ended Dr. Hills's dream of having a vocational high school on his family's homestead, Maude would gather 22 of her 4-H girls and teach the first class in the library of Dr. Hills's summer home, also named Alvirne. She ended up teaching a six-week course along with Principal Kenneth Gibbs, who taught agricultural classes to about a dozen boys. These students became the first graduating class of Alvirne on July 15, 1948. Maude still had to testify in court to prove the classes met the criteria to allow the school to continue, and she recalled being questioned long after everyone else had gone home and riding home on the bus alone, wondering if she had helped save or lose the school. Maude would go on to serve as the president of New Hampshire's General Federation Woman's Club. In 1971, she was named Hudson's Citizen of the Year. She was a longtime Alvirne trustee. Maude died in 1994 at age 90. (Courtesy *Hudson-Litchfield News*.)

Wilbur "Webb" Palmer

Wilbur "Webb" Palmer was born in Derry, New Hampshire, where he grew up on his family's farm and graduated from Pinkerton Academy in 1953. A graduate of the University of New Hampshire, he was a member of the Alpha Gamma Rho fraternity. He student taught at Alvirne High School in 1959 before being called to active duty in the Army. His first teaching assignment after being discharged from active duty was in Colebrook, New Hampshire. In 1963, Palmer was hired to teach math and science at Hudson Junior High School, now the Dr. H.O. Smith School. Due to space problems, the junior high was moved to Alvirne High School. His wife, Marge, taught English at Alvirne High School from 1963 through 1969, when she left to start a family. When Alvirne's agriculture teacher left, Webb was hired as his replacement but with the expectation that the program would be eliminated. Webb's tenacity and vision grew the program at Alvirne High School. Shawn Jasper recalls meeting Webb for the first time in 1972, when he and his father stopped by the high school on a Saturday to lend a hand to Webb, who was putting together a used greenhouse he had obtained for $500. The working farm and vocational programs are sources of pride for the community. Webb wrote a grant to the New Hampshire Department of Education, legislation was written, and the bill to provide $6.3 million for construction of the vocational center was signed into law. In 1993, the newly built Wilbur Palmer Vocational Center was dedicated to honor this hard-working man. The effort to name the center after him was a grassroots one; a petition was circulated around town by his former students and placed on the school district warrant. Although not initially supported by the school board, the article was adopted by a unanimous vote. Although Webb retired in 2001, he continues to serve Hudson as an Alvirne trustee. He has also been on the board of trustees for Eastern States Exposition (the Big E) for over 25 years, among other activities. Webb was a longtime officer in the Army Reserves; he retired with the rank of lieutenant colonel after 34 years of military service. Webb and his wife, Marge, still reside in Derry, where Webb is working on a book about his life. (Courtesy Alvirne High School.)

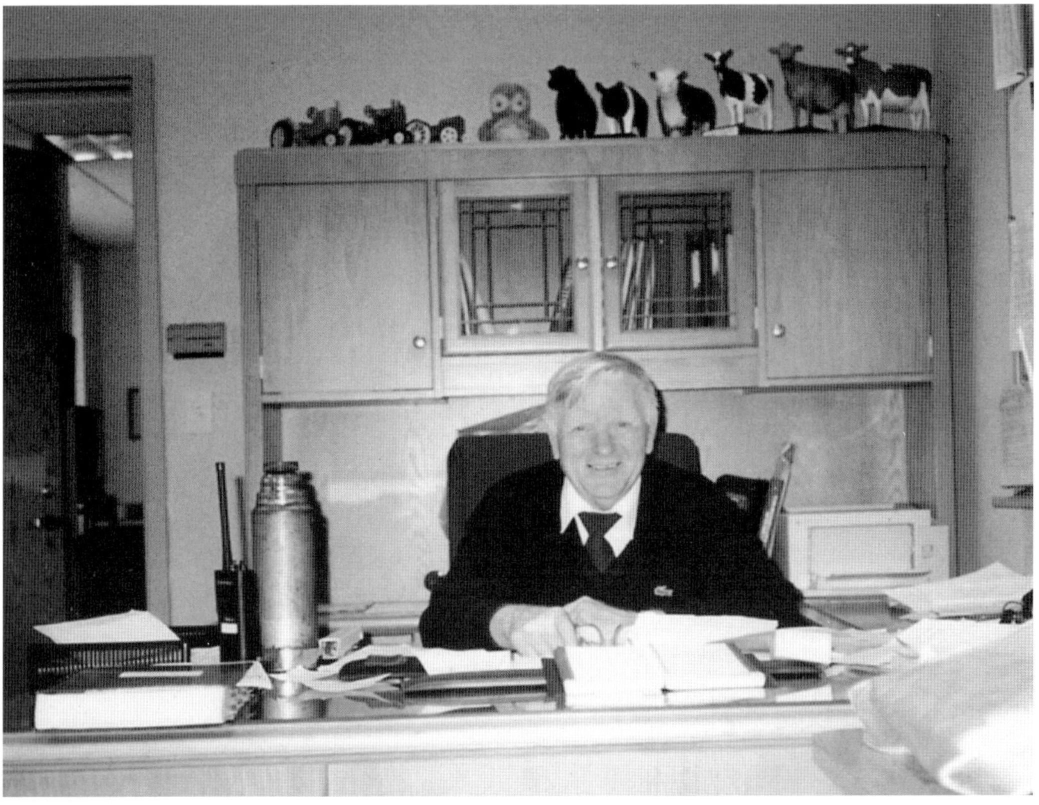

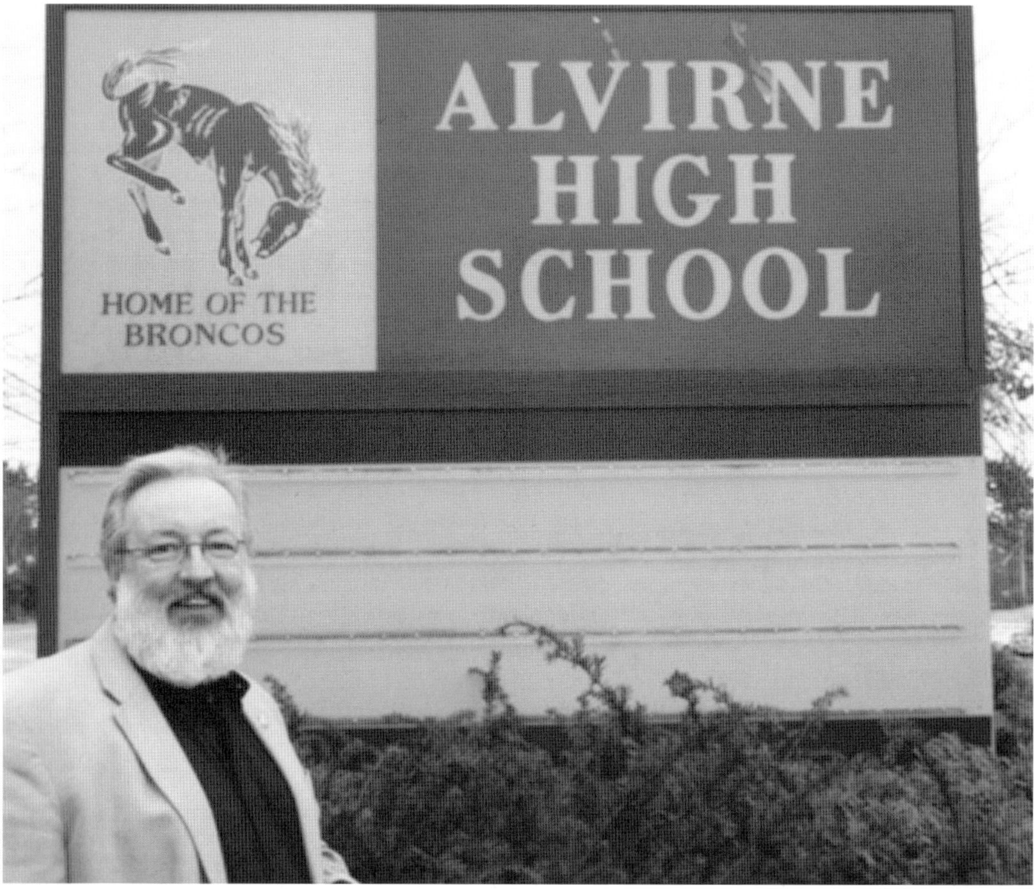
HOME OF THE
BRONCOS
ALVIRNE
HIGH
SCHOOL

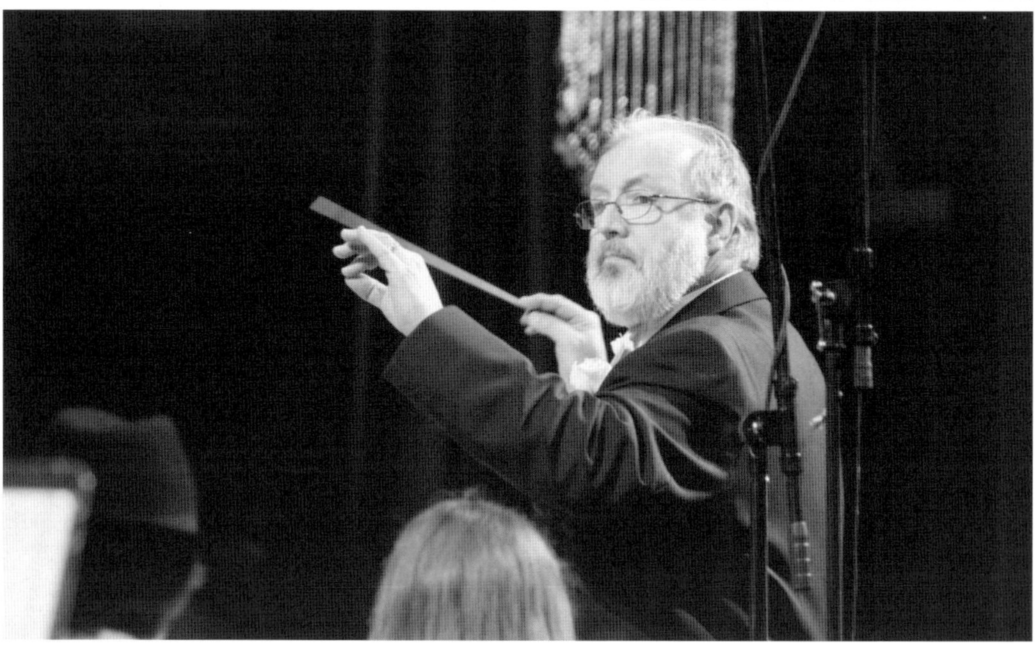

Gerry Bastien (BELOW AND OPPOSITE PAGE)
Gerry "Mr. B" Bastien has been Hudson School District's coordinator of music and director of bands at Alvirne High School since 1996. In addition to supervising, coordinating, and developing the district-wide program of music education and aligning the music curriculum with the National Music Education Standards and New Hampshire State Frameworks, Mr. B teaches marching, concert, symphonic, and jazz bands at Alvirne. With his amazing work ethic and energy, he has increased band membership from 32 in 1996 to 196 in 2014. He created and added the marching component to the band in 1997, and Alvirne High School's marching band works as hard as any sports team, starting with its annual band camp each August through Friday night football games and holiday parade seasons. Alvirne High School Bronco marching band and color guard have marched Main Street USA at Disneyworld (2002, 2006, 2010, and 2014) and performed their halftime marching show at Gillette Stadium in 2011. The concert band, jazz band, and newly formed symphonic band have traveled nationally and internationally to festivals and competitions, achieving superior ratings and many first place trophies. The jazz band has performed in Germany and Austria under Bastien's leadership. The band members also perform locally at town events, giving back to the supportive community. One of the most sought-after tickets in Hudson is to Alvirne High School's annual cabaret. For one weekend each spring, the school's gymnasium is transformed into a showcase for student talent. Each year it seems is the best cabaret ever, only to be outdone the following year.

Bastien is a charter and executive board member of the Alvirne Friends of Music Booster Organization and has received his own share of awards and accolades, including Distinguished Music Educator of the Year, Teacher of the Year from Wal-Mart, Sam's Club, and the Hudson Grange, and the VFW Loyalty Award three times. Alvirne High School band's motto is "Choose to. Want to. Love to."

Many Alvirne band alumni return to visit their mentor and keep in touch, and they have gone on to pursue degrees and work in the music field. He is very thankful to his loving wife, Dee, for all her help and support. Gerry and Dee became grandparents twice in 2013 with the birth of granddaughter Shelby Lee Bastien to son Dan and his wife, Liz, and granddaughter Catherin Pauline Bastien to son Jeff and his wife, Nicole.

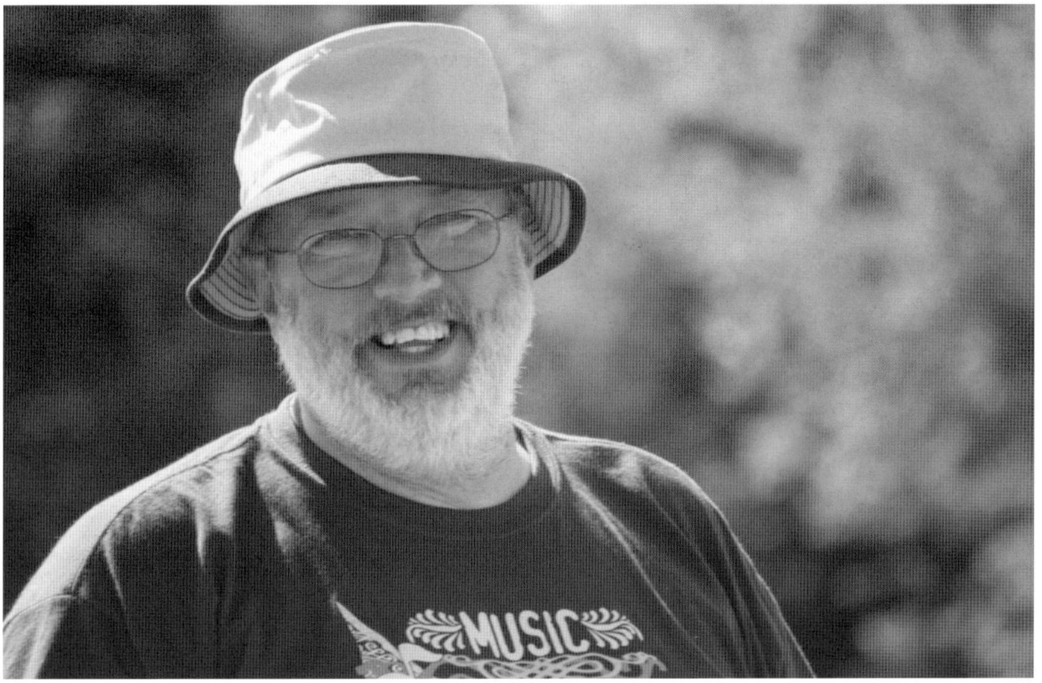

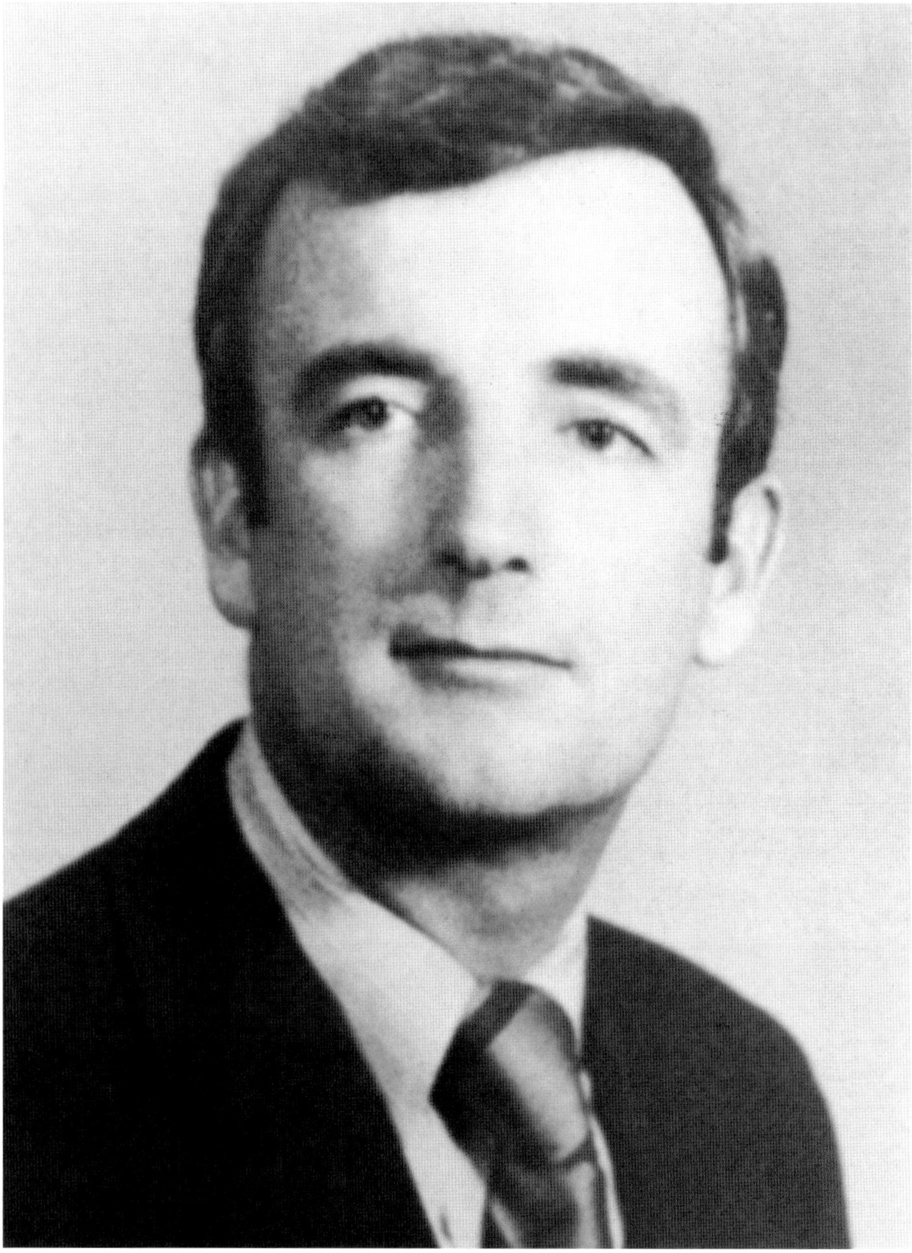

Peter Dolloff

Peter Dolloff was the superintendent of School Administrative Unit (SAU) 27, which combined Hudson and Litchfield School Districts, for 32 years. Hudson and Litchfield shared the SAU number until Hudson decided it was time for each town to be a separate entity and formed its own District 81 in 2003. During Peter's tenure as superintendent, he led the district's efforts to rebuild after the devastating Alvirne High School fire of 1974, accomplishing the entire process in just one year. He was also at the helm during the building of Nottingham West School in 1989. Retired since 1999, Peter Dolloff is an Alvirne trustee and is still active in Hudson activities. He resides in Hudson with his wife, Leona, and enjoys travel. (Courtesy HHS.)

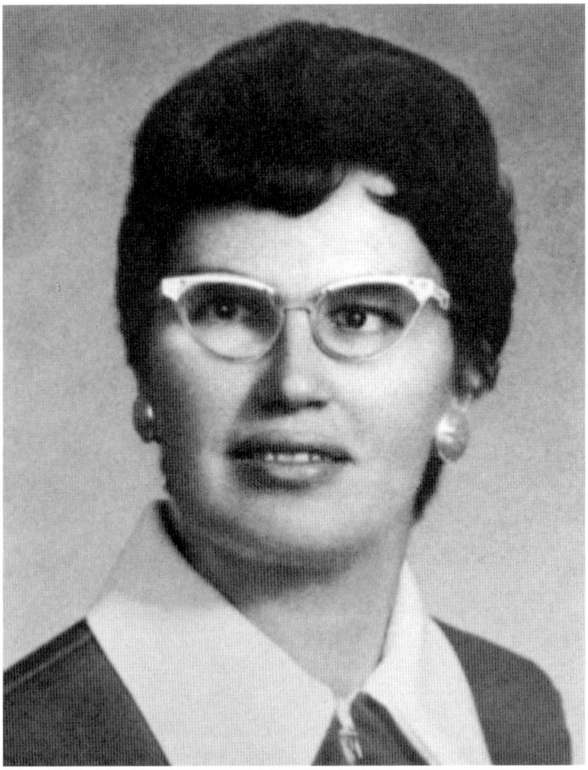

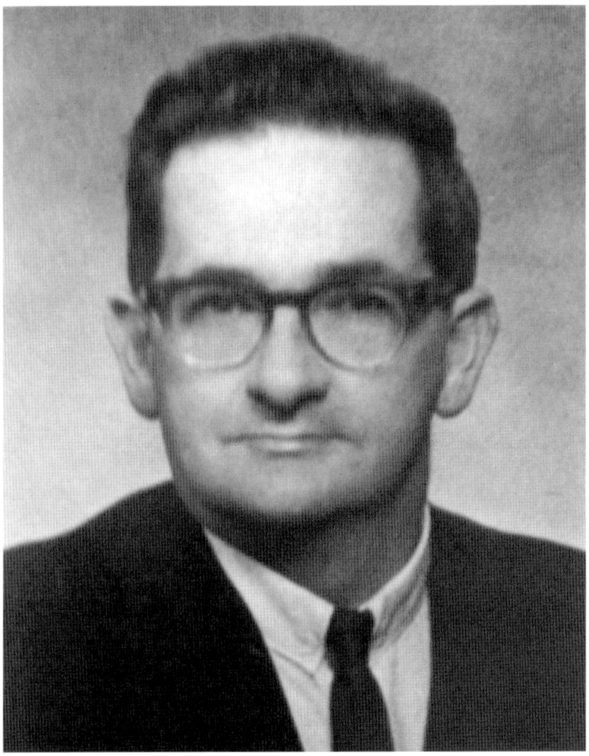

Ruth Grondin and Donald Shepherd
Ruth Grondin and Donald Shepherd are longtime Hudson residents. Both served on the school board together for many years, including the years during the Alvirne School fire and reconstruction. Both served as chairman of the school board at different times. Grondin and Shepherd are also current Alvirne trustees. That board is in charge of managing the money and the Alvirne Chapel bequeathed to Hudson by the late Dr. Alfred Kimball Hills and other members of his extended family. The Alvirne High School trustees work with the school board to provide extras to enrich high school curriculum and facilities. Recent projects accomplished with assistance from the Alvirne trustees include the new Alvirne elevator, the band room renovation, and the school's cupola.

Dalton Blodgett

Dalton Blodgett (show on right with New Hampshire commissioner of education Lionel Tracy) taught social studies and language arts for over 35 years before retiring from Hudson Memorial School in 1995. He was Social Studies Department chairman for 12 years and accompanied classes to Washington, DC, in 1987 and 1988. He was also the school's director of intramurals. In addition, Dalton was Hudson Memorial School's recreation director from 1962 to 1972. After his retirement in 1995, Dalton became an active school volunteer, averaging over 1,000 hours per year at Hudson Memorial School. In 2008, he received the Senior Volunteer of the Year honor at the annual New Hampshire Partners in Education Blue Ribbon Awards for his outstanding dedication and commitment. Dalton is one of the kindest, gentlest, and most giving people one could ever meet.

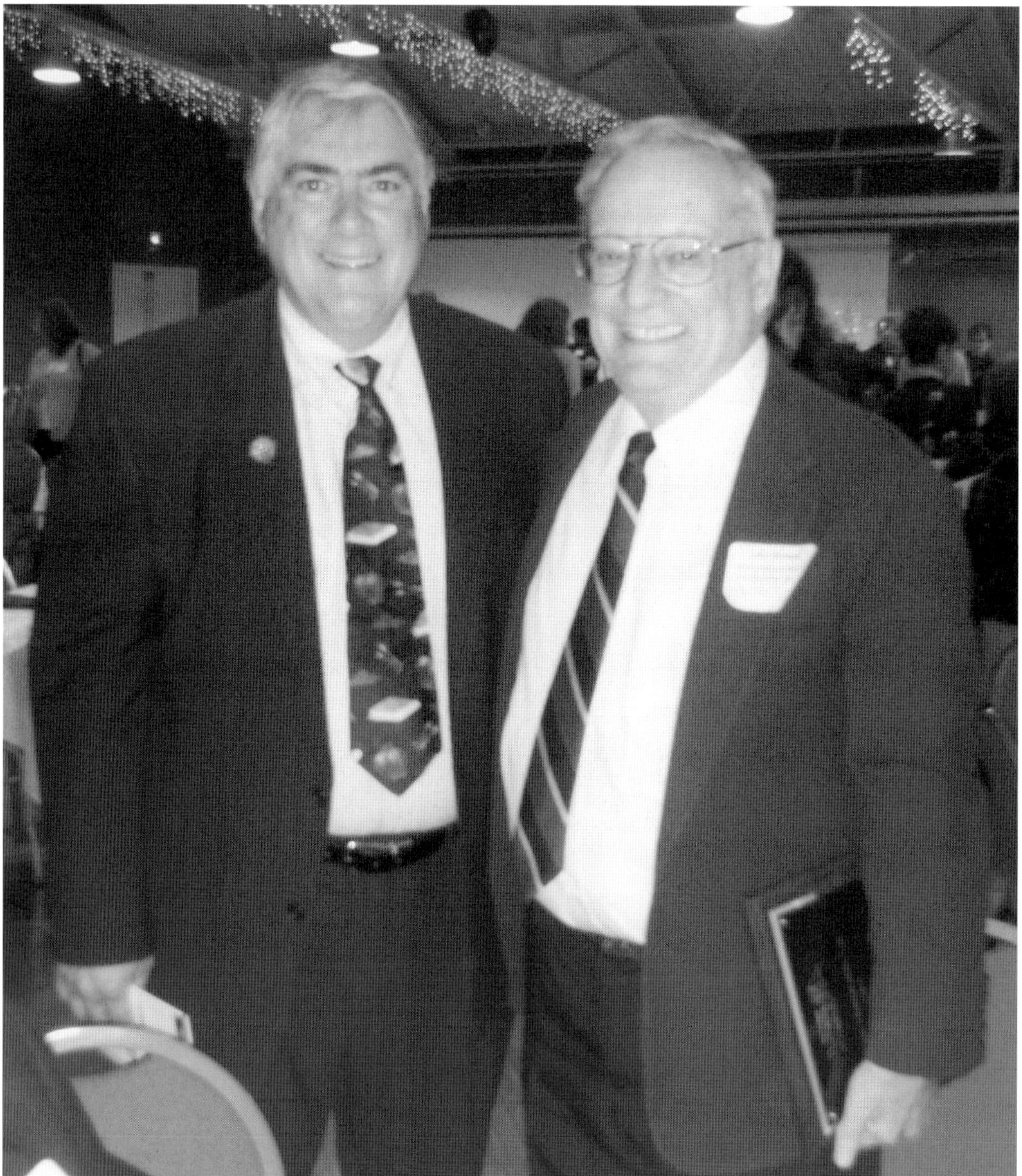

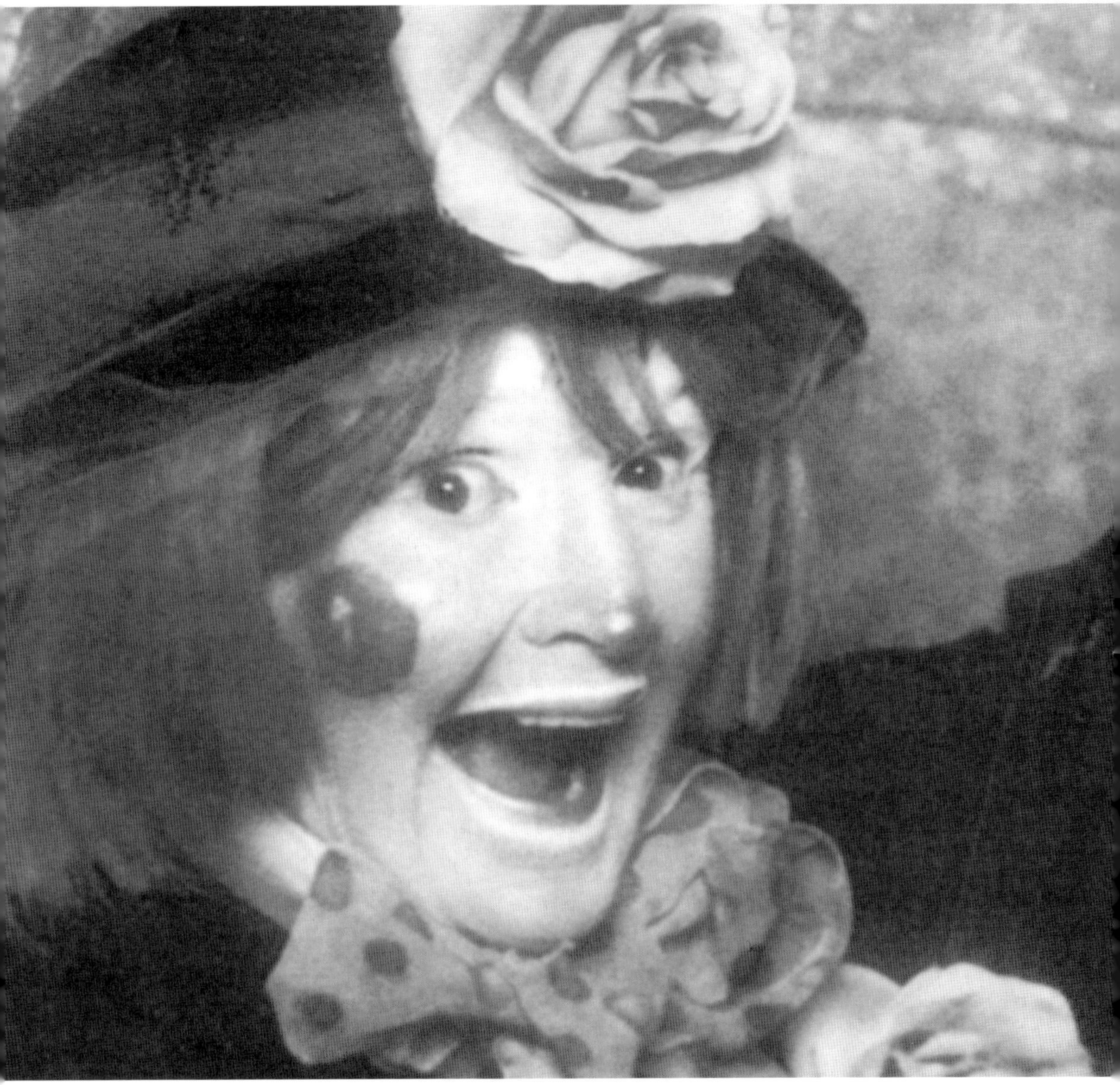

Beverly Landry
Beverly "Bev" Cluff Landry came to Hudson in 1968. She worked as a primary-grades teacher in the Hudson School District from 1969 to 1973. In 1973, she opened her own early childhood learning center on River Road, called Kinder World. What began as a small kindergarten for five-year-olds (there was no public kindergarten in Hudson at the time) expanded over time to offer readiness, pre-kindergarten, daycare, before- and after-school programs, summer camp, tutoring, music, and more. Bev retired in 2003 after 30 years, and the Kinder World building was torn down. However, the memories live on in the hearts of the parents and children who were served by dynamo Bev Landry. Bev continues to be active in town, substituting in the elementary schools and also volunteering her time at many children's events at Rodgers Memorial Library. Bev is also well known as Cluffee the Clown, a fun, energetic character she created in 1986. Cluffee (from Bev's maiden name, Cluff) continues to entertain at birthday parties and other venues, and Bev brings humor, fun, and happiness wherever she goes. (Courtesy B. Landry.)

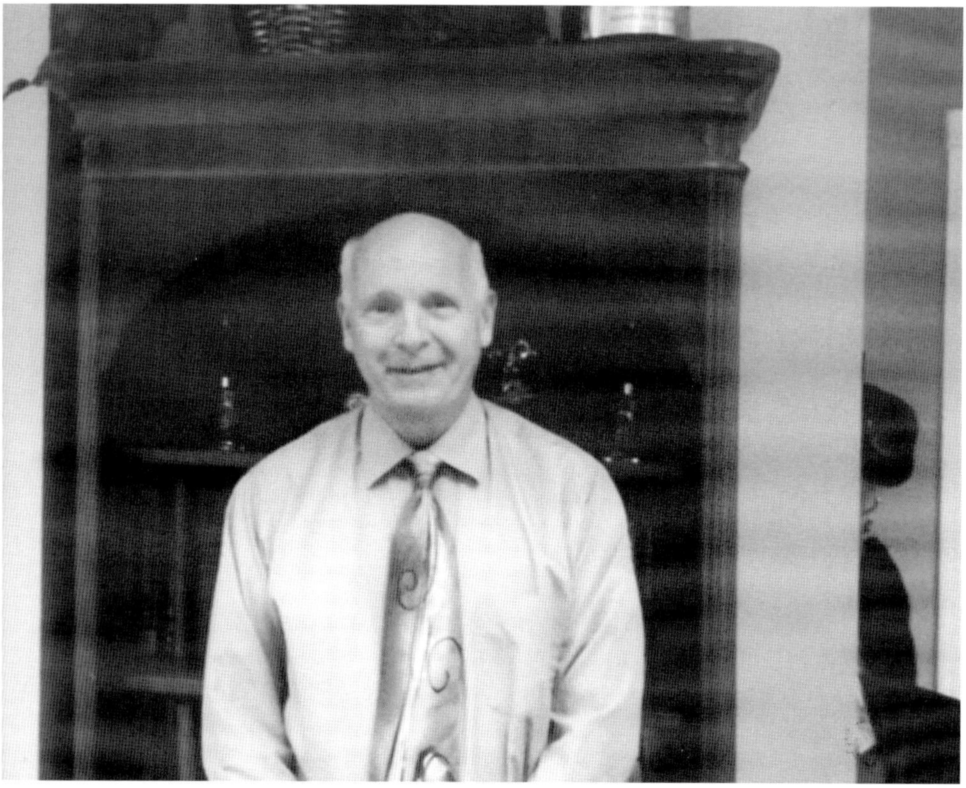

Bryan Lane

Bryan Lane was born February 12, 1957, to Leonard and Jean Lane in Pueblo, Colorado, and moved with his mother and brother Leonard to live with his maternal grandparents in New Rochelle, New York, in September 1957. He became an Eagle Scout at the age of 16 and earned varsity letters at New Rochelle High School in football, swimming, cross country, and track and field. Bryan's first job was as a lifeguard. Inspired by his third-grade teacher, Mrs. Sokol, he chose to attend Springfield College in Massachusetts, graduating in May 1979 with a degree in education and physical education. He began teaching in 1980 as a science teacher and coached football, diving, and track and field, primarily at Kingwood High School in Kingwood, Texas. In 1985, he married Pamela Sousa, whom he met in college. He earned his master's degree in educational administration in 1987 and became assistant principal of Kingwood High School in 1988. Bryan, Pamela, and their two children, Matthew and Allison, returned to New England, and Bryan became assistant principal at Salem High School in New Hampshire in 1991. He became assistant principal of Oyster River High School in Durham, New Hampshire, in 1995 and was selected the state's Assistant Principal of the Year in 1998. In May 1998, Bryan Lane was hired as the principal of Alvirne High School, a position he held for 14 years before being named superintendent of schools for the Hudson School District in May 2012. During his tenure at Alvirne High School, the school was twice selected as Secondary School of Excellence in the state, in 2001 and 2011, one of only two schools to ever receive the recognition twice. Bryan was named Principal of the Year for the state of New Hampshire in 2004. He was a firm but fair principal who considered each student his own. He was usually the first one to arrive at Alvirne, beginning every day greeting the students in the parking lot, regardless of the weather, and was often the last one to leave. During football game nights or band concerts, he could be found lending a hand with equipment, moving barrels out in the parking lot, and ensuring all was well at the school. Now as superintendent, the number of children in his care has increased, and he enjoys visiting all the schools as much as possible and is still a visible presence at many school events. (Courtesy Bryan Lane.)

CHAPTER FIVE

Relatively Speaking

Hudson has always been a place where people seem to stay. In the first 150 years after this side of the river was settled, it would be safe to say that nearly everyone in town was related to almost everyone else. One only had to go to a town meeting to experience a family reunion. The surnames may have changed, but the descendants of those pioneers are still here. In the years since women's suffrage, no doubt assisted by more modern appliances, which gave women some free time, Hudson saw a rise in the women's participation in all aspects of community life. Previously, fathers and sons were active in town, but beginning in the 1930s, the involvement of wives and daughters became more pronounced. Moreover, Hudson saw the rise of women's organizations. This chapter focuses on members of the same family, often husbands and wives, who have made a difference in Hudson. While many of them were active in different organizations, more than a few had shared interests.

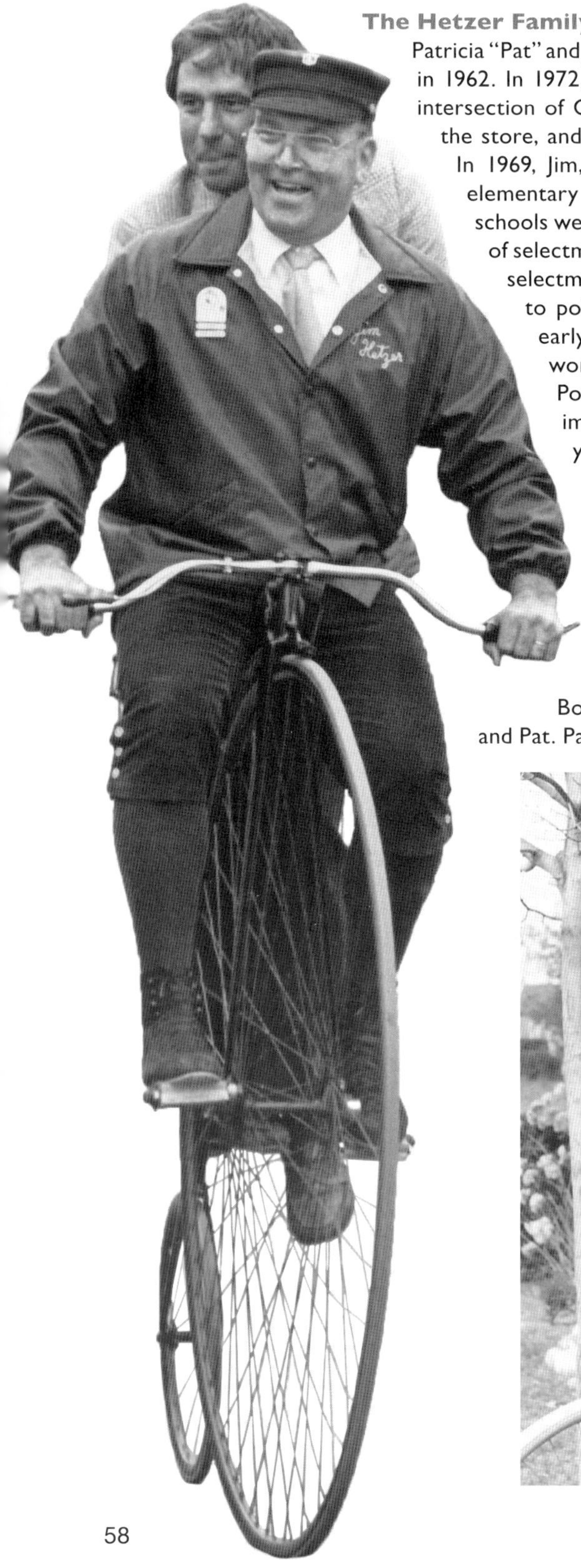

The Hetzer Family (LEFT, BELOW, AND OPPOSITE PAGE)
Patricia "Pat" and James "Jim" Hetzer moved to Hudson from Wisconsin in 1962. In 1972, they opened a bike shop on Lowell Road near the intersection of Central Street. Their son Mark eventually took over the store, and they worked for him until the shop closed in 2005. In 1969, Jim, as a concerned parent, became a member of the elementary school study committee; this was at a time when the schools were bursting at the seams. He was elected to the board of selectmen in 1970, serving one term and realizing that being a selectman could be bad for business, but in 1979, he returned to politics as a member of the budget committee. In the early 1970s, Pat and Jim devoted much of three summers working as part of a group that developed the Robinson Pond Recreation Area, which immediately became an important asset to the town. Pat volunteered for several years as a librarian at the Dr. H.O. Smith School. In more recent years, Pat served as a cemetery trustee and was instrumental in locating the Town Poor Cemetery, overseeing the repair of gravestones, and mapping out the cemeteries. Both Pat and Jim, along with other family members, were members of the Wheelmen Antique Bicycle Club and were seen on their high wheel bicycles in parades and events all over New England. Jim gives a ride to Boston sportscaster Bob Lobel at left. Opposite are Jim and Pat. Pat is ready to ride below. (All, courtesy the Hetzers.)

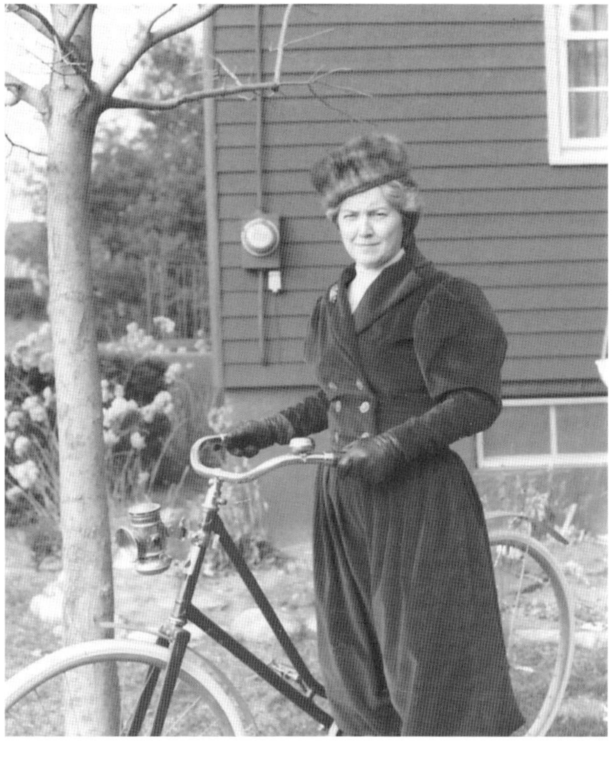

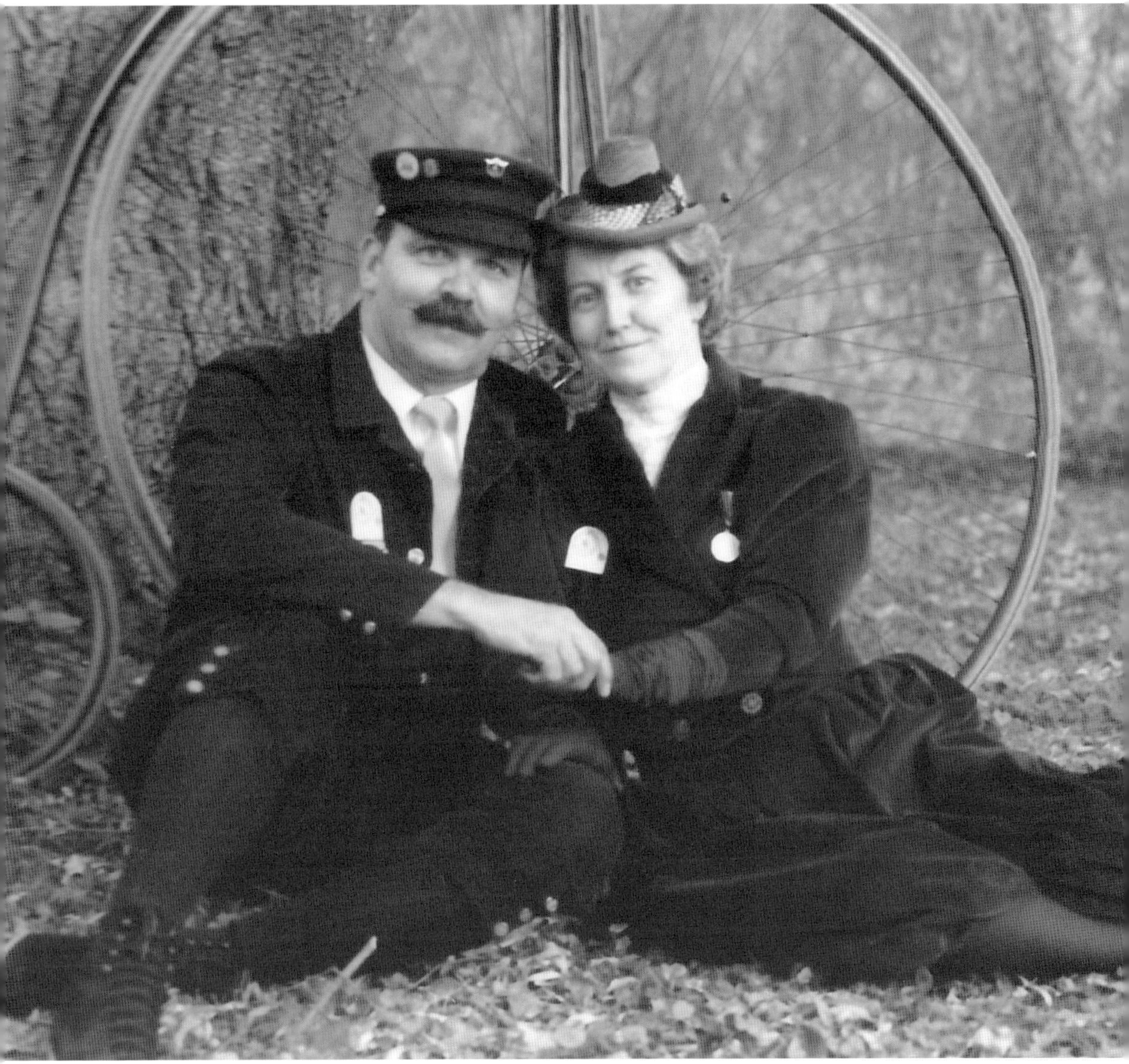

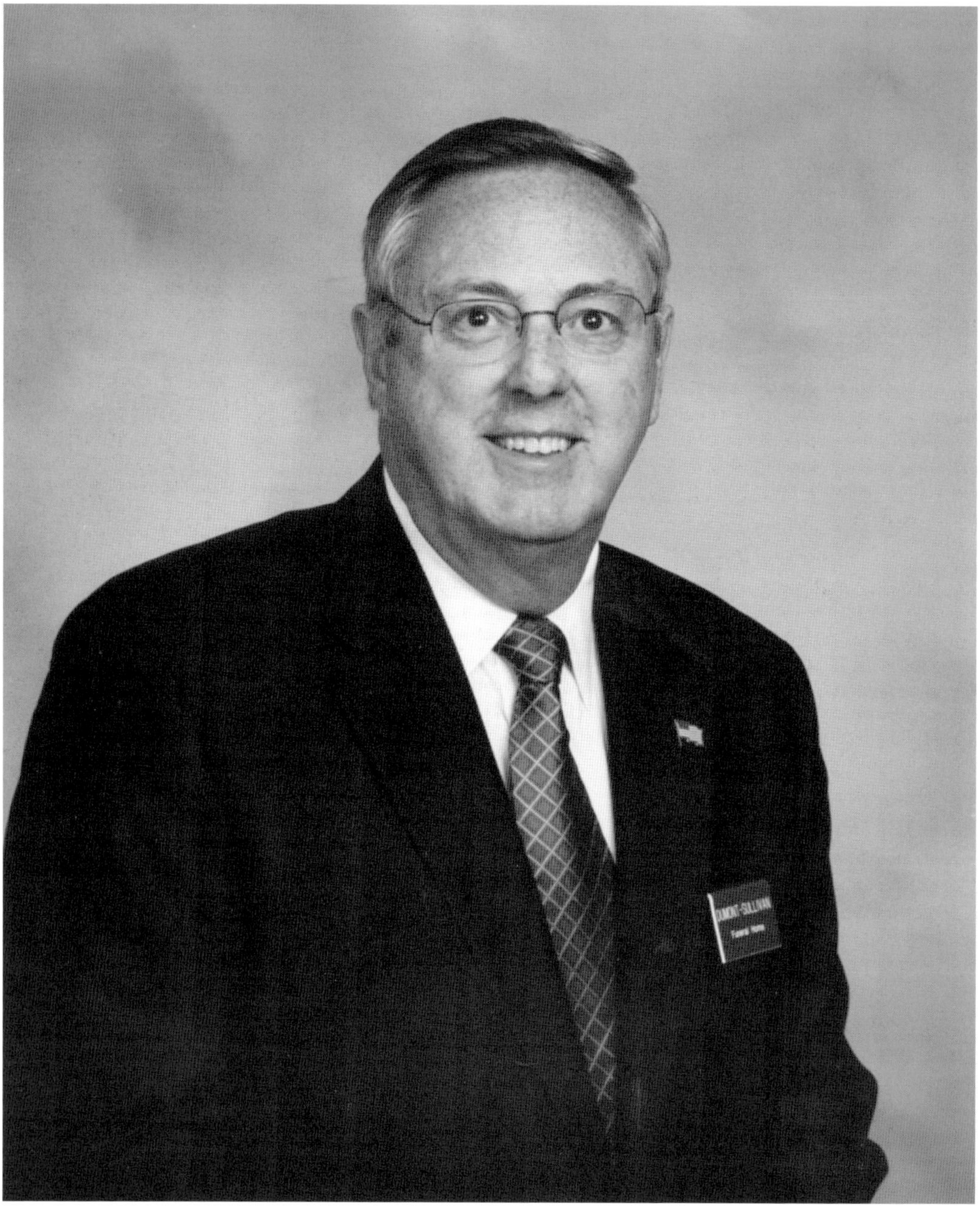

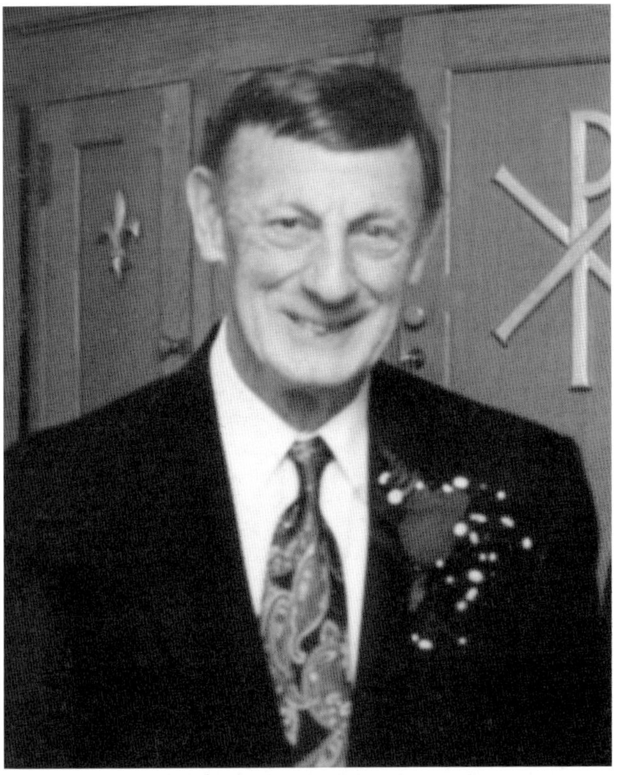

The Dumont Family
(RIGHT AND OPPOSITE PAGE)
The Dumont family has been in the funeral business for three generations. Leo Dumont Sr. (above right) graduated from Nashua High School and served in World War II in the Army Medical Corps as a staff sergeant from 1942 to 1945. Returning home, he attended New England Institute of Anatomy and Mortuary Science (NEI). In 1949, he constructed a funeral home at his residence on Ferry Street in Hudson. In 1967, a second Leo A. Dumont Funeral Home opened on Kinsley Street in Nashua, where it remained until 1978. The Sullivan Funeral Home in Nashua was purchased, and Dumont's son Leo Jr. (opposite) joined him in the business in 1969, after graduating from Alvirne High School in 1967 and NEI. Leo Dumont Sr. died in 2000. Leo Jr.'s son Leo III (below right) graduated from Bishop Guertin High School in 1993 and St. Joseph's College in 1997 with degrees in English and psychology before attending NEI. In 2000, he joined the family business, which still has locations in both Hudson and Nashua. The Dumont-Sullivan Funeral Home has cared for local families for over 64 years and has always offered excellent service. Trust, respect, and personal care continue to be the motto of this well respected Hudson business. (All, courtesy the Dumont family.)

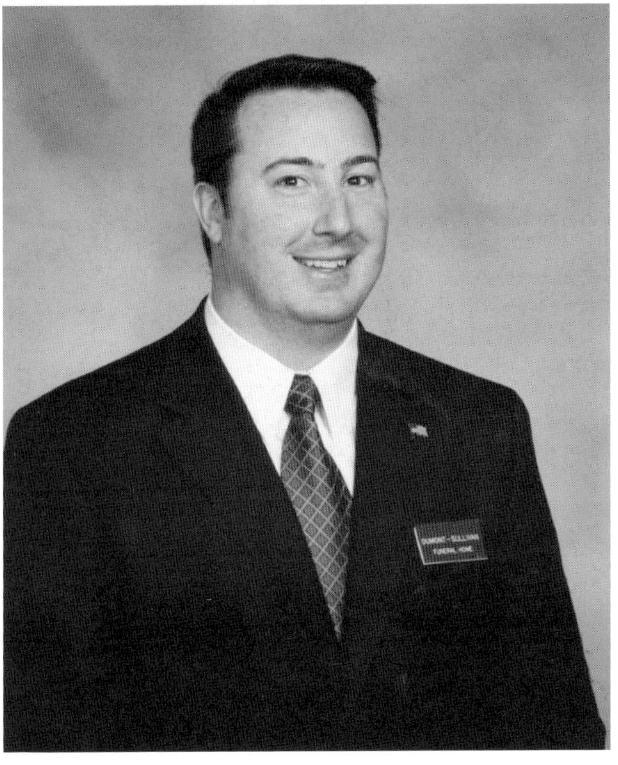

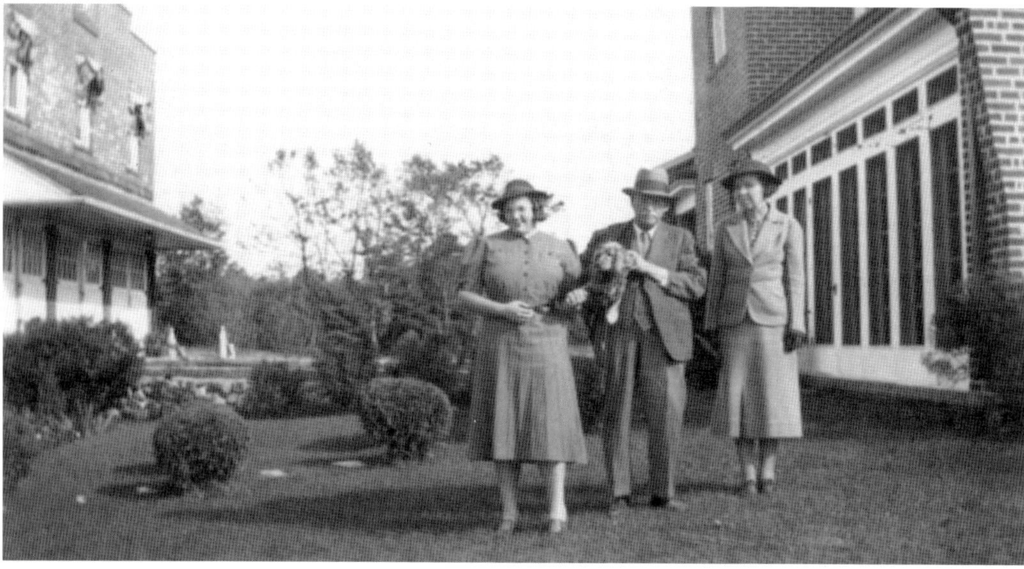

Dr. H.O. Smith

Dr. Henry Onslow Smith was born in Hudson in 1864, a son of Dr. David Onslow Smith. He and his father served at the same time on the town's board of health in the late 1890s. Dr. H.O. Smith was one of the most civic-minded individuals in town. In 1913, he was the only resident practicing physician in town. Dr. H.O. Smith also served for many years as a member of the school board on and off from the early 1900s through 1930. The 1945 town report was dedicated to him. He is pictured above at the Brick House, a function hall at the time and now a private home at 2 Old Derry Road, with members of the 1933 Bicentennial Committee. The three men in the photograph below are celebrating Dr. H.O. Smith's birthday. From left to right are Dr. Frank Kitteredge, Dr. H.O. Smith, and Rev. Stanley E. Anderson of Hudson Community Church. (Both, courtesy HHS.)

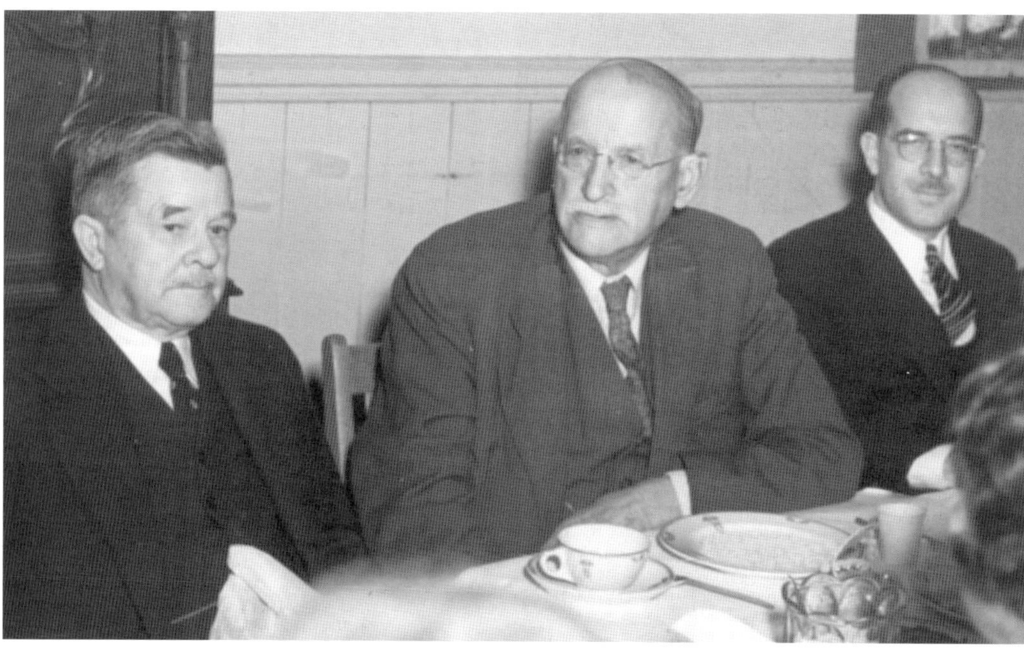

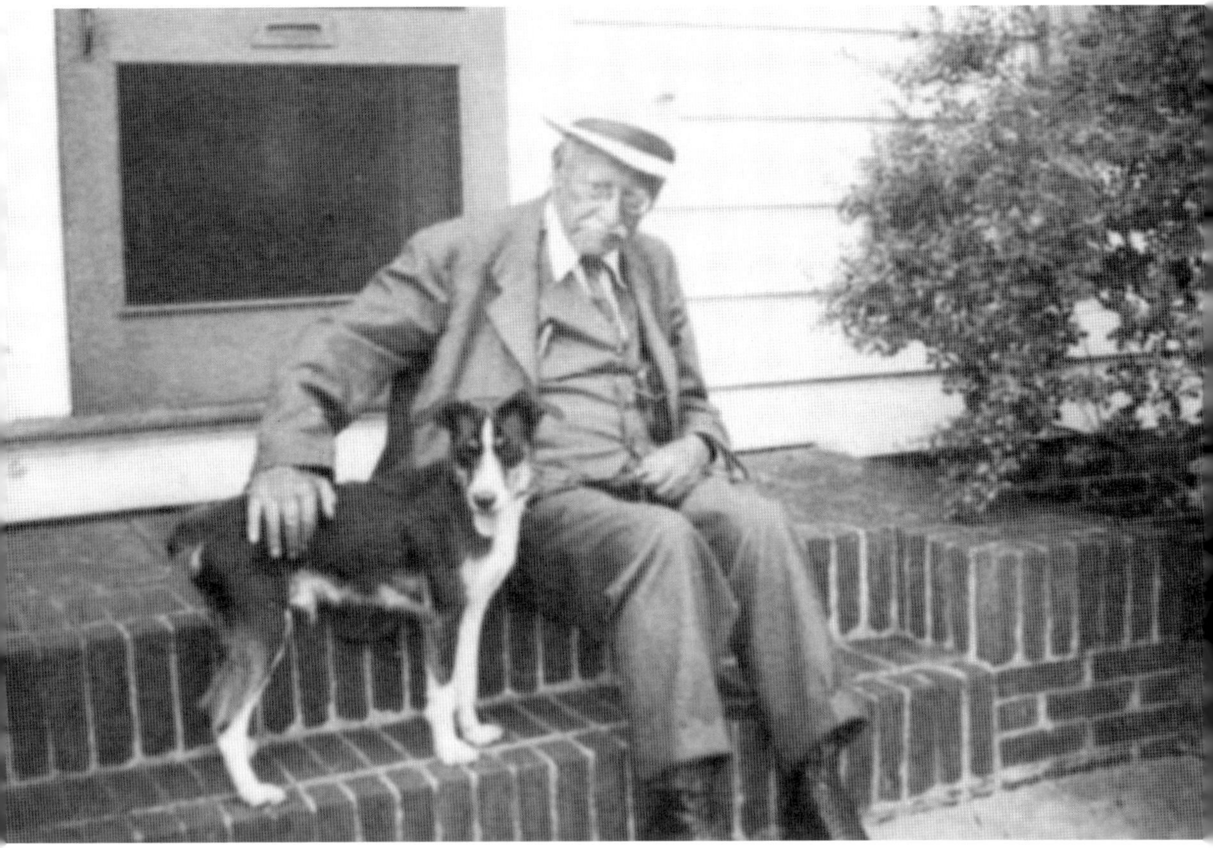

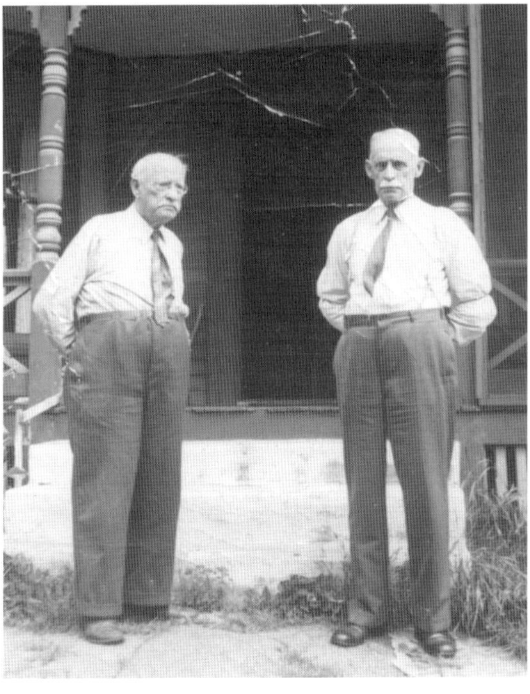

Smith and Friends

The Smith family had been in Hudson since before the Revolution and was distantly related to Kimball Webster. His mother was a sister of Dr. Adoniram Greeley, who left a collection of books to start a public library. In 1893, prior to his uncle's bequest, the selectmen appointed Dr. Smith as a trustee of the yet-to-be-established free public library. As a result of the gift, the library was named the Greeley Public Library. Upon the opening of the Hills Memorial Library, he continued as a library trustee of the new library and served until his death in 1945. Above, Dr. H.O. Smith and his dog Fala are shown. In the photograph at left, John Abner Robinson (right) and Dr. H.O. Smith (left), friends who shared many interests, including genealogy, are seen around 1940. (Above, courtesy HHS; left, courtesy the Parker family.)

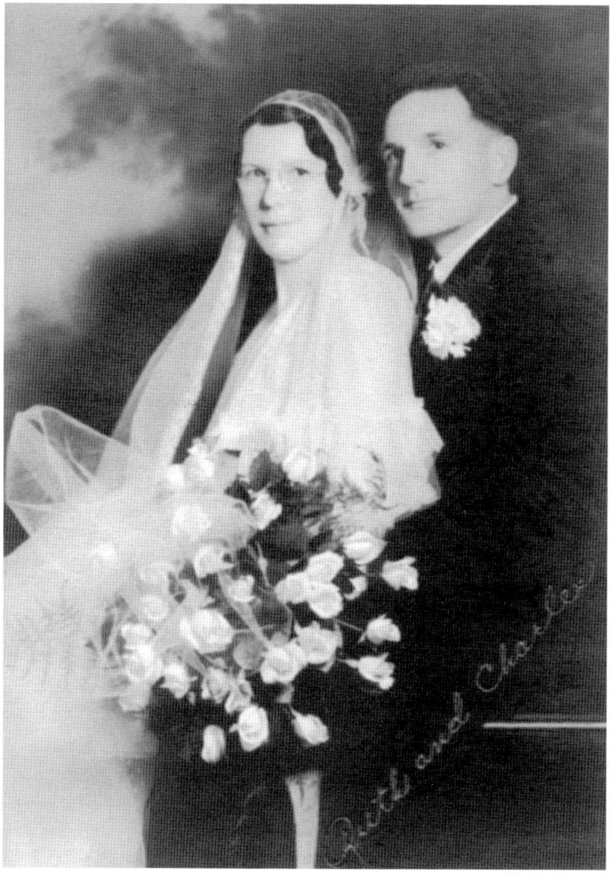

Parker Family (ABOVE AND OPPOSITE PAGE)
The Robinson/Parker family has resided on the same property for nine generations since 1763. Originally part of Londonderry, the property was purchased by Peter Robinson; the farm was annexed to Nottingham West (now Hudson) in 1788. Charles "Charlie" Parker was a son of Hattie Robinson and Rev. Clarence Parker. Charles married Ruth Blood from Nashua in 1933. Charlie milked cows on the farm until the mid-1960s. He also operated a sawmill near the pond in the area that is now Parker Drive. Charlie was a longtime library trustee and member of the board of adjustment.

Both he and his wife, Ruth, were active members of the Baptist Church, the Grange, and the Hudson Historical Society. Ruth was cochairman of the society's Hudson history update publication, completed in 1977. Ruth was a part-time Latin teacher at the Hudson Junior High School and a correspondent for the *Nashua Telegraph*. Ruth and Charlie's two daughters, Marilyn and Ruth M., attended Hudson schools and graduated from Alvirne High School. Marilyn graduated from Plymouth State College and married James Rollins of Ashland, New Hampshire, and they had four children. Ruth M. graduated from the University of New Hampshire in 1961; at the same time, her mother received her master's degree. The photograph above opposite shows the two scholars. Ruth M. Parker has continued the family tradition of community service. She is the first graduate of Alvirne High School to serve as an Alvirne trustee and continues to do so. She is a charter member of the Hudson Historical Society, has had several positions in the society over the years, and volunteers to assist in family outreach and Hudson history. In 2006, she was honored as Hudson's Citizen of the Year. Marilyn's children and grandchildren represent the 10th and 11th generations of the family since they settled the homestead. The town's recreation area and wildlife sanctuary at Robinson Pond were part of the original farm. The Parkers' Butternut Hill Farm is distinguished as a Bicentennial Farm, one of only two in Hudson. (Courtesy the Parker family.)

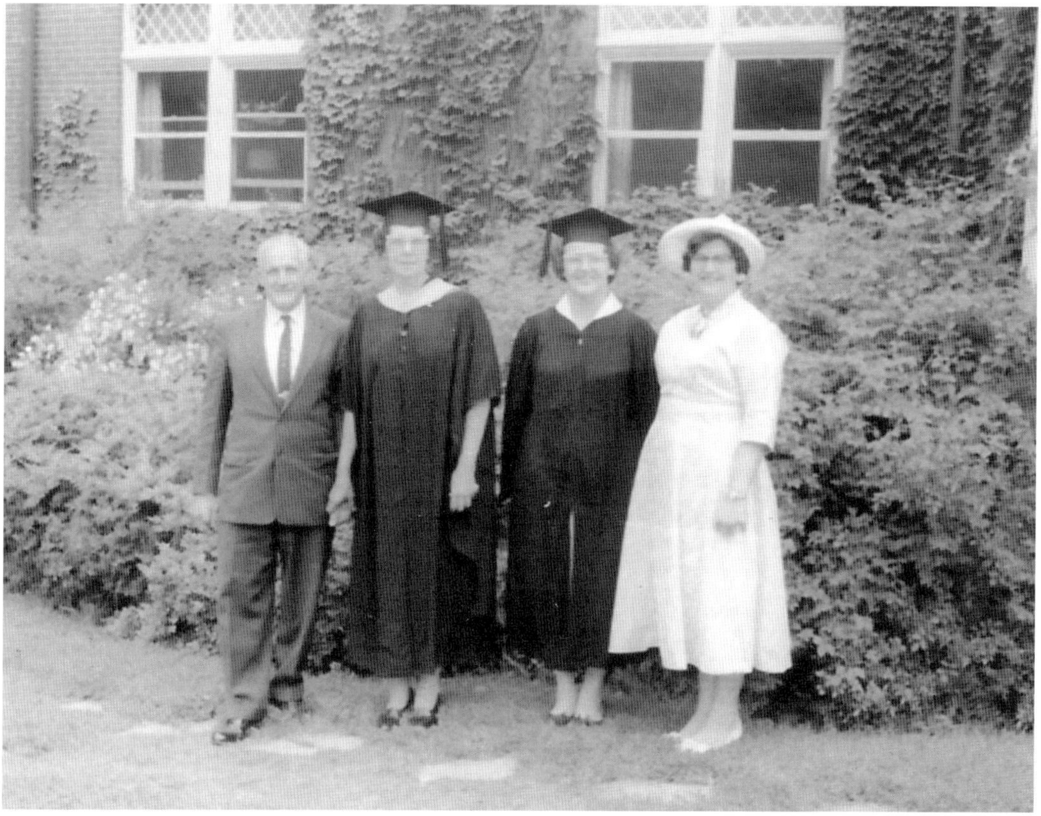

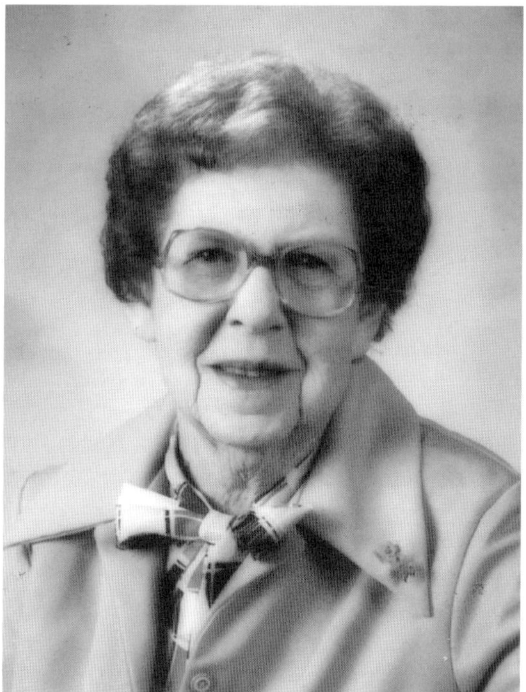

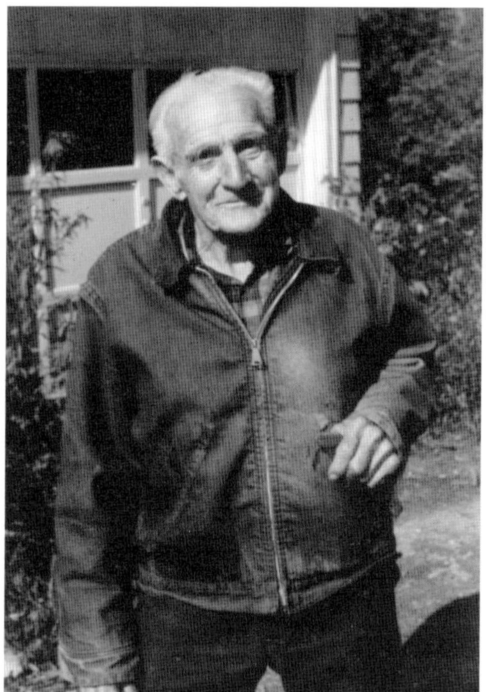

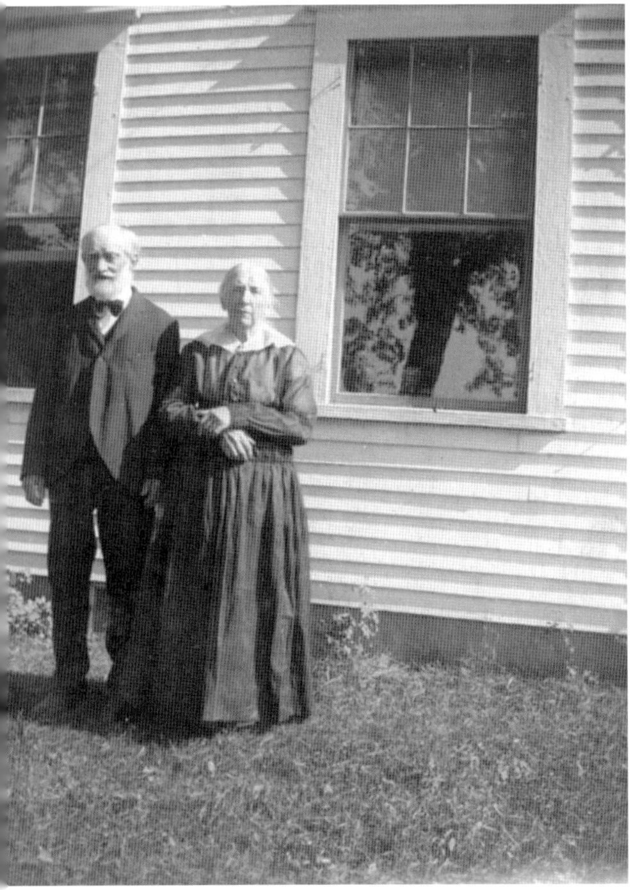

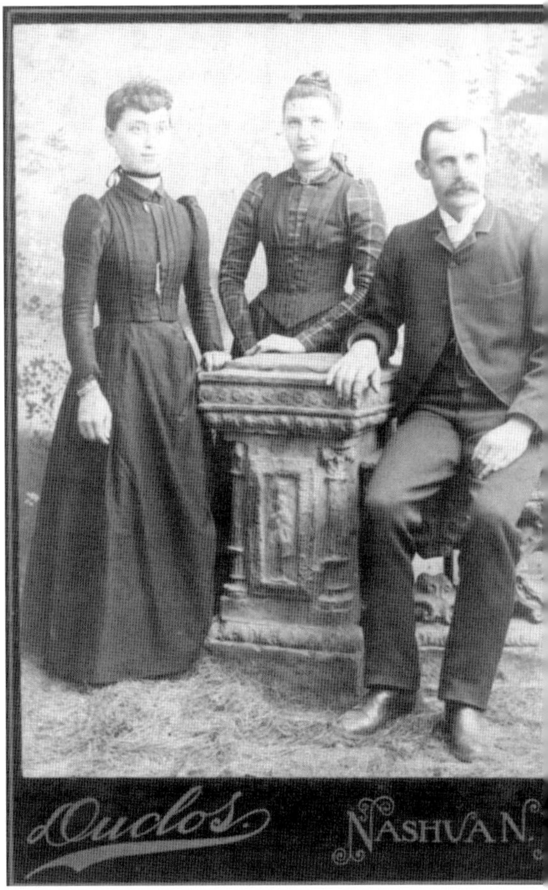

Alfonso and Louisa Robinson

Alfonso and Louisa Robinson are shown in the right photograph about 1910. Alphonso Robinson was the sixth generation to live on the farm; he was a respected member of the community and married to Louisa Haselton. Their son John Abner Robinson was born in 1863 and married Julia Ann, a daughter of Kimball Webster. John served the town for at least 22 years and is still the longest-serving selectman in the town's history. He also served as a state representative. John's sister Hattie Louisa married Rev. Clarence Parker in 1889. Hattie died at age 40 in 1912, and after her death, her children came to live on the family farm with their grandparents. Hattie's son Charles never left the farm. On the right, from left to right, Julia, Hattie, and John are pictured around 1890. (Both, courtesy the Parker family.)

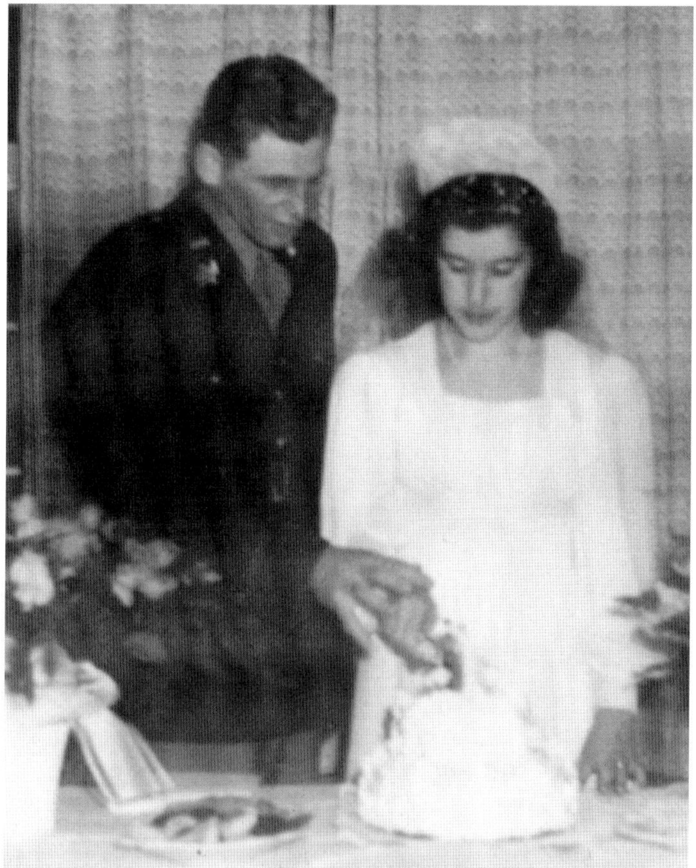

Leonard and Claire Smith
Leonard "Lenny" Smith grew up on Baker Street in Hudson, and Claire Richard grew up nearby on Highland Street. Lenny served in the Army Corps of Engineers during World War II, and he and Claire were married in 1942. After the war, they returned to Hudson and lived with his parents on Baker Street, where their son was born in 1948. They purchased the Kenrick House, the stately Second Empire mansion across from Library Park, which remains in the family. Lenny remodeled the house, turning the single-family home into an apartment house. He moved his family into an apartment in the building and began his career as a homebuilder. The first home he built was on Leslie Street; the Smiths moved into it and remained there for the rest of their lives. Their daughter Ann Brooke was born after their move to Leslie Street. Claire was a member of the Hudson Players (a theatrical group), the Hudson Fortnightly Club, and the Hudson Historical Society. Lenny was known for high-quality work, and he and his brother Gordon joined the fire department at the same time in 1950. Gordon retired in 1978 and Lenny in 1979. Having received his degree in architectural construction, Lenny designed and helped build the Central Fire Station (now named for him) as well as town hall and its first addition. He served as the clerk of the works for the rebuilding of Alvirne High School; there is little doubt that his expertise and practical methods were primary reasons the project was completed less than a year after the fire. Smith served 10 terms in the state legislature beginning in 1972. He also served on the Nashua Regional Commission, the town planning board, and the building board of appeals. He was a library trustee and an Alvirne trustee, along with service on numerous committees. He was named citizen of the year in 1991. It is safe to say that no one served Hudson in more capacities over a longer period. He died at 87 while still serving on three boards, and the 2002 annual report was dedicated to him. (Courtesy Ann Brooke Smith.)

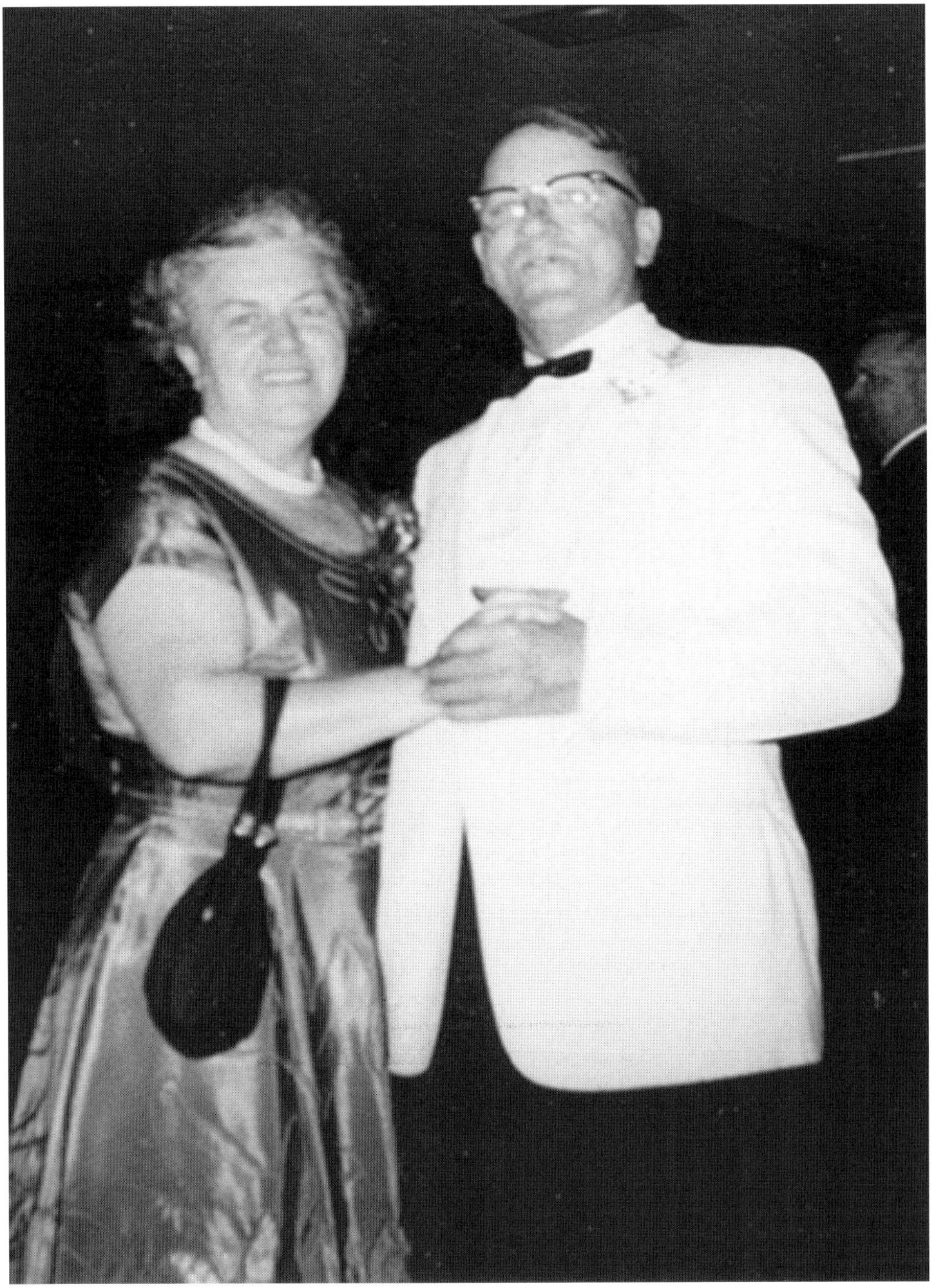

George H. and Ella M. Rodgers

George and Ella (Landry) Rodgers were the parents of five sons, G. Philip, Alvin, Kenneth, Joseph Duane, and Ronald. They married in Nashua in 1927 and moved to Stuart's Corner near Eayrs Pond in Hudson to raise their family. George was a textile millworker in Nashua and a mechanic, and they ran a family store and filling station. They also taught their children the value of hard work and giving back to the community. Their sons G. Philip and Alvin donated $4 million to build a beautiful new library in their parents' names, which was completed in 2009. (Courtesy Rodgers Memorial Library.)

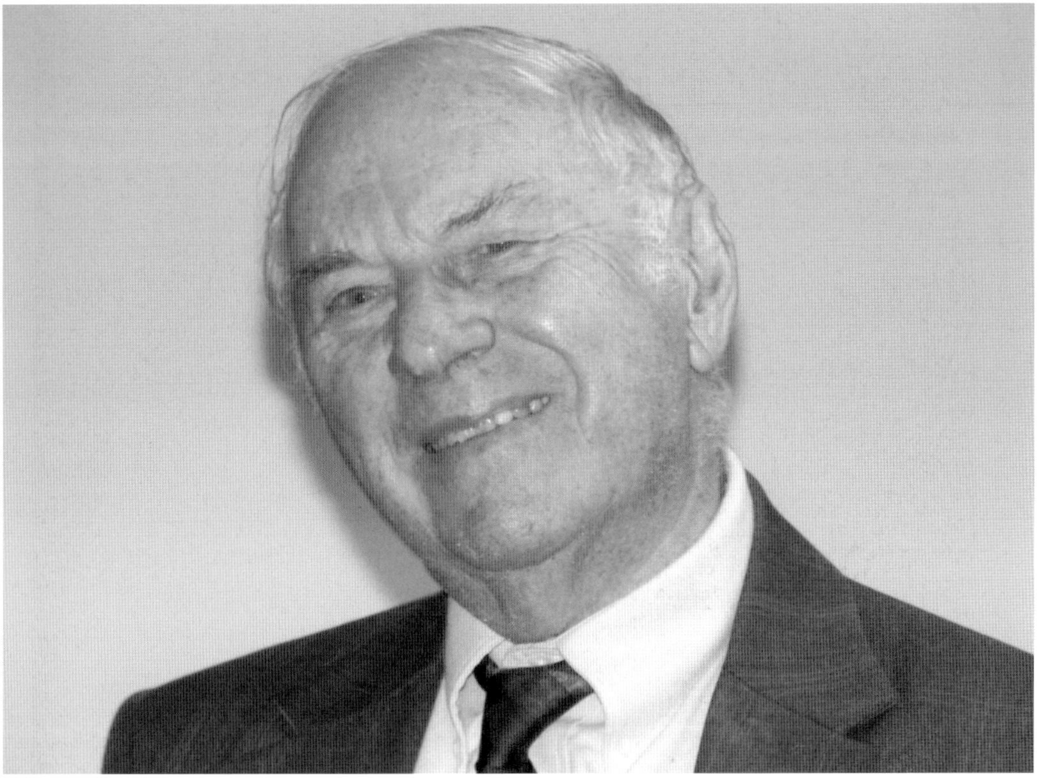

G. Philip Rodgers

Philip Rodgers, the eldest of five sons of George and Ella (Landry) Rodgers, started Rodgers Brothers Home Builders with his brothers. He was also a state representative, a member of the Hudson Planning Board, and a repeat recipient of Hudson Chamber of Commerce Citizen of the Year, among many other activities. Philip and his brother Alvin Rodgers donated $4 million to build a new library for the town, named in memory of their parents, which was dedicated in June 2009. Sadly, Philip died in 2011 at 82, but not before seeing his dream fulfilled. (Courtesy Rodgers Memorial Library)

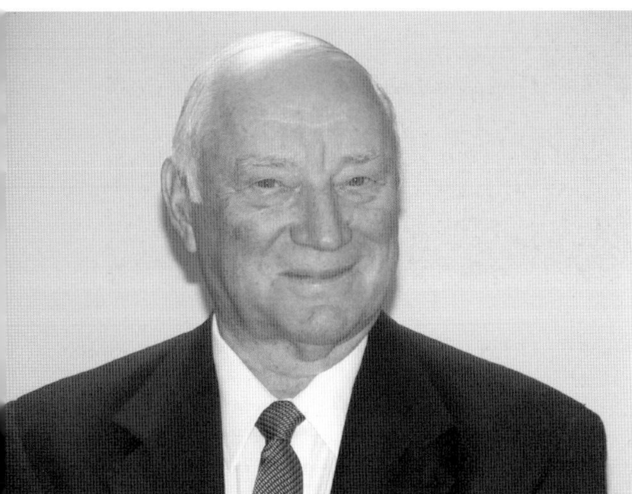

Alvin "Al" Rodgers

Alvin Rodgers and his brothers started Rodgers Brothers Home Builders shortly after his return from the US Air Force. The father of Gary Rodgers (see page 38), he, too, is a member of the Lions Club and received Hudson Citizen of the Year award twice, most recently sharing the honor with his brother G. Philip in 2007 in grateful recognition of their donation of $4 million to build Rodgers Memorial Library for the town of Hudson. Al was the Lions Club district governor in 1975–1976 and is a Melvin Jones Fellow, the highest Lions Club honor. Al and his wife, Betty, enjoy golf and travel. (Courtesy Rodgers Memorial Library.)

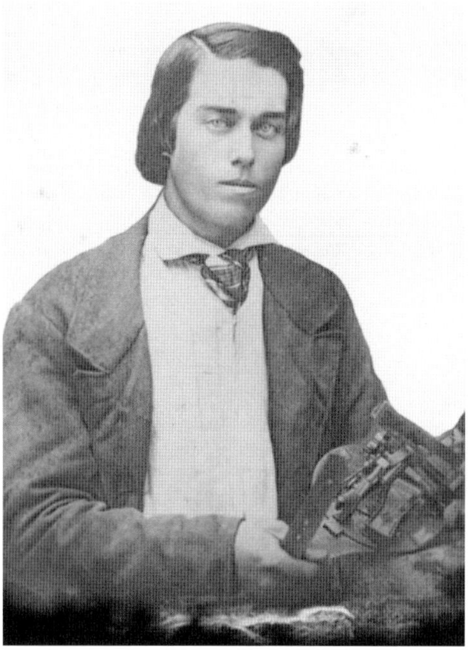

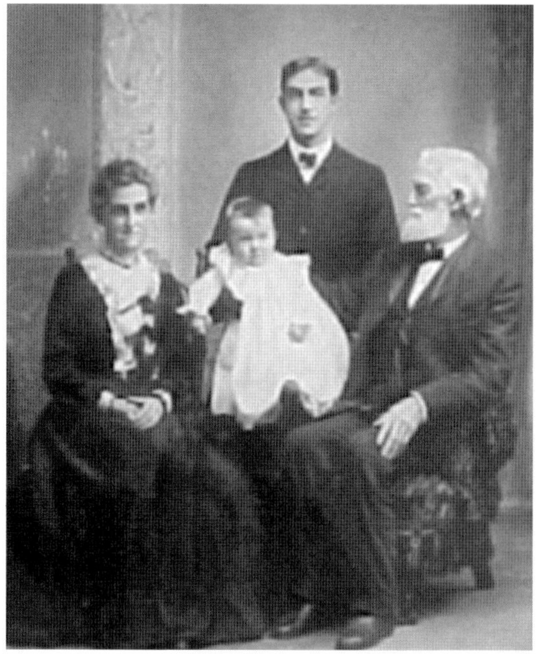

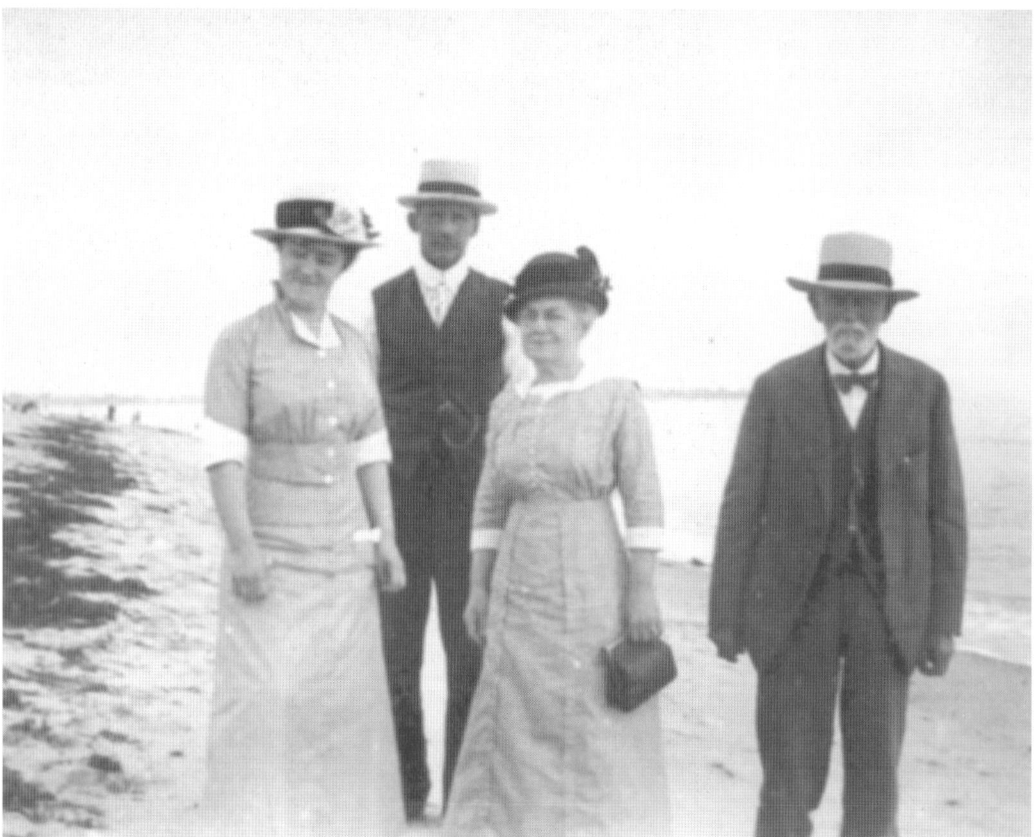

Kimball Webster (BELOW AND OPPOSITE PAGE)
Kimball Webster was born in Pelham on November 2, 1828, to John and Hannah (Cummings) Webster and attended Pelham and Hudson schools. He went out to California during the Gold Rush of 1849 and wrote a book about his experiences, called *The Goldseekers*. Although he did not find the fortune he sought, he learned the surveying trade, earning the title of deputy surveyor in Oregon. He arrived back in Hudson in 1854. In 1857, he married Abiah Cutter, and they had several children. He was a surveyor and engineer. In addition, he served as town selectman, state representative, school board member, and an original trustee of the public library. He was also a justice of the peace, a bank trustee in Nashua, member of Rising Sun Lodge, F.&A.M., of Nashua, and the local Grange's master for 10 years. Webster was always interested in history and landmarks and responsible for erecting several historic markers around town. In 1884, Kimball Webster was approached to write a 20-page history of Hudson for inclusion in a Hillsborough county book. Thus began his comprehensive research and writing of the Hudson's history from 1673 to 1913. Webster's *History of Hudson* is a detailed compilation of Hudson and its people. He died on June 29, 1916. The photographs show a young Kimball (opposite left); Kimball and A.W. Gale in a 50th anniversary portrait entitled *California Pioneers,* dated 1909 (right); Kimball and members of his family at the beach (opposite bottom); and Kimball and his daughter and family (opposite right). (All, courtesy HHS.)

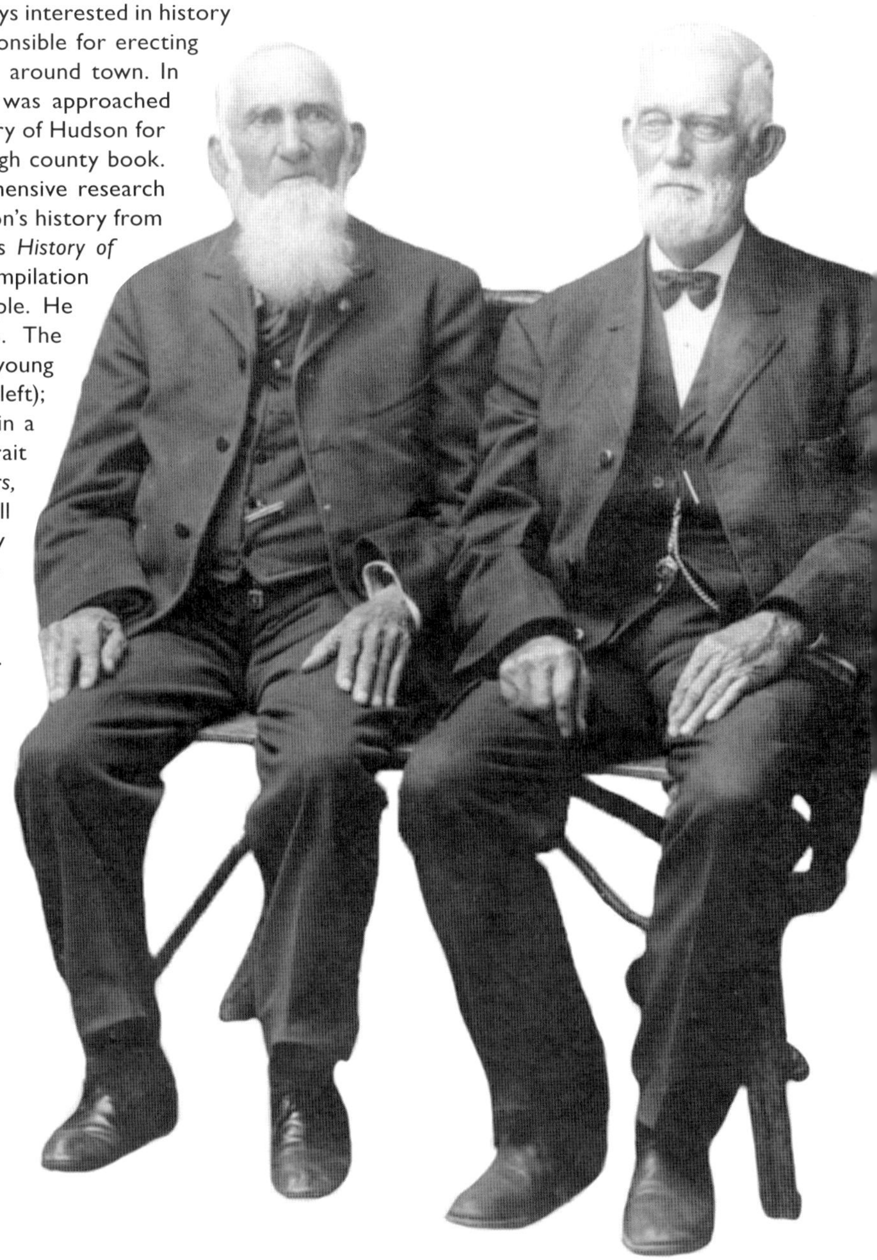

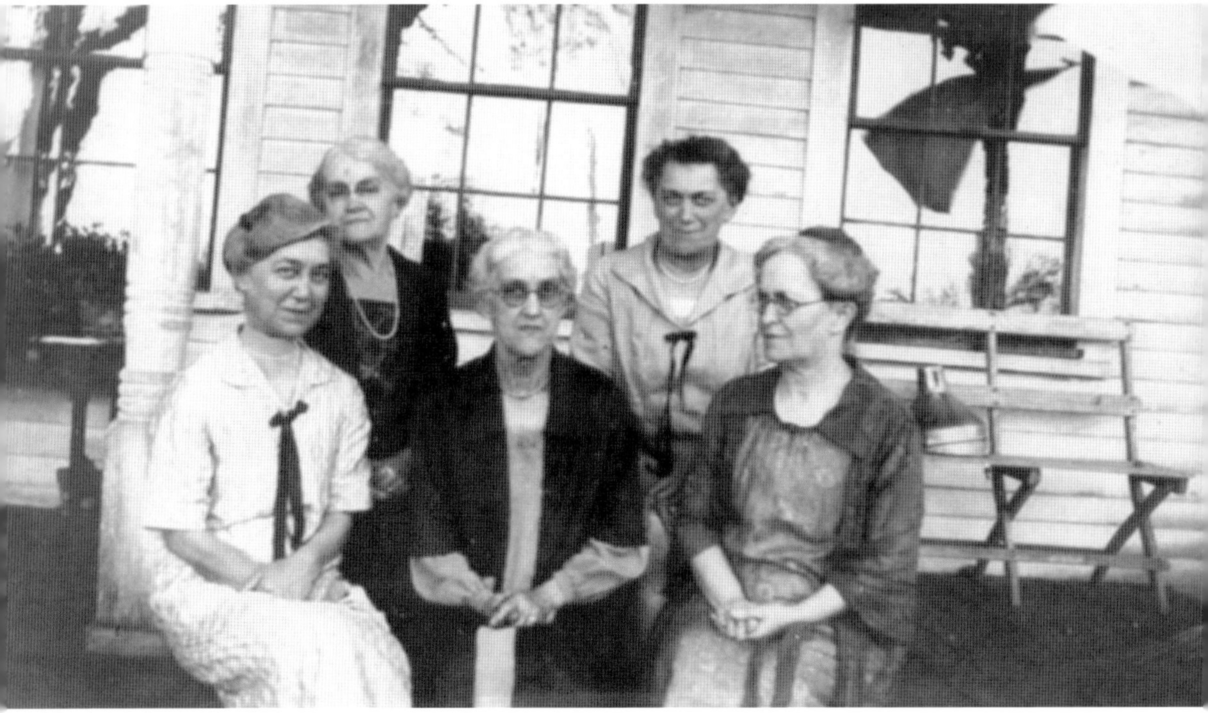

Daughters of Kimball Webster

Kimball Webster and his wife, Abiah (Cutter), were married on January 29, 1857. They had 10 children, four of whom died in infancy (twin boys and another set of twins, a girl and a boy), and one daughter who died at age 22. Kimball Webster lists his children in his book *The History of Hudson*. The children were as follows: Lizzie Jane, born on January 11, 1858, and married to Horace A. Martin; Ella Frances, born on August 19, 1859, and married to Frank A. Walch; twin boys, born on June 26, 1861, and died a short time later; Eliza Ball, born on July 14, 1862, and married to Charles C. Leslie; Latina Ray, born on July 26, 1865, and died on November 12, 1887; Julia Anna, born on October 26, 1867, and married to John A. Robinson; Mary Newton, born on August 9, 1869, and married to George H. Abbott; and twins, a boy and girl, born on June 10, 1876, and died the same day. This photograph shows five of his adult daughters. (Courtesy HHS.)

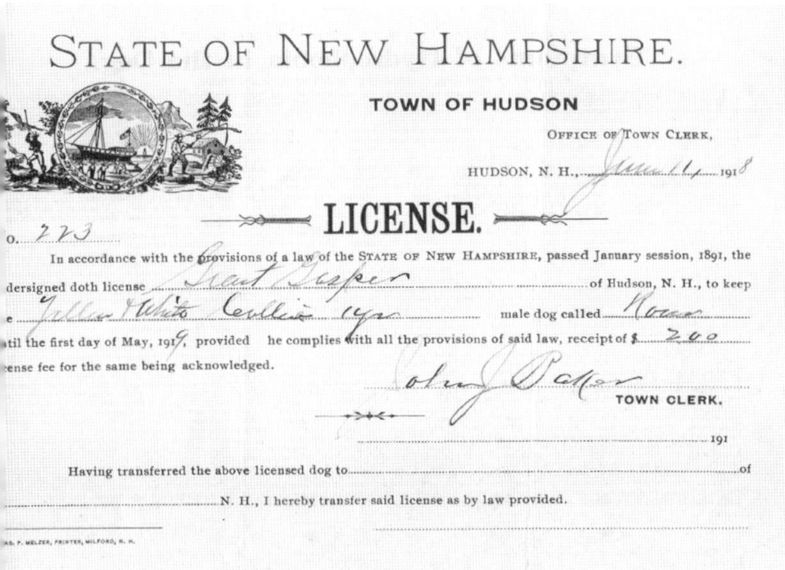

STATE OF NEW HAMPSHIRE.

TOWN OF HUDSON

OFFICE OF TOWN CLERK,

HUDSON, N. H., 191_

LICENSE.

No. 223

In accordance with the provisions of a law of the STATE OF NEW HAMPSHIRE, passed January session, 1891, the undersigned doth license ____ of Hudson, N. H., to keep ____ male dog called ____ until the first day of May, 1919, provided he complies with all the provisions of said law, receipt of $2.00 license fee for the same being acknowledged.

John J. Baker
TOWN CLERK.

____ 191_

Having transferred the above licensed dog to ____ of ____ N. H., I hereby transfer said license as by law provided.

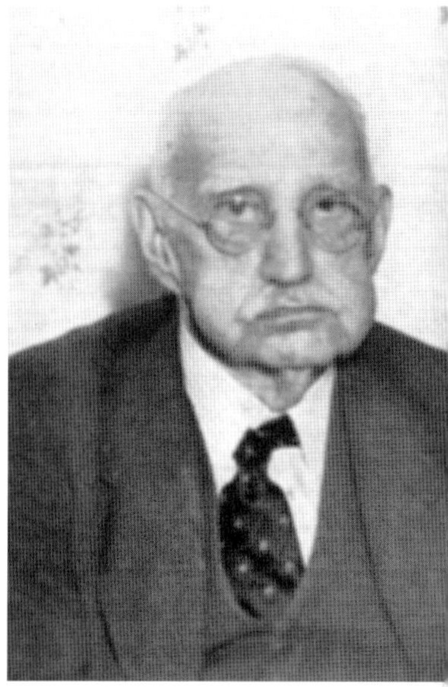

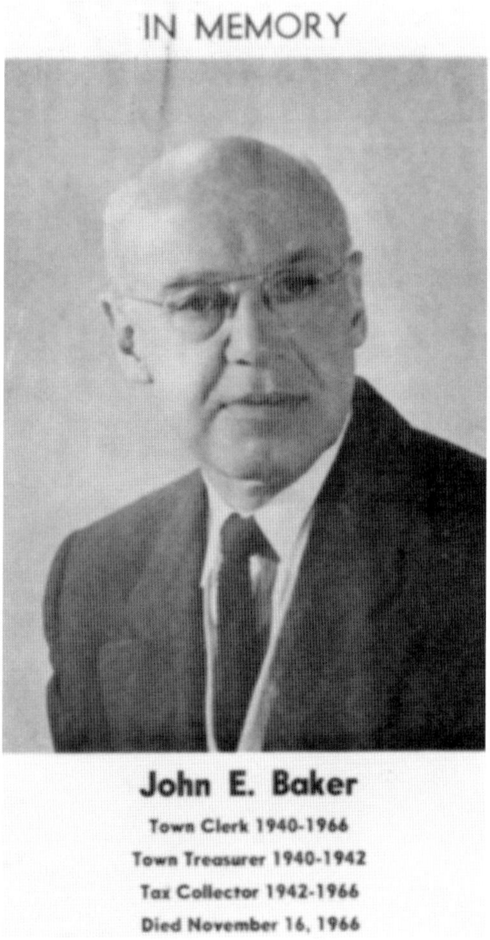

The Bakers
John Julian and William Wallace Baker were known as the Baker brothers, and together they established a general store near the Taylor's Falls Bridge. Their mother was a sister of Kimball Webster. John served as postmaster for several years in the 1890s and was a member of the state legislature in 1899. He is best known for his long service as the town clerk from 1891 to 1894 and again from 1902 to 1939. He also held the position of tax collector in 1886 and town treasurer from 1902 to 1939. The town report of 1939 was dedicated to him upon his retirement, and this was the first time a town report had been dedicated. John Julian Baker died in 1942 at age 85. Upon his retirement, William's son John E. Baker became the town clerk and treasurer. In 1942, he gave up the job of town clerk, but he served as tax collector until his death in 1966 at age 65. The town report was dedicated to him that year. His widow, Frances S. Baker, took over both positions, holding them until 1971. (Above left, courtesy the Jasper family; above right and below left, courtesy HHS.)

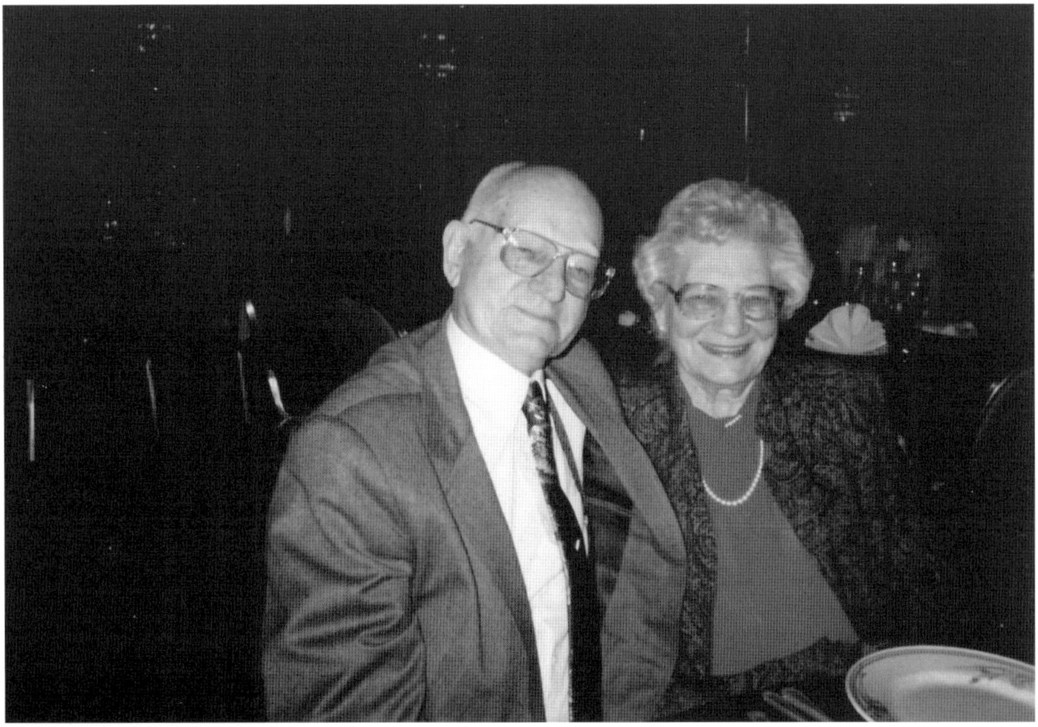

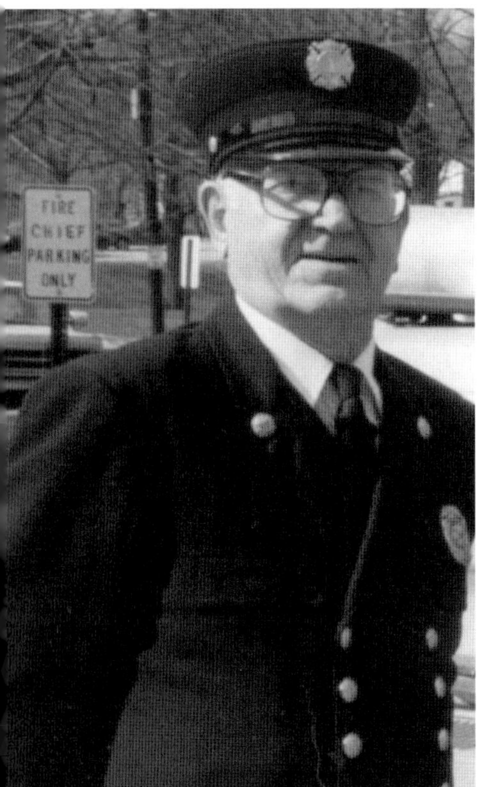

Leon and Geri Hammond (ABOVE, LEFT, AND OPPOSITE PAGE)
Leon and Gertrude "Geri" Hammond were married in Nashua in 1936 and were soon living in Hudson; by 1942, they were living on Central Street in the Colonial house they would call home for over 60 years. Leon served on the budget committee beginning in 1950. He was a member of the fire call department from about 1960 to 1977. He continued to be an active member of the Firefighters Relief Association for the remainder of his life. The association named a community service award in his honor, and he was the first recipient of that award. Leon's was a familiar face at elections for decades, where he served as an assistant moderator. Leon and Geri were active members of the Hudson Historical Society, and he continued to man the grill at Old Home Days well into his 80s. Geri was the first secretary to the board of selectmen, serving from 1958 to 1975. She also assisted as a dispatcher for the fire department and served as the police secretary. Geri was the secretary for the chamber of commerce, and she was active in the Hudson Baptist Church, the Fortnightly Club, and several other organizations. The 2003 town report was dedicated to both of them.

Hammond Park, on the corner of Lowell Street and Central Street, the location of the Hudson Firefighters' Memorial, was named after Leon and is located across the street from Leon and Geri's former home on Central Street. (Above, courtesy the Jasper family; left, courtesy Hudson Fire Department.)

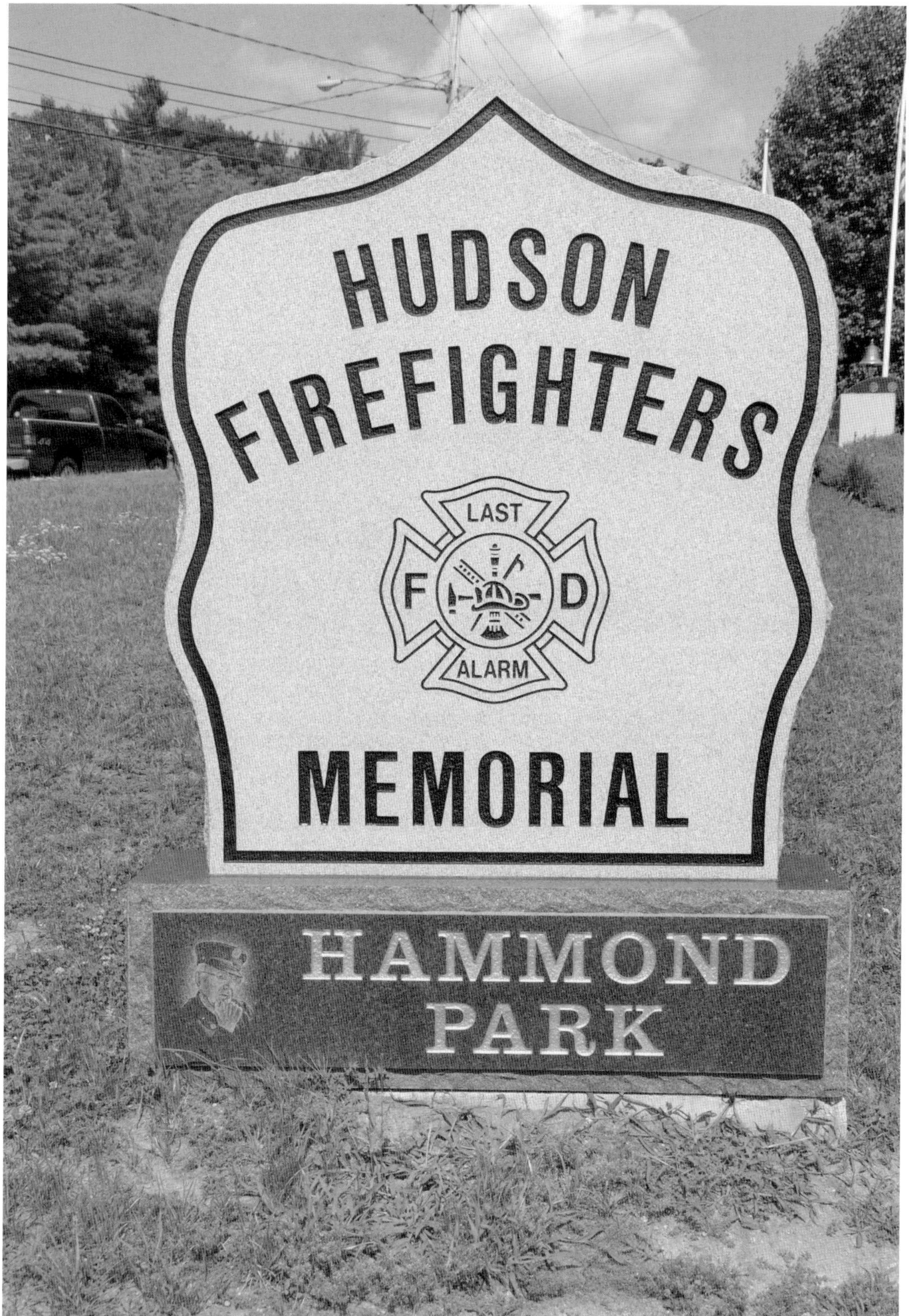
HUDSON
FIREFIGHTERS
LAST
F
D
ALARM
MEMORIAL
HAMMOND
PARK

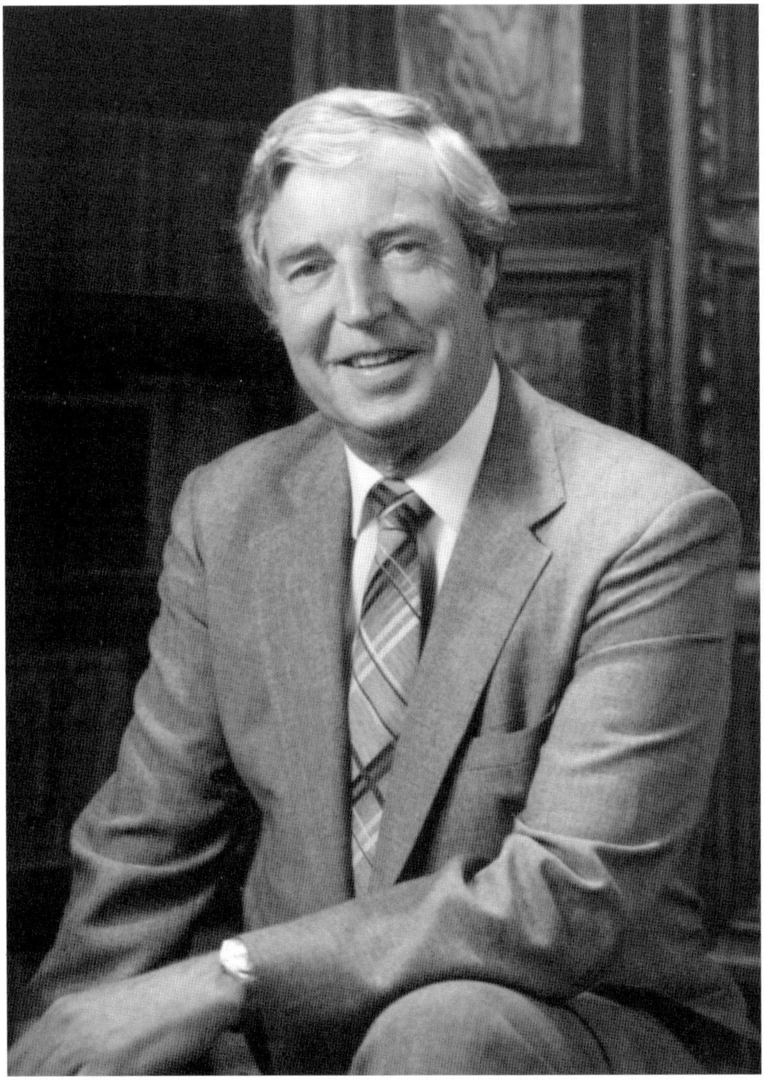

Gerald Q. Nash

Gerald "Jerry" Q. Nash died peacefully on July 25, 2014, at the age of 90, truly a life well lived as a member of the Greatest Generation. Born in Nashua, New Hampshire, on October 6, 1923, Jerry was the fourth of five sons who each served his country during World War II. Jerry joined the Army as a member of the 10th Mountain Division, and he trained in Colorado as a member of this elite group. The famed 10th Mountain Division's missions in the mountains of Italy in early 1945 were crucial to the Allied victory. Returning to New Hampshire, he graduated from Boston University and went to work for his father at Nashua Box Company, eventually purchasing the business with his brother. Next, Jerry became interested in real estate, and he and business partner Samuel Tamposi greatly contributed to southern New Hampshire's economic growth and development. Jerry was a 52-year member of the Nashua Rotary among many other organizations. He had a strong work ethic and also enjoyed travel, skiing, tennis, and genealogy. He made several return trips to Italy with family and friends for 10th Mountain Division reunions. He, Sandra Martinson, and Roland Marchand compiled *The Vital Records of Hudson, New Hampshire 1734–1985*, a listing of births, deaths, and marriages in one complete volume. Jerry and his wife, Lucille, were married 64 years and had six children. (Courtesy the Nash family.)

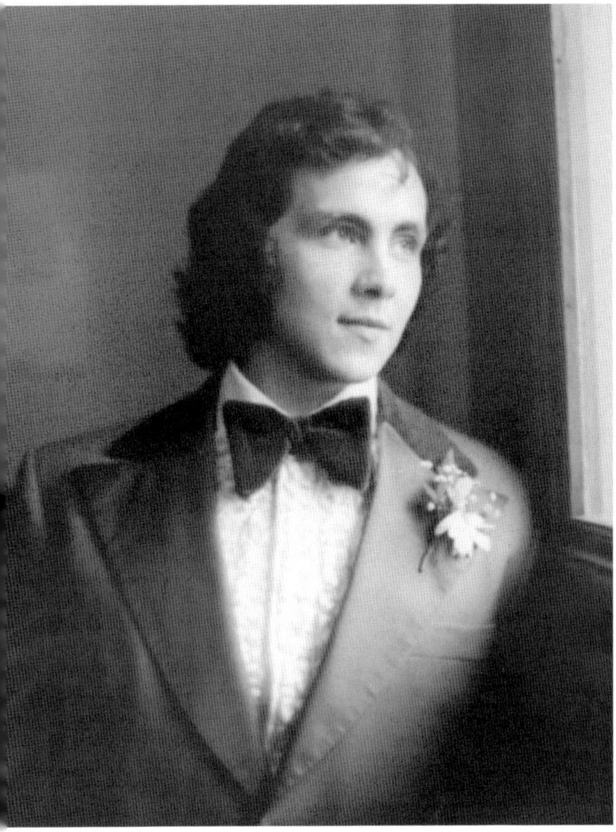

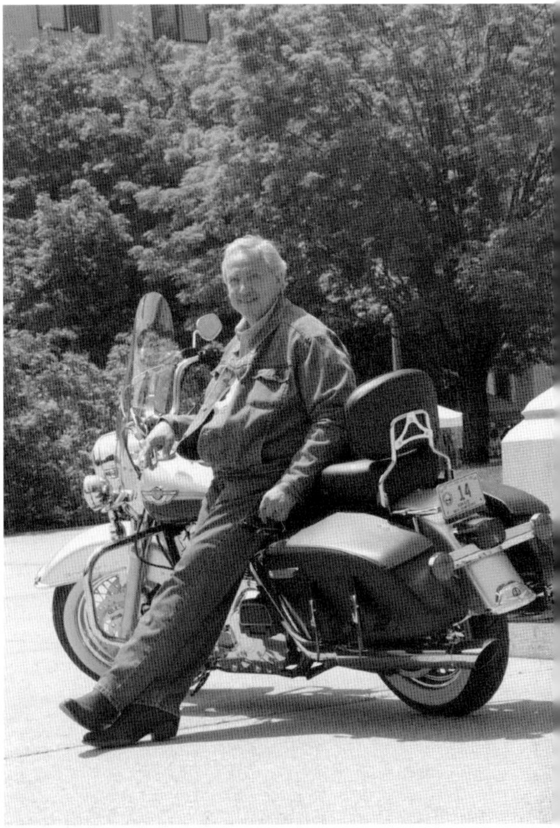

Robert "Bob" Clegg

Robert "Bob" Clegg has had a successful career in the construction business as well as in politics. During his four terms in the New Hampshire House of Representatives, he served in several leadership positions including speaker pro tempore, assistant majority leader, and majority caucus whip. The National Republican Legislators Association and Home Builders and Remodelers Association of New Hampshire named him legislator of the year. He was also elected to represent District 14 in the state senate in 2002. Bob has always felt it was important to be a good member of the local community. Over the years, he has served on the town council, board of selectmen, budget committee, building board of appeals, economic development committee, and charter study committee. He was recognized as the Hudson Chamber of Commerce Citizen of the Year in 1993 and has been recognized by Hudson Post No. 48 for his work on behalf of veterans. In 2008, Bob retired from the senate and is now a partner at Legislative Solutions. Bob and his wife, Priscilla (Nash) Clegg, have two adult children. Bob's father-in-law was Gerald Q. Nash. (Both, courtesy the Clegg family.)

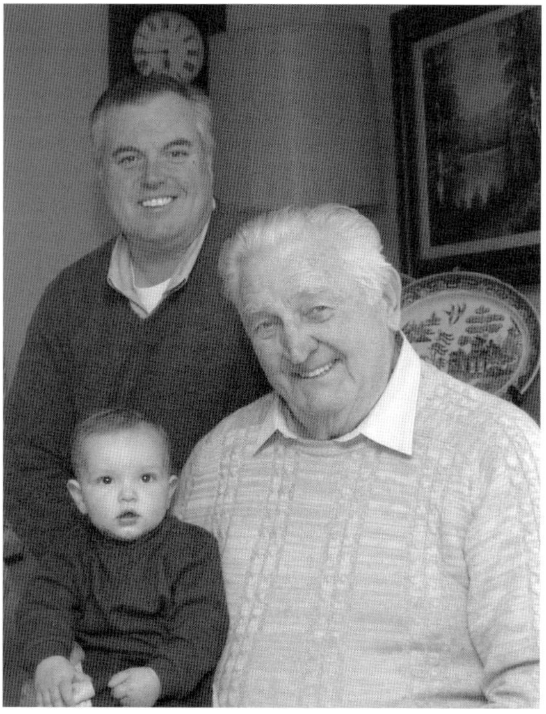

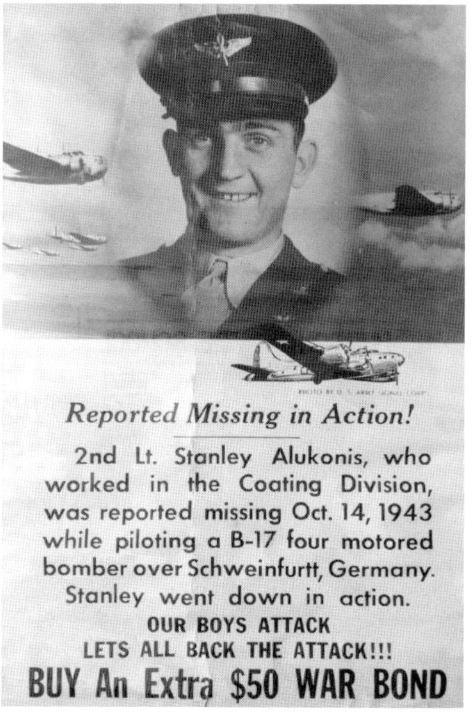

The Alukonis Family

The Alukonis family has resided on the family farm on Central Street for over 100 years. The farm was purchased by Stevens Alukonis and operated as Granite State Dairy for many years. Stevens's son Stanley was a bomber pilot during World War II; he was shot down over Germany but evaded capture and was reported as missing in action. While missing in action, his face was used on posters to help sell war bonds. He retired from the Air Force with the rank of lieutenant colonel. Stanley was a land developer and served the town as a selectman from 1969 through 1971; he also served as a state representative from 1973 to 1974. Stanley died at age 88 in 2006, and the town report was dedicated to him. Stanley's son David resides on the homestead with his family; he is a 1978 graduate of Alvirne and a graduate of Boston College. His wife, Michele (Roome), has taught in the Hudson school system for many years. Their son Seamus was born in 2003. David has served on the town council and as chairman of the school board. He served six terms as a state representative. He is a lifetime member of the Hudson Historical Society and has served as chairman of the board and president of the society. He took over the grill at Old Home Days from Leon Hammond but has since moved on to the job of making lobster rolls at the event. Pictured above on the left around 2006 are three generations of Alukonis men: Stanley, his son David, and his grandson, Seamus. (Both, courtesy the Alukonis family.)

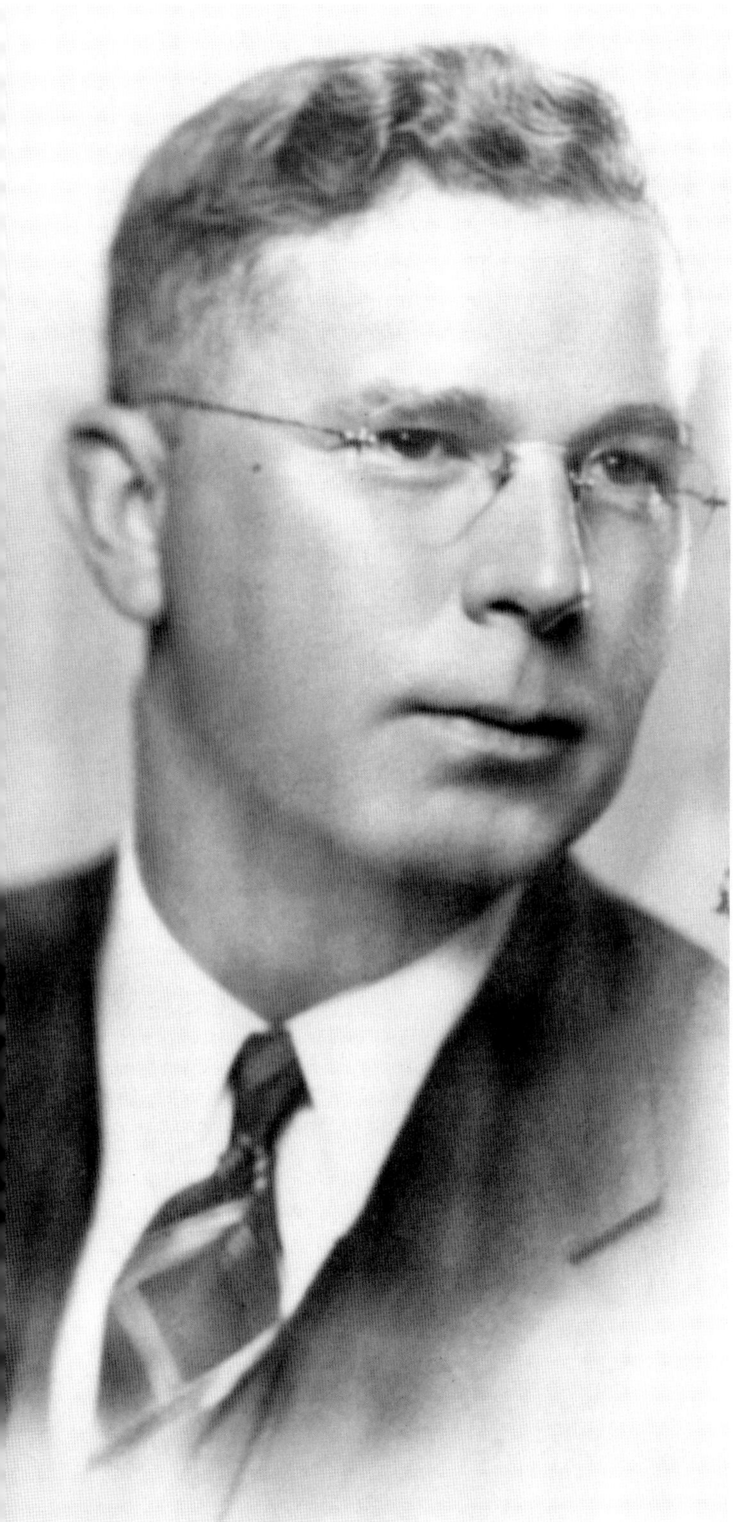

Grant Jasper

Grant Jasper was born in Amsterdam, New York. He purchased a small poultry farm on the Derry Road in 1916 for $6,000. Over the next 30 years, he expanded the business, making it the third-largest poultry operation in the state, by purchasing the Nathaniel Hills Jr. Farm, the Henry Hills Jr. Farm from the Dooley family, and the Andrews Farm, all on what is now the Derry Road. He produced his own line of chickens and sold hatching eggs and baby chicks. His hatchery was capable of hatching 20,000 baby chicks a week. By 1950, those four farms were among the 10 properties in town with the highest assessment. Grant played a large role in the leadership of the poultry industry in the Northeast, which at the time was a very important part of the economy of the state and the region. Grant served as president of the Northeast Poultry Producers Council and the New Hampshire Poultry Growers Association. He was an active member of the Hudson Community Church, heading up fundraising for both the parsonage and the addition to the church. He was elected to the first town budget committee in 1932 and served on the municipal budget committee from 1939 to 1950. In 1938, he purchased the No. 9 Schoolhouse from the school district for $250. He was a 32nd-degree Mason and a member of the Shriners International. He was an Alvirne trustee at the time of his death in 1956. The 1956 town report was dedicated to him. (Courtesy the Jasper family.)

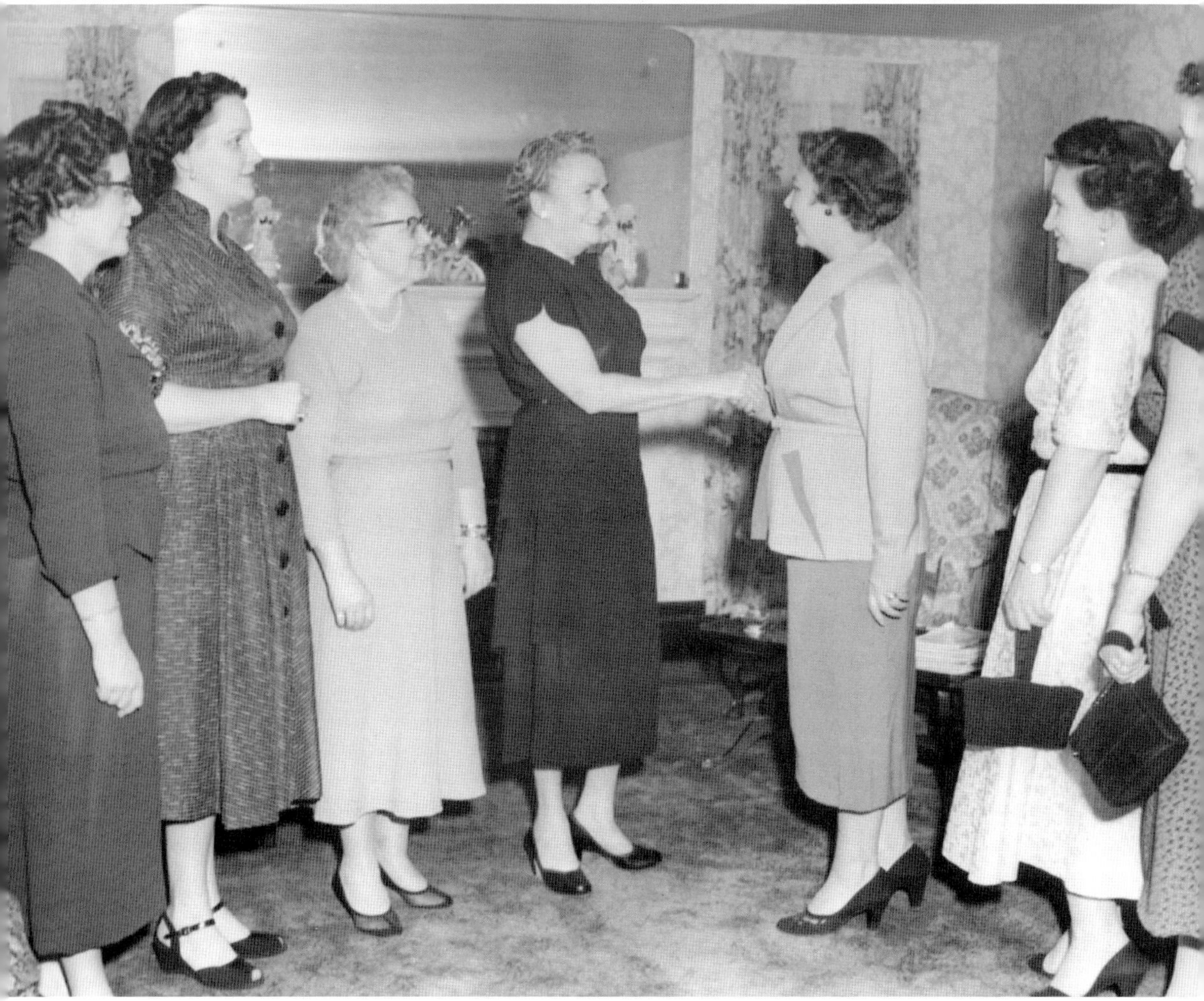

Fortnightly
The ladies of the Fortnightly Club gather at the home of Grant and Bernice Jasper about 1948. Pictured here from left to right are Hazel Austin, Josephine Steckevicz, Bernice Jasper, Maude French, Mildred Claveau, Madeline Adhrendt, and an unidentified woman. (Courtesy the Jasper family.)

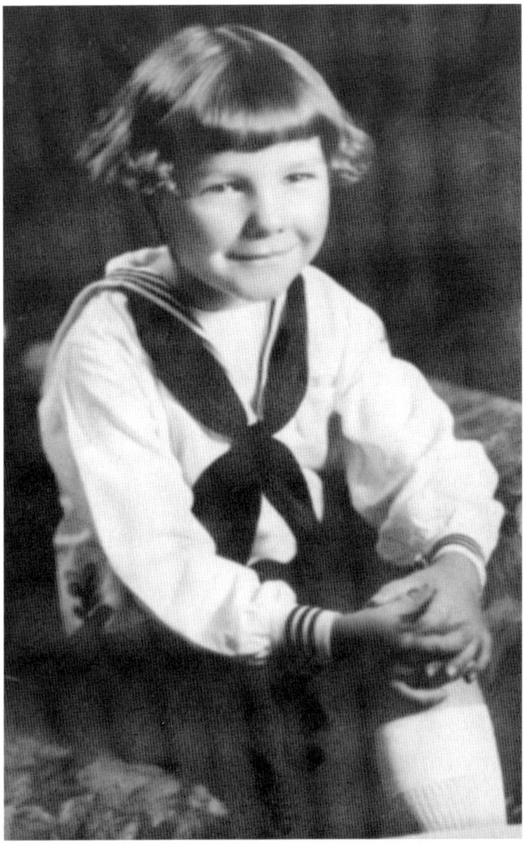

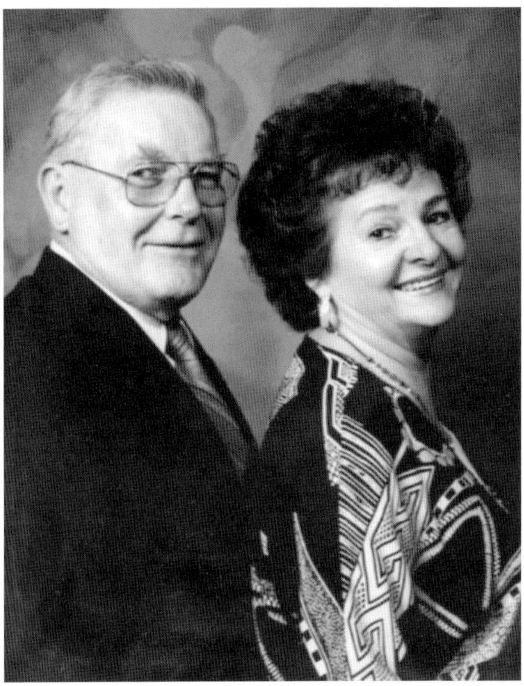

Robert "Bob" Jasper

Bob Jasper was a son of Grant Jasper and was brought up on the family farm. Prior to his father's death, he had taken over the day-to-day operations of the farm. In 1969, there were 40,000 laying hens and 20,000 replacement pullets on the four farms. Production hit a high that year with 6.5 million eggs. Most of production on the farm was in hatching eggs. Bob, like his father, served as president of the New Hampshire Poultry Growers Association. The association used to have an omelet booth at fairs around the state at which he worked, even wearing a rooster suit one year to attract business. Bob closed down the poultry operation in 1972 and developed a campground and later a mobile home park. He served the town as a member of the school board during the 1950s and represented the school board on the budget committee. He stated that closing the Center School was the hardest vote he ever had to take, as parents and students were so fond of it. He served as an Alvirne trustee for over 25 years. Bob served on the planning board during the late 1970s and early 1980s. He was a life member of the Hudson Historical Society, a 32nd-degree Mason, and a member of the Shriners. He and his wife, Reita, pictured below, had two children, Shawn and Maria (Jasper) VanderWoude. Bob died at age 89 in 2012, and both the 2012 town and school district reports were dedicated to him. (Courtesy the Jasper family.)

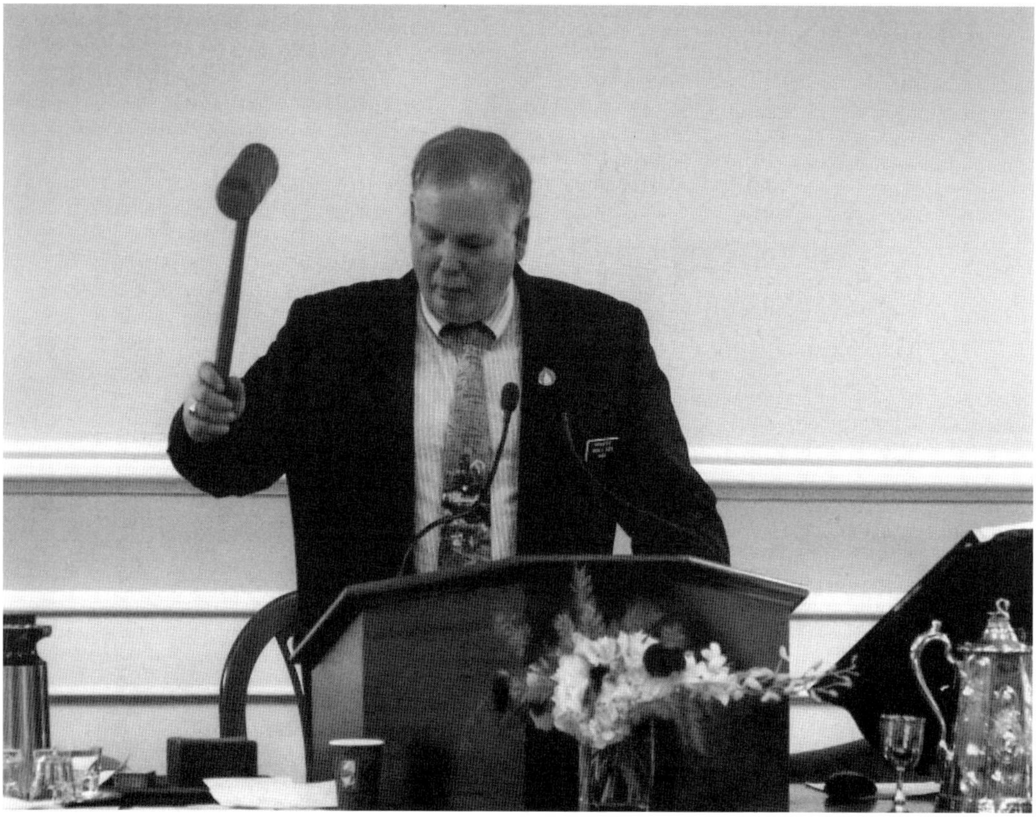

Shawn Jasper

Shawn Jasper is the son of Robert and Reita Jasper. The family lived on what was the old Andrews Farm, currently 55 Old Derry Road, until the death of Shawn's grandmother in 1974, when they moved to the family homestead. Shawn married Laurie (Lyons) in 1992, and they have a daughter, Sarah. They now live in the family homestead, and Shawn is an Alvirne graduate. While at Alvirne High School, he was active in the Future Farmers of America (FFA), and he holds a life membership. He received his associate's degree from the University of New Hampshire, where he was a member of Alpha Gamma Rho, the agricultural fraternity. He has served his fraternity as chapter advisor for the past 26 years. In 1979, at age 20, Shawn went into the poultry business with 7,500 breeding hens. He operated the farm for four years. By the time he closed the farm, the family had produced 150 million eggs on the farms. He currently runs the family business, renting apartments, commercial space, and self-storage. In 2012, he was elected to his 10th term in the state legislature, where he has served in various leadership roles over the past five terms. On December 3, 2014, Shawn was elected speaker of the New Hampshire House of Representatives. He served 17 years on the board of selectmen, chairing that board several times. He is currently serving as chairman of the budget committee, on which he has served many terms since he was first elected to that body in 1980. He has also served as town and school district moderator and chairman of a charter study commission. He was the first junior member of the Hudson Historical Society and helped write the update of the *History of Hudson* in 1977. He is currently a life-member of the society and has served as its president and the chairman of the board. For many years he was chairman of the society's Old Home Days Committee. He served the town for 20 years as a call firefighter. Shawn played an important role in the redevelopment of Benson's Wild Animal Farm as a town park, and currently he is a member of the town's Benson Park Committee and a member of the board of directors of the Friends of Benson Park. He is a 32nd-degree Mason and a Shriner. (Courtesy *Concord Monitor.*)

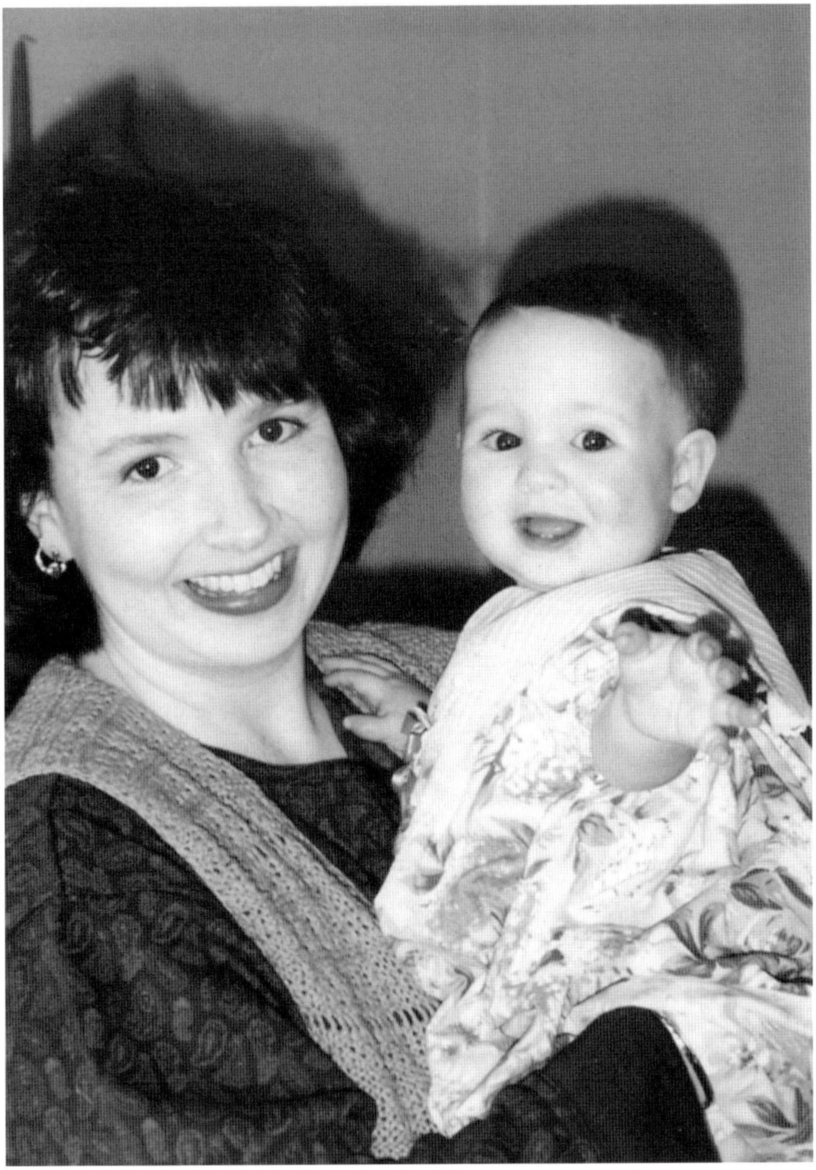

Laurie and Sarah Jasper

Laurie (Lyons) Jasper was born and raised in Andover, Massachusetts. A graduate of the University of Massachusetts at Lowell with a degree in English, she married Shawn Jasper on October 3, 1992, and moved to Hudson. She is a member of the Hudson Historical Society and was clerk from 1993 to 2002. She was an original member of the Benson Park Committee. She and Shawn have one daughter, Sarah Jean, who was born in 1994, and she is seen with Laurie in this photograph. Sarah is a student at the University of New Hampshire. In 1999, Laurie's book Images of America: *Hudson, New Hampshire* was published by Arcadia Publishing. She also helped write the history of St. Kathryn Parish for its 40th anniversary in 2008, the first written history of the parish. She worked as a reading tutor for the Hudson School District and works at Rodgers Memorial Library. She also contributes to the *Hudson-Litchfield News*. One of her favorite activities is accompanying the third-grade classes on the Hudson History Tour each year.

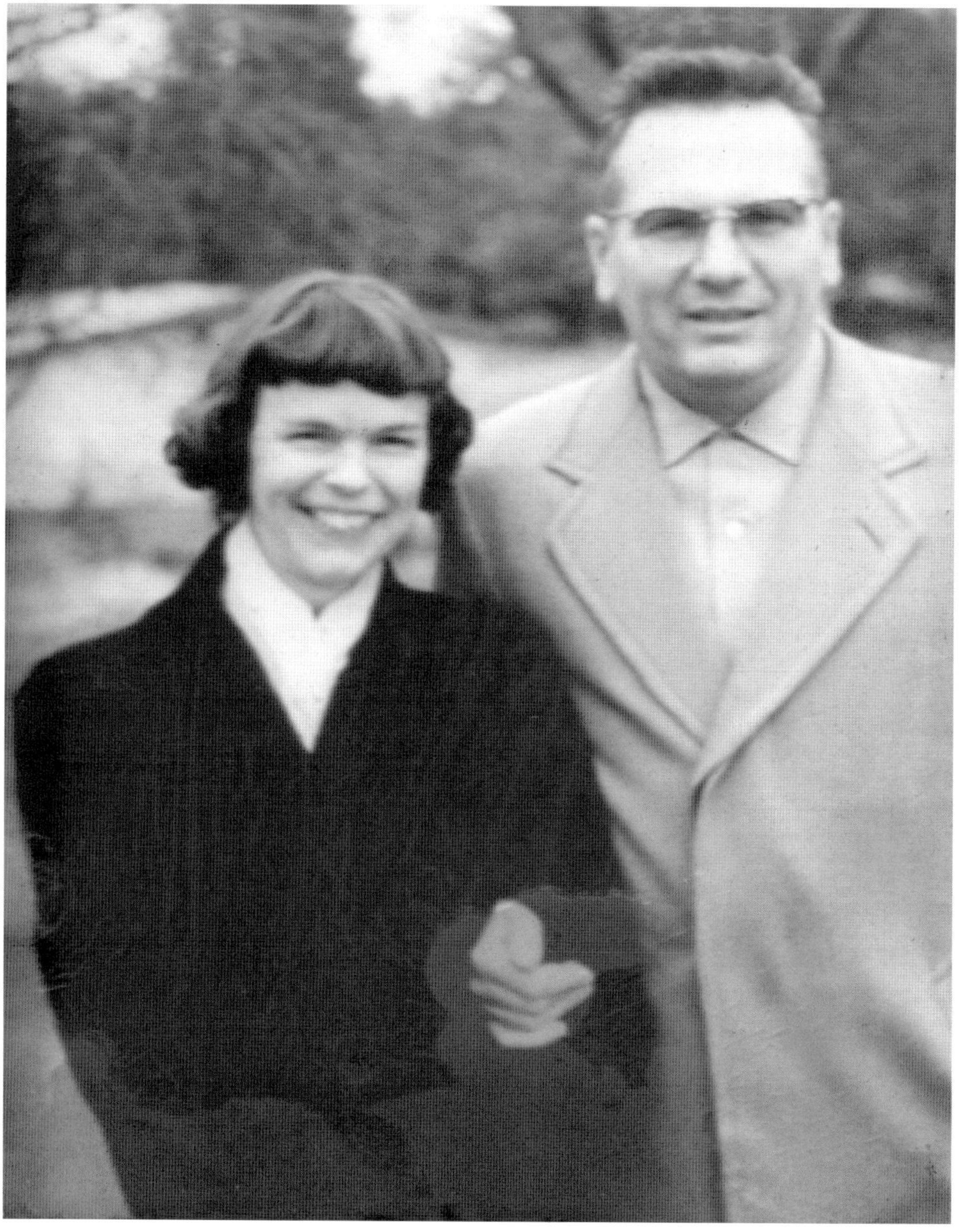

French Family (ABOVE AND OPPOSITE PAGE)
Harold French was born in 1899, a son of Menzell French of Hudson. In 1928, he started the French Insurance Agency, which was run by his son Gordon for many years. Today his grandson Richard "Rick" and granddaughter Roberta "Bobbi" continue the family business. Harold was active in community affairs and a longtime Alvirne trustee, as was his son Gordon, who died in 2009. The French family has always been active in the community and is a highly respected family. Above, Gordon and wife, Bette French, are pictured. The next image shows, clockwise from left, Harold, Maude, Gordon, Bette, and Rick French. In the last image, pictured from left to right in back are Harold French, Patricia Rogers (Harold's daughter), Maude French, Rick French, Roberta "Bobbi" French, Bette French, and Gordon French. In front of Maude French is Carol French. The five children in front are not identified. (All, courtesy the French family.)

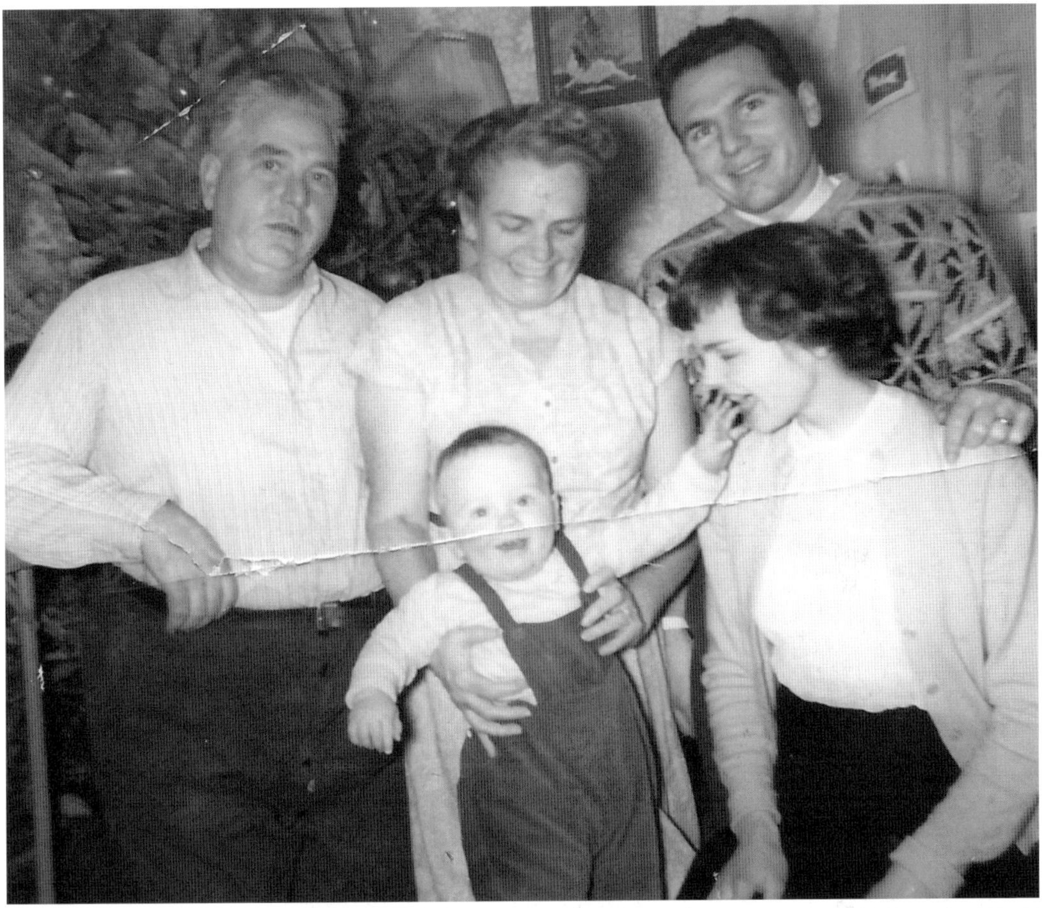

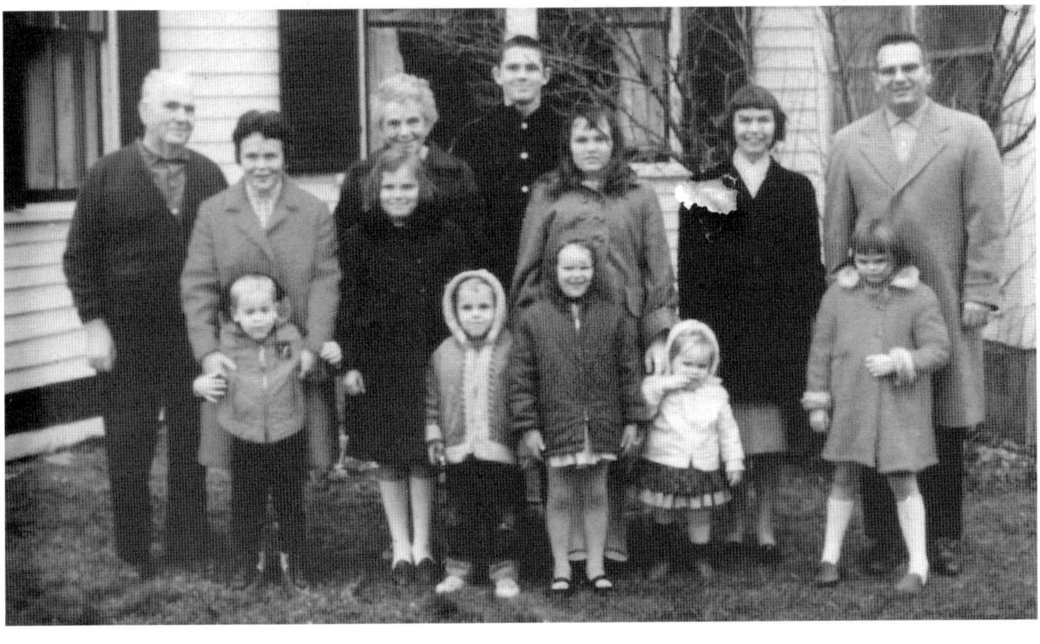

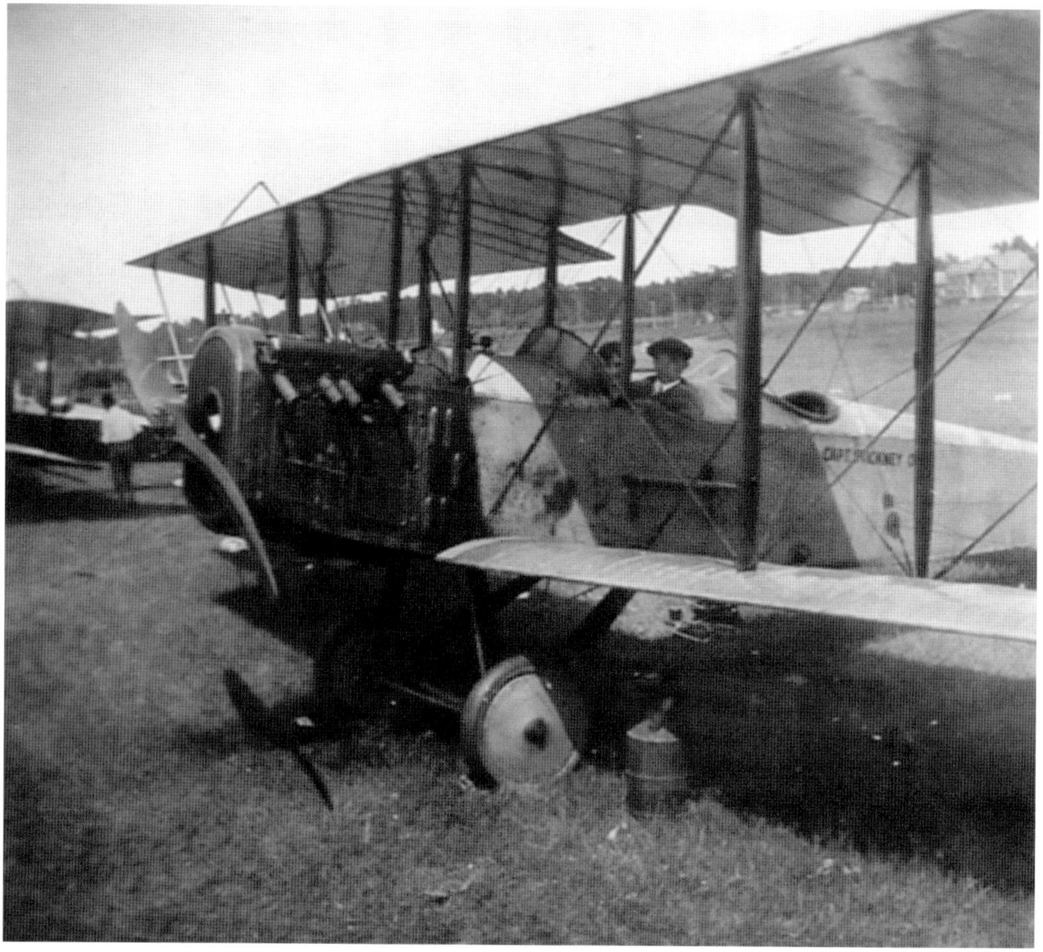

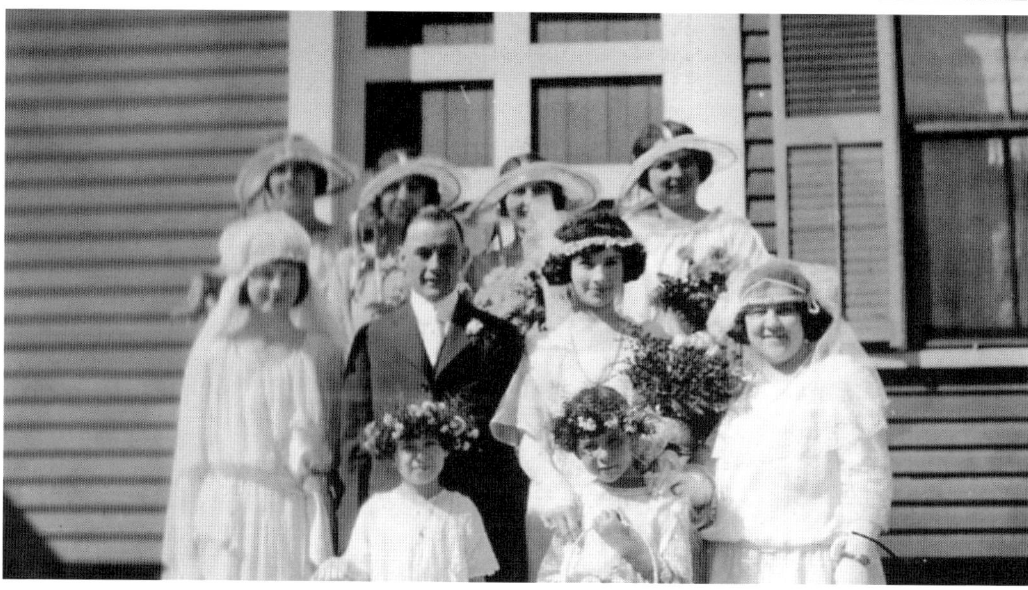

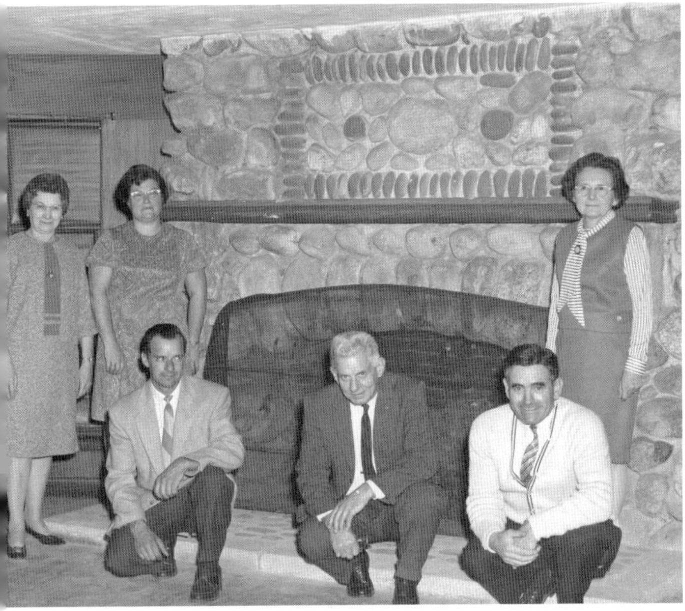

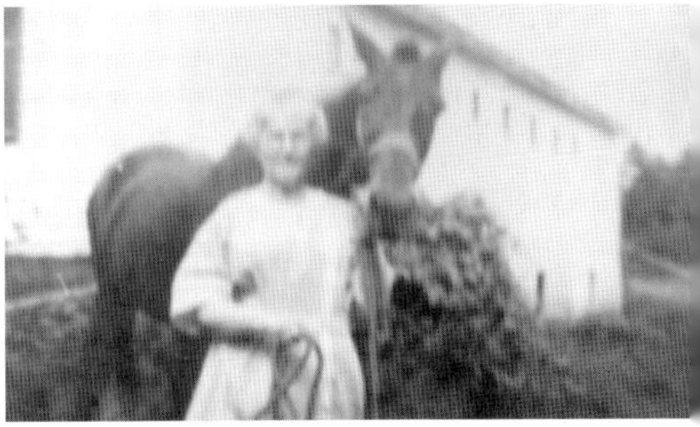

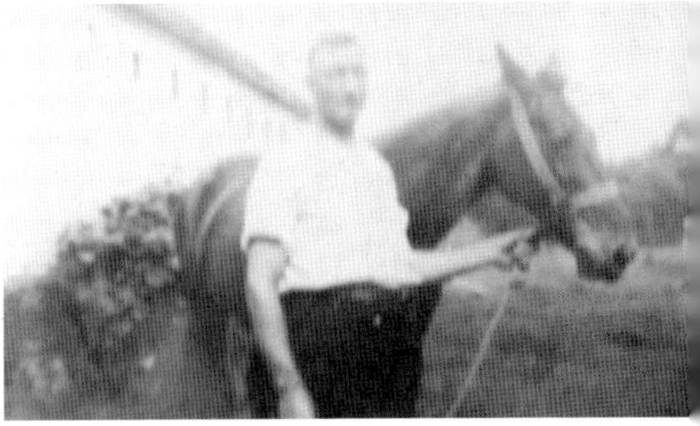

The Ferryall/Rowell Family (ABOVE AND OPPOSITE PAGE)
In the late 1890s, Abraham Ferryall purchased one of the finest homes in town on what is now Webster Street. That farm was part of the original Joseph Hills Farm. By World War I, the farm was owned by Abraham's son Fred, and he allowed a portion of the property near the Merrimack River to be used as a landing field for planes. It was included on government maps and known as Ferryall Field, and early air shows were held there. The plane on the opposite page is shown there around 1920. More can be learned about the field from the *History of Hudson Update*, published in 1977 by the Hudson Historical Society.

Zoula Ferryall was the daughter of Fred; she married Harold Rowell (shown on the opposite page with their wedding party in 1923), and they eventually took over the family farm. Zoula had a long and distinguished record of community service. She served on the Recreation Committee for 27 years and was involved in both 4-H and Scouting. She served as president of the Fortnightly Club, of which she was a member for over 50 years, and was the first president of the Women's Guild at St. John's Parish in Hudson. She was an active member of the Hudson Historical Society and assisted in writing the update to the *History of Hudson* in 1977. Zoula died in 1978 at age 75. Upon the death of her son Fred, the farm passed out of the family. The stately home was demolished, and the farmland was developed for housing.

Zoula's parents, Fred and Augustine Ferryall, are pictured in the 1920s. The 1968 photograph above at left shows members of the Hudson Historical Society. From left to right are Zoula Rowell, Doris Provencher, Fred Rowell (Zoula's son), Robert Hill (the first society president), Louis Pecce, and Gretta Pecce. The Pecces were the first caretakers of the society's Hills House. (All, courtesy HHS.)

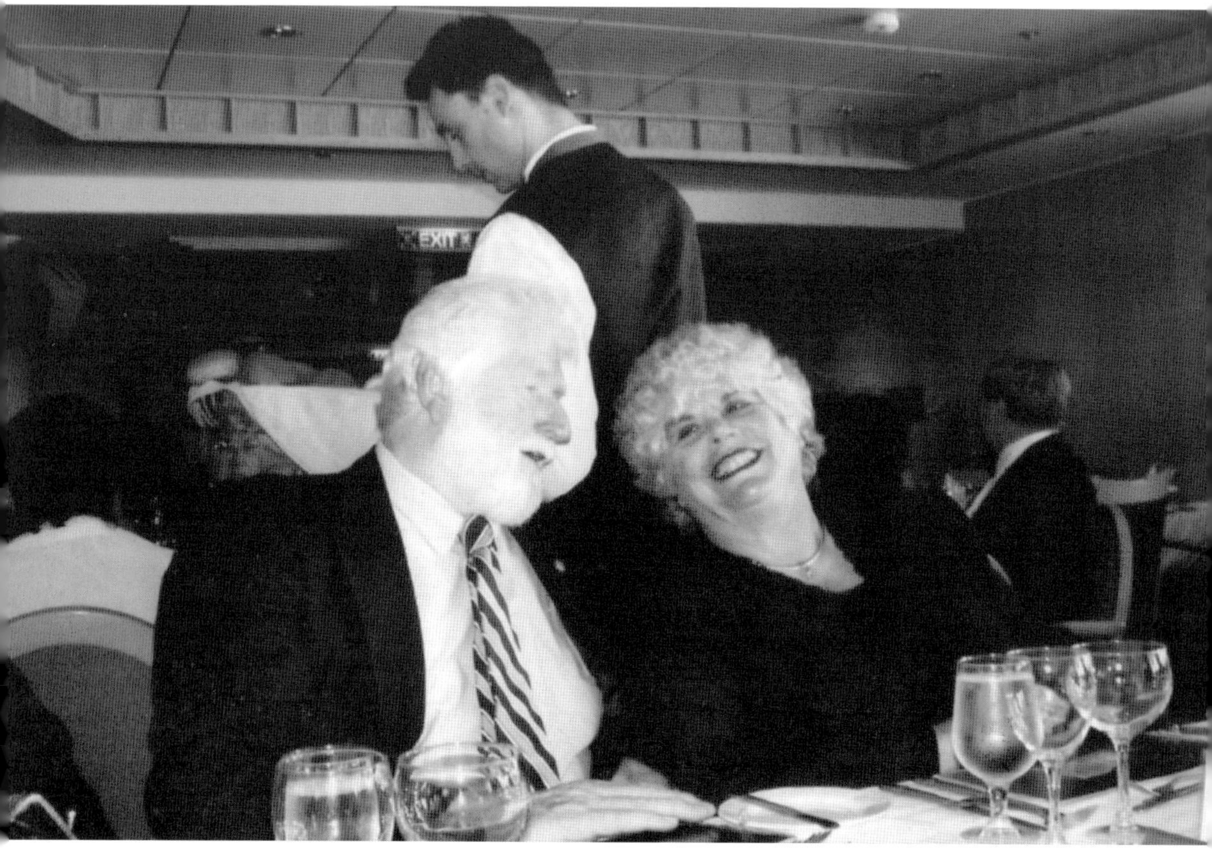

Bradford and Ann Seabury

J. Bradford "Brad" and Ann Seabury moved to Hudson in 1964. They were both born in Maine but were living out of the New England area when family obligations brought them to Hudson. While their children were young, both Brad and Ann were involved in Scouting. Brad became an alternate member of the zoning board of adjustment in 1982 and has served as a regular member since 1983. He has been chairman for well over 25 years. The 2013 town report was dedicated to Brad for his years of dedicated service, only the second report dedicated to a living person. Brad has also held the position as school district clerk for many years. Ann went to the school district looking for a job as a secretary, but instead, she was told she should be a substitute teacher. It was a job she loved, and her students loved her; for 25 years, she substitute taught at Hudson Memorial School. Ann was very active in civic organizations, including Hudson Junior Women's Club, the Hudson Fortnightly Club, and the Hudson Community Club. She ran for selectman in 1984 and won a seat on the board. In 1991, Ann became the school district clerk, a position she held until her death. In 1992, Ann served on the last town council and then on the new board of selectmen. Over her years on the board of selectmen, Ann served as the liaison to nearly every department. Ann died in 2005, and the school district and town reports were combined into one volume and dedicated to her. A study room at Rodgers Memorial Library was named for Ann Seabury, as is the Ann Seabury Meeting Room at the Hudson Police Department. Those who knew her will always remember her infectious laugh. (Courtesy the Seabury family.)

CHAPTER SIX

Community Leaders, Locals, and Legacies

Many of the people in this chapter could no doubt fit neatly into other chapters, and many of those in others chapters could have been placed here. It is safe to say that numerous residents through the years have worn many different hats in town. It seems that running a business in Hudson was only part of their job; serving the community was the other part. Others found here served the town in various ways on many different, boards, committees, or civic organizations. Hudson has always relied on volunteers to get things done. That continues to be evidenced in the wonderful work a large group of dedicated volunteers has done and continues to do at Benson Park. Many people have fond memories of the former Benson's Wild Animal Farm, and the town's passive recreation park, the pride of the town, is a legacy to John T. Benson and Arthur Provencher and all who worked and enjoyed the one-of-a-kind location.

In addition to business leaders and volunteers, Hudson has been fortunate to be led by men of strong faith who have helped the community grow spiritually. During hopeful, joyful times, as well as times of deep sorrow, Hudson has been fortunate to be led by kind, capable leaders. The town of Hudson always seems to come together in the sad times, as in the loss of a community member who has gone too soon but who was a vibrant part of the community.

All have a story to tell, and all leave a legacy behind.

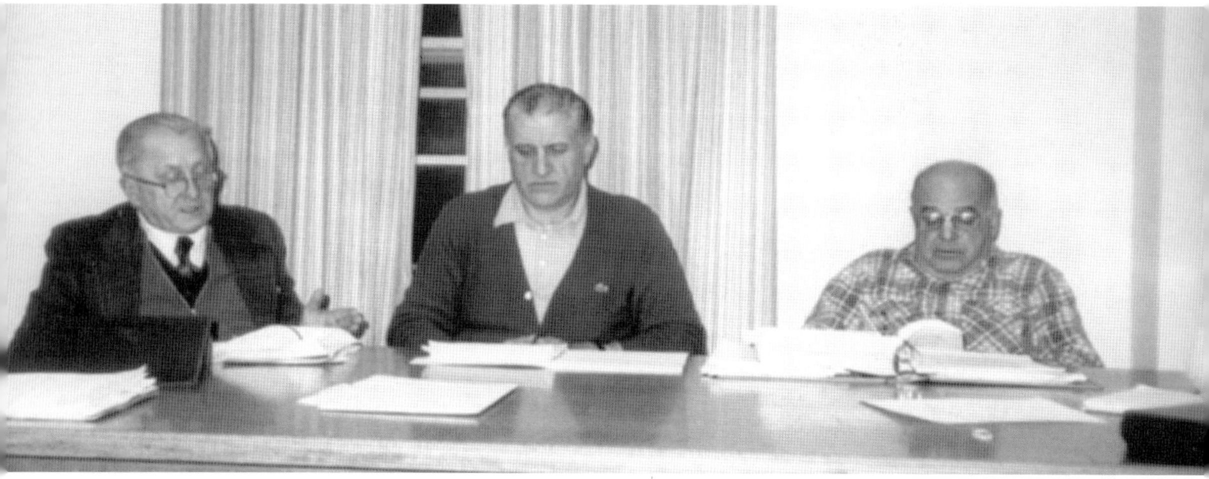

John Bednar

John Bednar moved to Hudson in 1949 and opened a restaurant. John was a blunt individual who angered easily. He served in the legislature and sponsored "The Right to Know" Law. He inspired strong feelings and once was the only candidate for town clerk and tax collector when signs sprang up for someone else, and John lost to the write-in candidate. He was town moderator in the early 1960s and was elected in 1966 to the board of selectmen, where he served four nonconsecutive terms. He petitioned for and chaired the Charter Study Commission. This photograph shows the last of the three-member board of selectmen, in 1983: from left to right, John Bednar, Leon Malouin, and John Lawrence. (Courtesy HHS.)

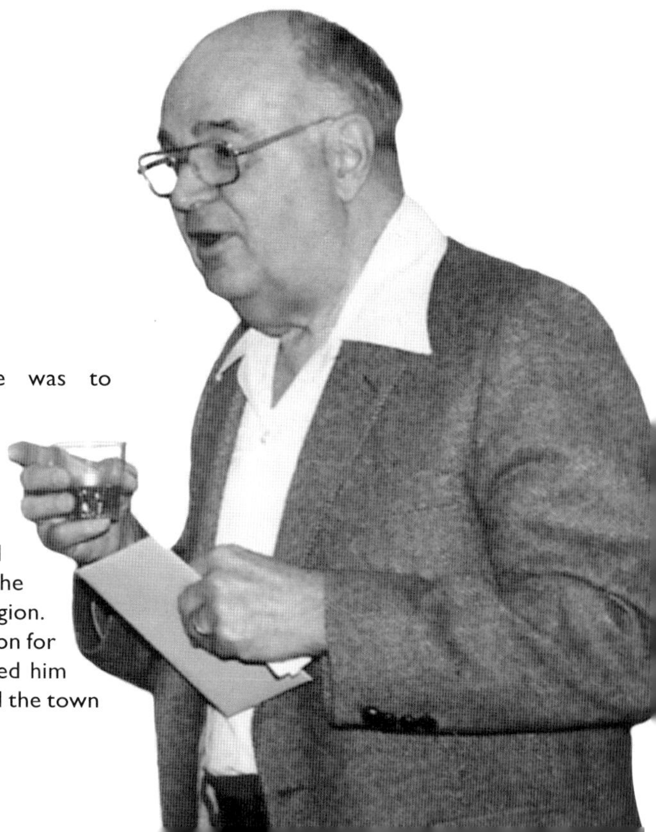

John Lawrence

John P. Lawrence's first elective office was to the school board in 1959. He served as the town clerk and tax collector, supervisor of the check list, selectman, and state representative. John worked for IBM and acquired an early computer from them which, while out of date, was still serviceable. He began a business servicing the accounting needs of many towns in the region. many years, he provided that service to Hudson for free. His daughter Karen Wisnoski succeeded him as town clerk. John died in 2007 at age 91, and the town report was dedicated to him.

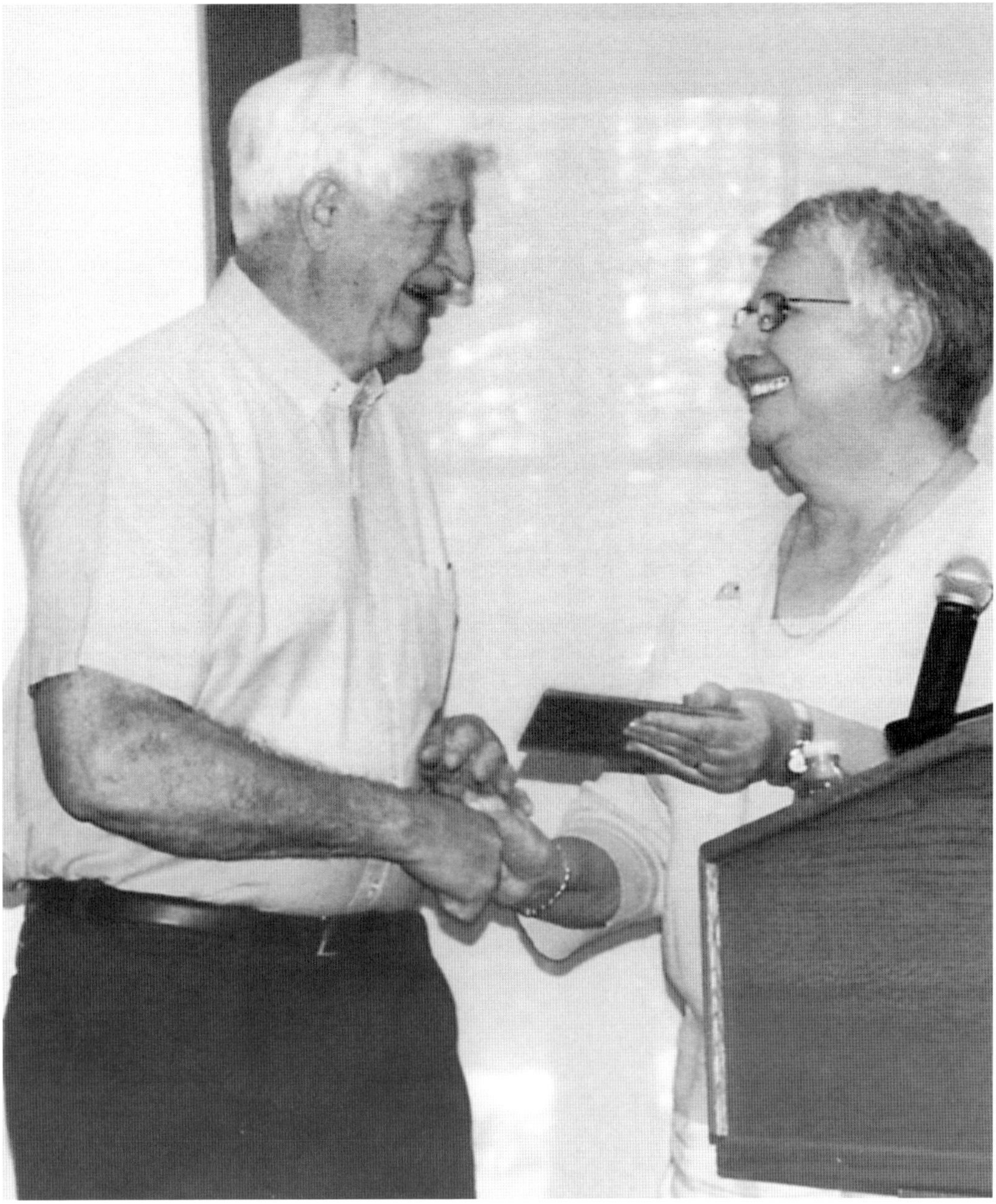

Bernard "Bernie" Manor

Bernie Manor has been "clerk of the works" for many town projects, including Rodgers Memorial Library, Hills Garrison School, and the recently completed North Barn Senior Center at Benson Park. He also oversaw the contract work on the Benson Park buildings. The library's archival room was named in his honor in 2013. He has worked on the Hudson Historical Society's 1911 Maxwell restoration, was on the planning board and water utility committee, and is a genuinely nice man who has always looked out for the taxpayers of Hudson. Here Bernie is shown with Elaine Brody. (Courtesy Rodgers Memorial Library.)

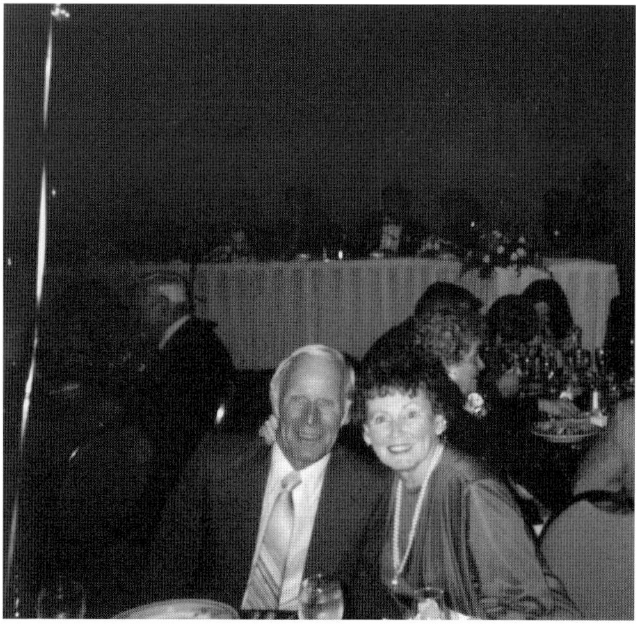

Leslie and Margaret Erb

Leslie "Les" and Margaret Erb lived at Sky Farm Orchard at the top of Bush Hill Road, the farm on which Les grew up. While Les ran the apple orchard and later served on the zoning board of adjustment in the 1980s, Margaret began a successful career as an award-winning photographer in the 1960s. She also took a turn as a racecar driver. In the 1980s, Margaret jumped into town politics, serving first on the budget committee and then as a member of the school board and town council simultaneously. The home now belongs to James Mills, who operates a sawmill on the property.

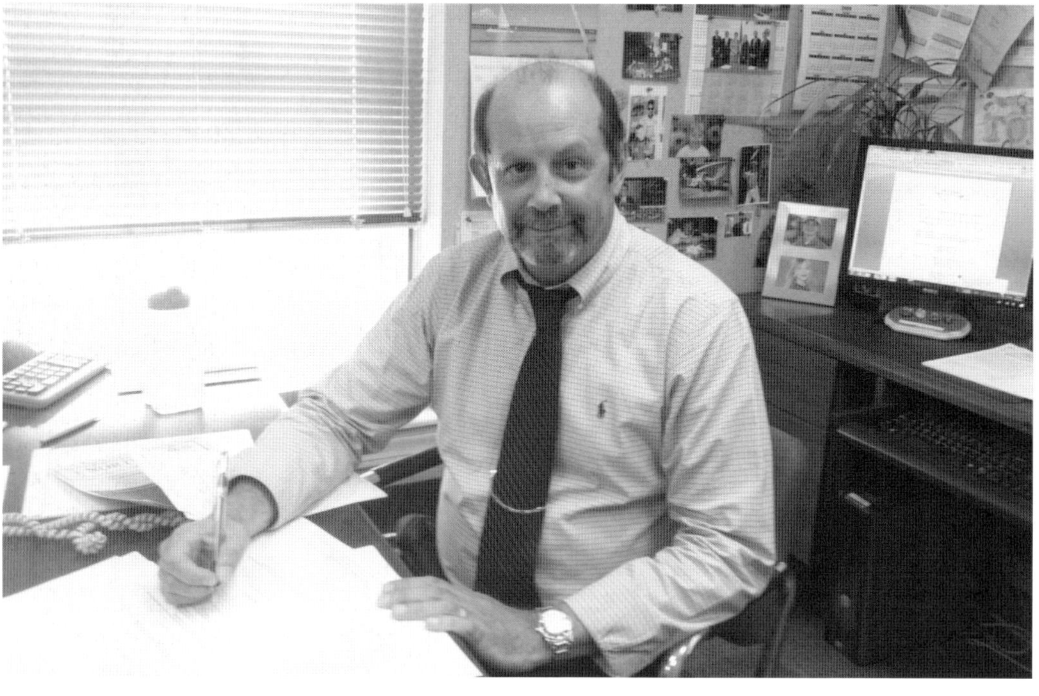

Steve Malizia

Hired by the Hudson Board of Selectmen on January 6, 1997, as the town's second finance director, Steve Malizia has been Hudson's town administrator since April 9, 2003. Steve works closely with the board of selectmen and town department heads and runs the day-to-day operations of the town with great care and efficiency. He holds a bachelor of science degree in business administration from the University of Massachusetts at Lowell. He and his wife, Deanne (Chaisson), live in Hudson with their two children, Daniel (15) and Lara (11). (Courtesy Steve Malizia.)

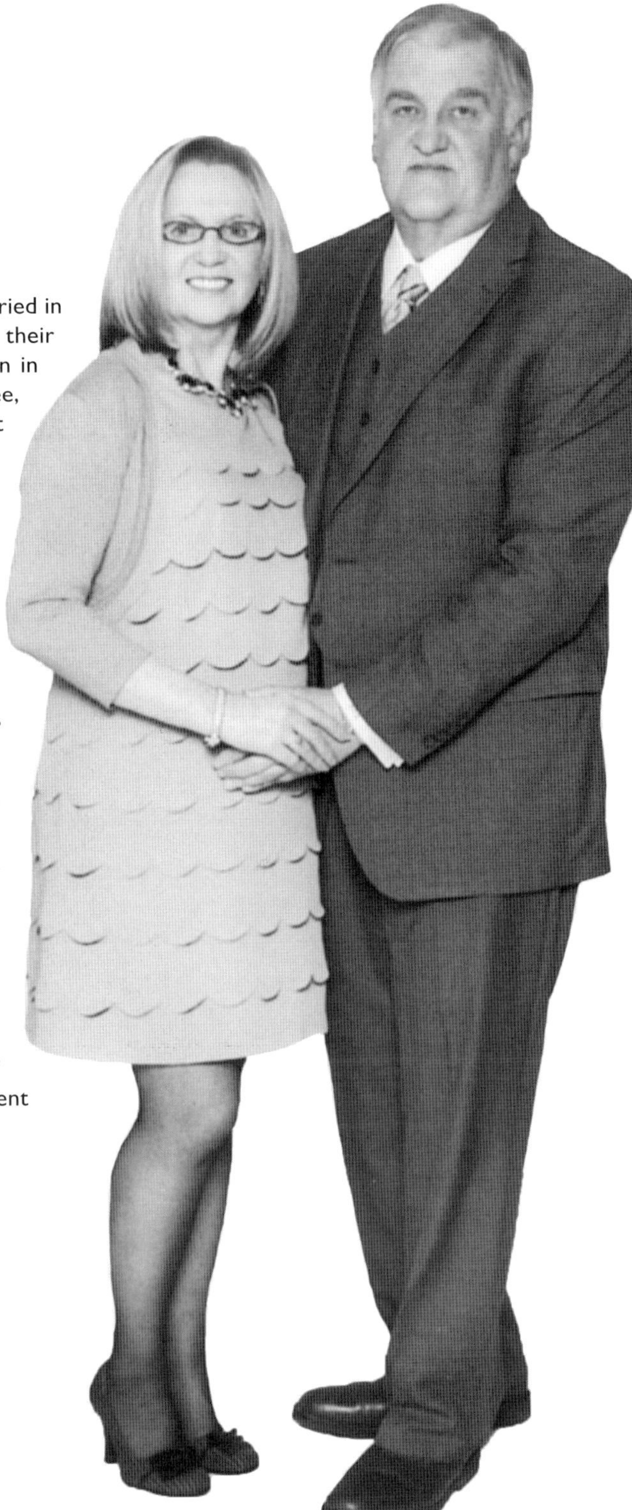

Leonard and Eileen Lathrop

Leonard "Len" Lathrop and Eileen Moore married in 1975 in Lowell, Massachusetts. They adopted their daughter Sarah in 1981 and moved to Hudson in 1985. Len served on the recreation committee, zoning board of appeals, and the budget committee. He also served on the selectmen's ad hoc committee for Hudson seniors and was a member of the Merrifield Playground Development Committee and Presentation of Mary Field Development Committee. In 2000, Len purchased the local weekly paper, the *Hudson-Litchfield News*, from longtime owner Fidele Bernasconi. He developed the *Pelham-Windham News* in 2003 and the *Salem Community Patriot* in 2007. Currently, Len is a member of the Presentation of Mary Board of Advisors, the Greater Salem Board of Directors, Hudson Historical Society Board of Directors, Zach Tompkins Memorial Field Executive Committee, SAU 81 Business Advisory Committee, and the Regional Economic Development Committee Advisory Board. Len was named Hudson's Citizen of the Year in 2009, received the Salem Kiwanis Community Award in 2009, the Greater Salem Boys and Girls Club Communication Award in 2010, and Enterprise Bank Celebration of Excellence Award in 2010. Len is also an excellent photographer. (Courtesy the Lathrop family.)

Dr. Bernard and Elaine Brody

Dr. Bernard "Buzz" L. Brody and Elaine (Poskanzer) Brody, friends throughout high school in Albany, New York, married in July 1968 and moved to Hudson in 1976. Dr. Brody was a prominent veterinarian in town for 25 years. He and his wife have given back to the community in many ways. They opened Countryside Animal Hospital first at 148 Webster Street in 1976 before construction in 1978 of the new hospital building on Derry Road, where Dr. Brody cared for countless Hudson-area animals until retiring in 2001 and selling the business. In addition to being the business manager for Countryside Animal Hospital, Elaine volunteered in the Hudson schools, assisted in the renovation of Alvirne High School's farmhouse, and was cochairman of the Hills Garrison School building committee. She is presently an Alvirne trustee and a longtime member of the Friends of the Library. Elaine will always be remembered as the person who received the call from the Rodgers family stating they wished to donate money to build what would be called the George and Ella Rodgers Memorial Library. Elaine played an important role in the successful completion of the beautiful new library and was administrative coordinator for the project. The Elias Brody Memorial Concert, held at Alvirne High School, is sponsored by the Brodys each spring in memory of Dr. Brody's father, Elias, who died in 1984, loved the arts, and had been a musician and music teacher. The Brodys have four daughters, four granddaughters, and three grandsons. (Courtesy the Brody family.)

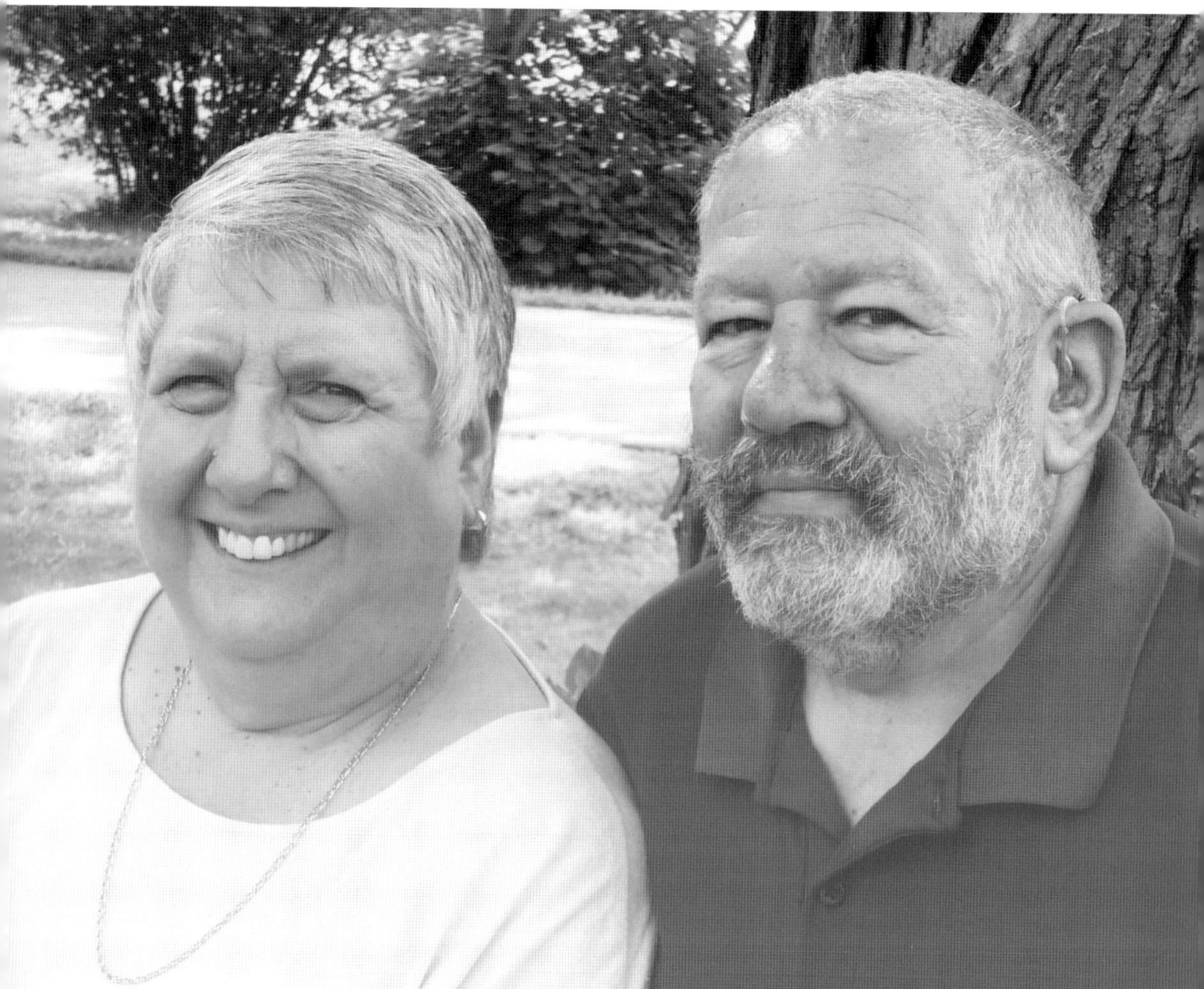

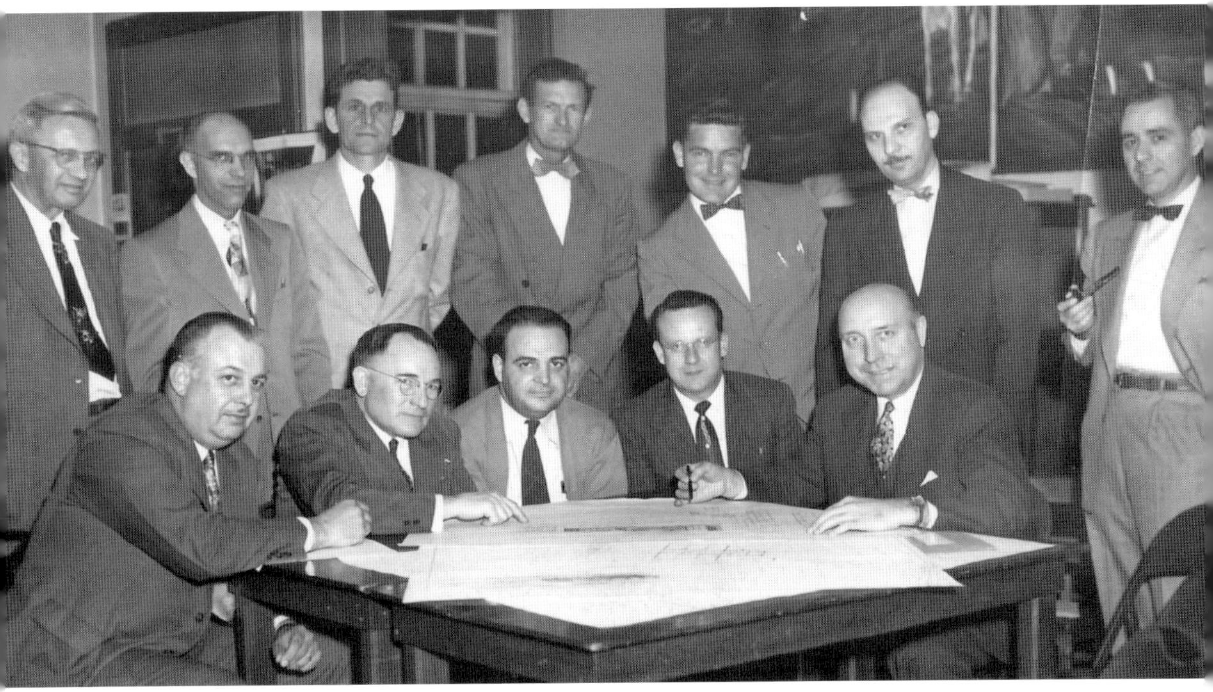

Dr. H.O. Smith School Building Committee

Members of the Dr. H.O. Smith School Building Committee are seen reviewing the plans for the new addition in this April 1954 photograph. Pictured here from left to right are (first row) Arthur Lougee (school board), Paul Buxton, John Lawrence, Robert Thompson, and Albert Richmond; (second row) Herbert Canfield, Henry Hastings (superintendent of schools), Leonard Smith, Arthur Smith, Robert Jasper (school board), and architects Herbert Glassman and John Carochia of Perley Gilbert Associates. (Courtesy the Jasper family.)

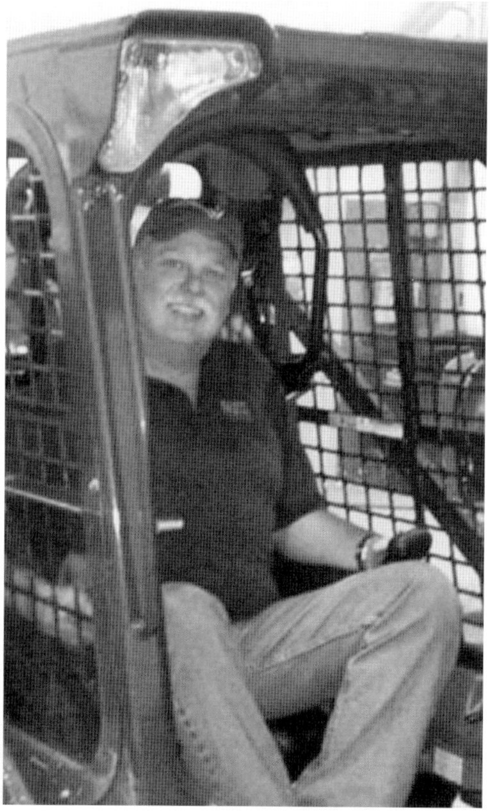

Kevin Burns

The Hudson Highway Department has been under road agent Kevin Burn's capable leadership since 1999. Born and raised in Lowell, Massachusetts, he began working with the highway department after the Air Force in 1983, becoming a foreman in 1987. One of the highlights of his career was the construction of the new highway facility that opened in 2000 for $950,000. Under Kevin, the town adopted the successful automated trash and recycling program and modernized the fleet, always staying within his budget. Hudson's highway department has played a major role in the revitalization, care, and upkeep of Benson Park and takes great pride in its work decorating Library Park for each season, especially at Christmas with festive lights, former Benson's Wild Animal Farm soldiers, and the town's Nativity scene. Kevin is quick to point out that he could not have accomplished these items without such a great group working along with him, especially his longtime right-hand man Jess Forrence, a lifelong Hudson resident who has been with the department since 1987. Hudson is fortunate to have such a dedicated group on the highway department who treat every part of Hudson as their own. (Both, courtesy Kevin Burns.)

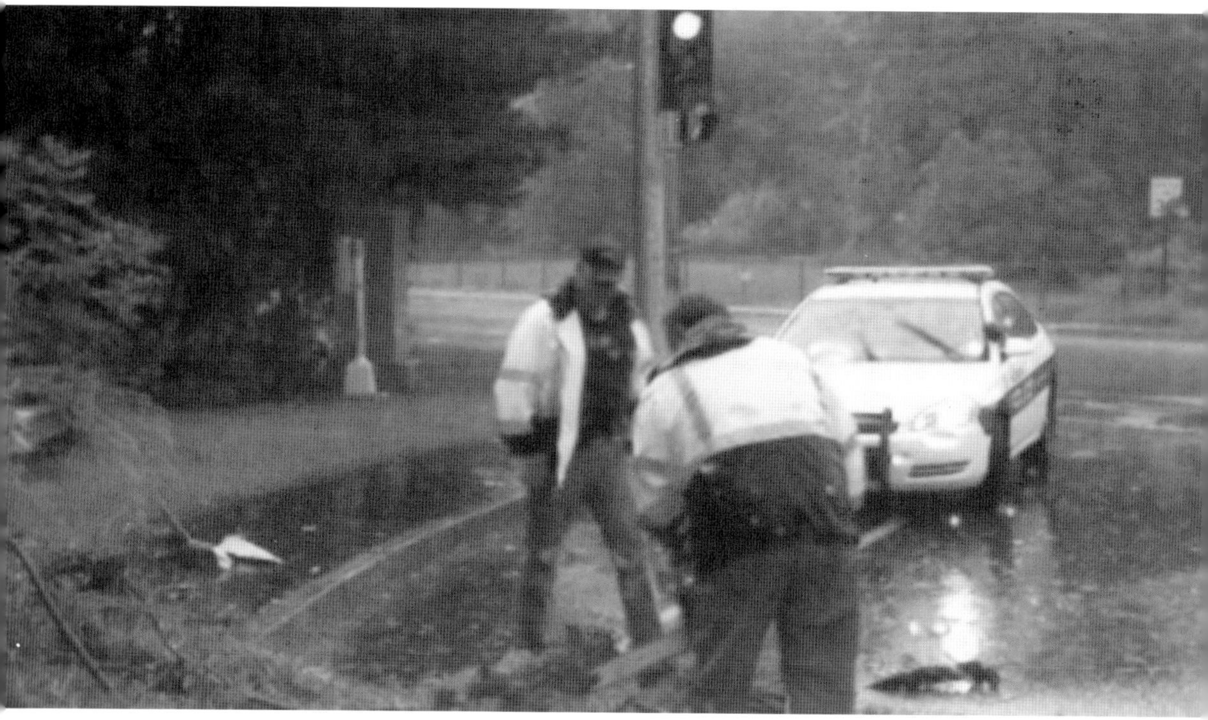

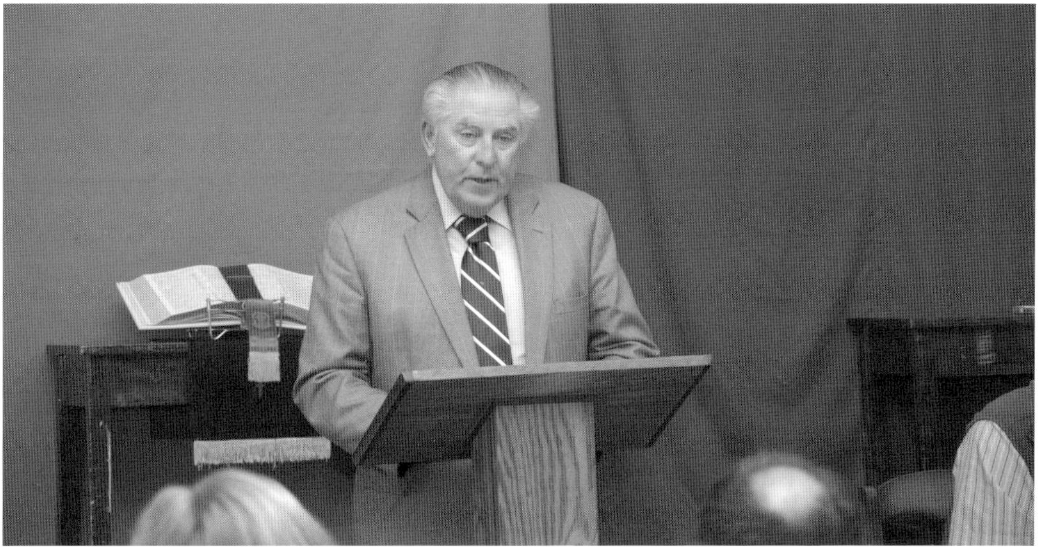

Rev. David Howe

Rev. David L. Howe has been pastor of the United Pentecostal Church for over 30 years. Reverend Howe's father established the church on the corner of Derry Road and Phillips Drive in 1963 and was the first pastor, with his son David succeeding him. The church changed its name in 2013 to the Sanctuary United Pentecostal Church. The Reverend Howe is a respected member of the Hudson community and has been the police and fire departments' longtime chaplain. (Both, courtesy Hudson Fire Department.)

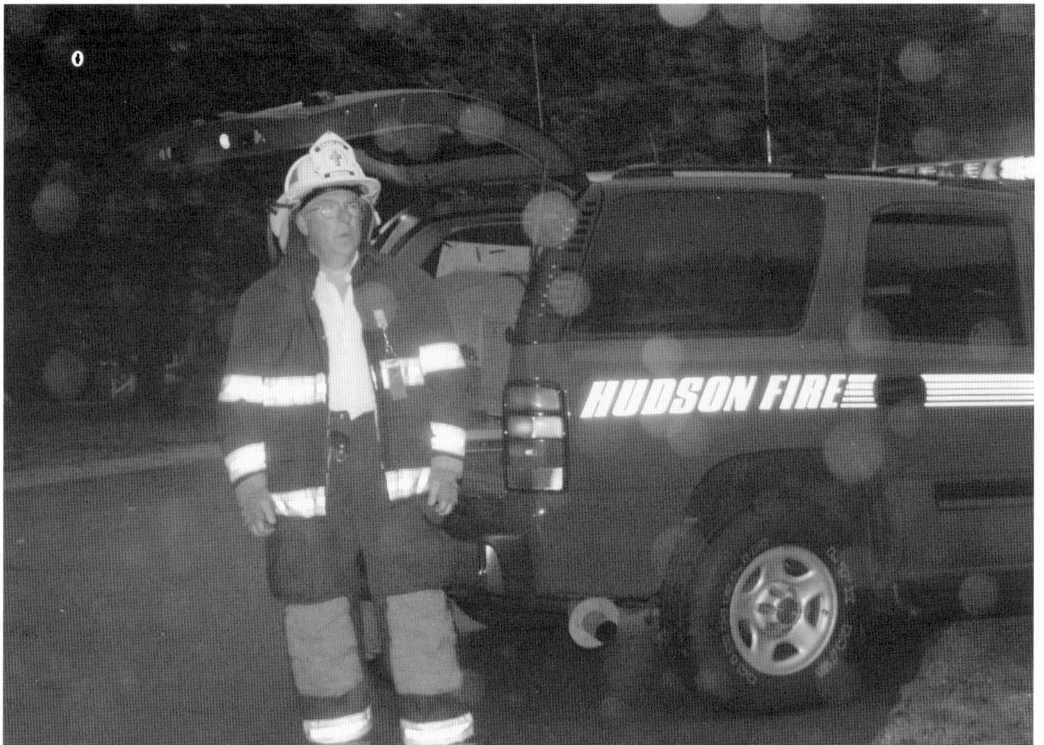

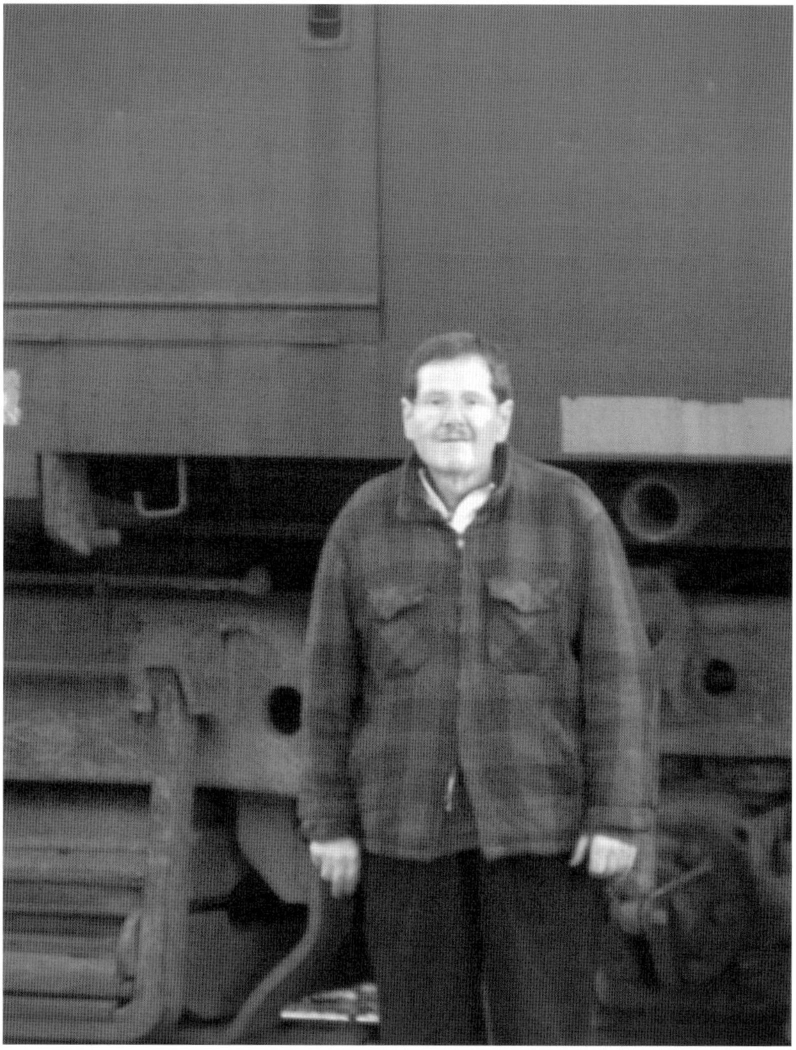

Howard Dilworth Jr.
Howard Dilworth Jr. moved with his family to Hudson in the 1960s. He graduated from Alvirne High School in 1972, having been an active member of the FFA, with which he served as a chapter and state officer. Howard was proud of the fact he was the first person in the state of New Hampshire to become a life-member of the FFA National Alumni Association. Howard joined the fire department as a call firefighter and emergency medical technician in 1975, and he would serve for 25 years. Howard was first elected to the budget committee in 1992 and served there until being elected to the board of selectmen in 1994. While on the board of selectmen, he served as the board's representative to the planning board and budget committee. After leaving the board of selectmen, Howard was elected to the budget committee in 1999 and served multiple terms as its chairman, leaving the committee in 2007 to become the Litchfield town manager. He also served for several years on the sewer utility committee. He was a longtime member of the Hudson Historical Society, having served as its president for several years. Howard had always hoped to help write the next update of the *History of Hudson* and diligently saved materials for that project for decades. Howard died at age 58 in 2012, and the town report was dedicated to him. This photograph shows Howard in his favorite well-worn red plaid jacket. (Courtesy the Dilworth family.)

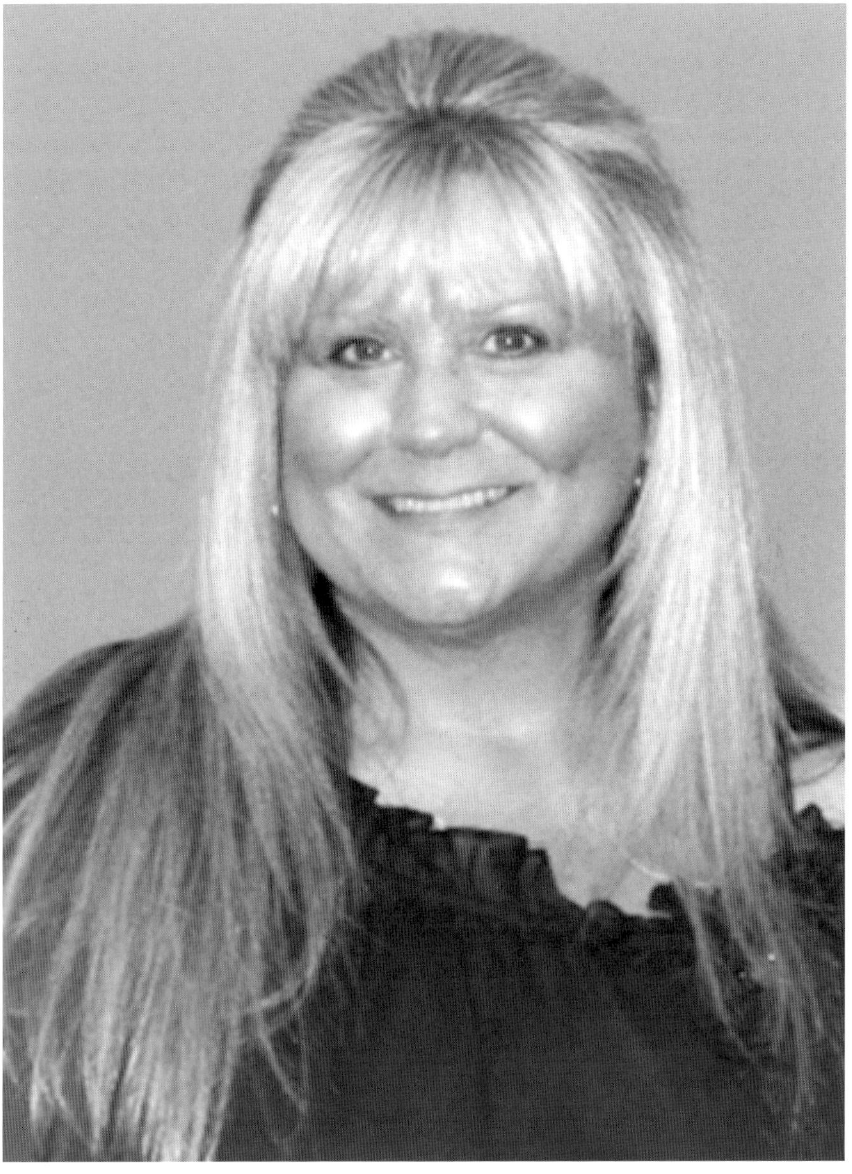

Brenda Collins
Brenda Collins was born and raised in Hudson, graduating from Alvirne High School in 1982 and Rivier College in 1986. She and her husband, Bill, have been married for 27 years and have two children, Olivia and Patrick. Many will recognize Brenda as the face of the Greater Hudson Chamber of Commerce, a position she has held since 1998. The chamber has grown from 85 members to over 185 members, and Brenda cheerfully organizes and attends to every detail of the many chamber events. For the past 13 years, the chamber of commerce has hosted a silent auction and dinner in December to benefit the St. Vincent de Paul Society. The chamber hosts an annual community exposition, the annual Citizen, Business, and Jr. Citizen of the Year Dinners, and many networking opportunities. Brenda is a member of the Hudson Historical Society, and for the past three years she has served as vice president of the town's Hudson Old Home Days Committee. Brenda was recognized as one of Greater Nashua's 25 Exemplary Women in 2014. (Courtesy Brenda Collins.)

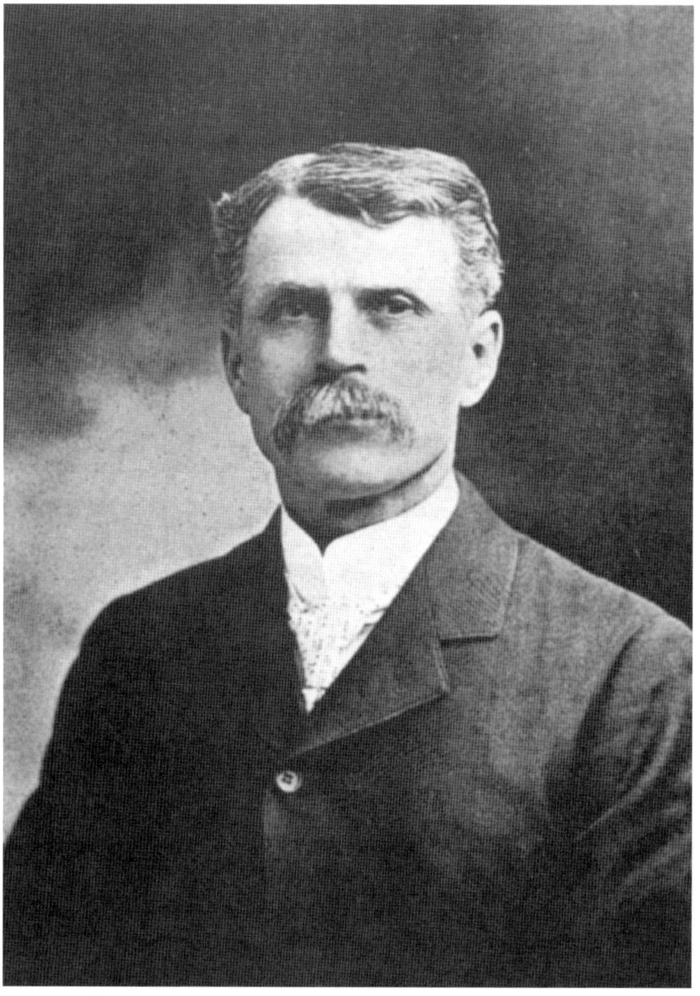

The Cummings Family (ABOVE AND OPPOSITE PAGE)
Willis Putnam Cummings was born in Lowell, Massachusetts, on January 27, 1850, and moved to Hudson with his family when he was six years old. Like his father before him, he was a builder by trade. He and his brother Charles bought the local wheelwright shop from James Carnes in 1882. Cummings Brothers manufactured and sold quality horse-drawn carriages. When the automobile became more popular, the business built commercial truck bodies. Willis was a musician throughout his life. During the Civil War, he, his father, and his uncle provided marching music as they escorted the 13th Regiment from their camp to the train station in Nashua to join the war, Willis playing a snare drum and his father and uncle playing fifes. He later learned to play the cornet and continued to pursue his love of music. He was a member of the Hudson Community Church, the Hudson Lodge of Odd Fellows, and the Hudson Grange. He was honored as the oldest male resident of the town and presented with the Boston Post Cane. In 1909, the *Boston Post Newspaper* distributed to 700 towns in New England a gold-headed ebony cane with the request that each be presented to the oldest male citizen of the town, to be used by him as long as he lives (or moves from the town), and at his death handed down to the next oldest citizen of the town. The cane would belong to the town and not the man who received it. Willis's father had previously held the cane. Willis died on June 15, 1939. Shown in the photographs are: Willis Cummings, a Cummings carriage, and a receipt from Cummings to Grant Jasper. (Above and above opposite, courtesy HHS; below opposite, courtesy the Jasper family.)

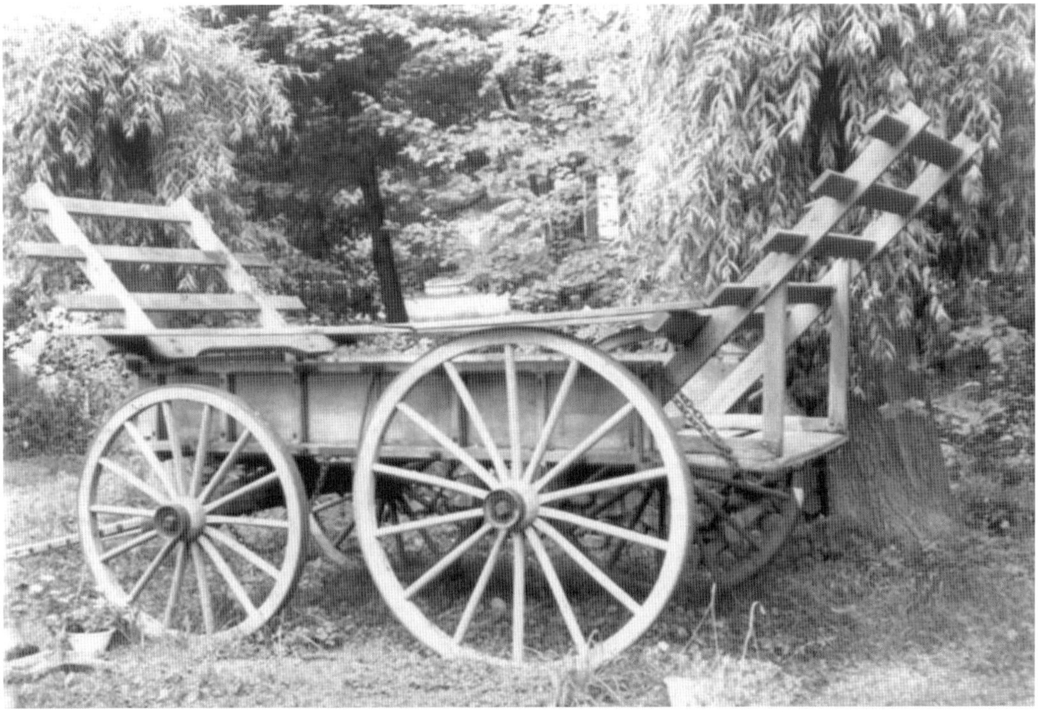

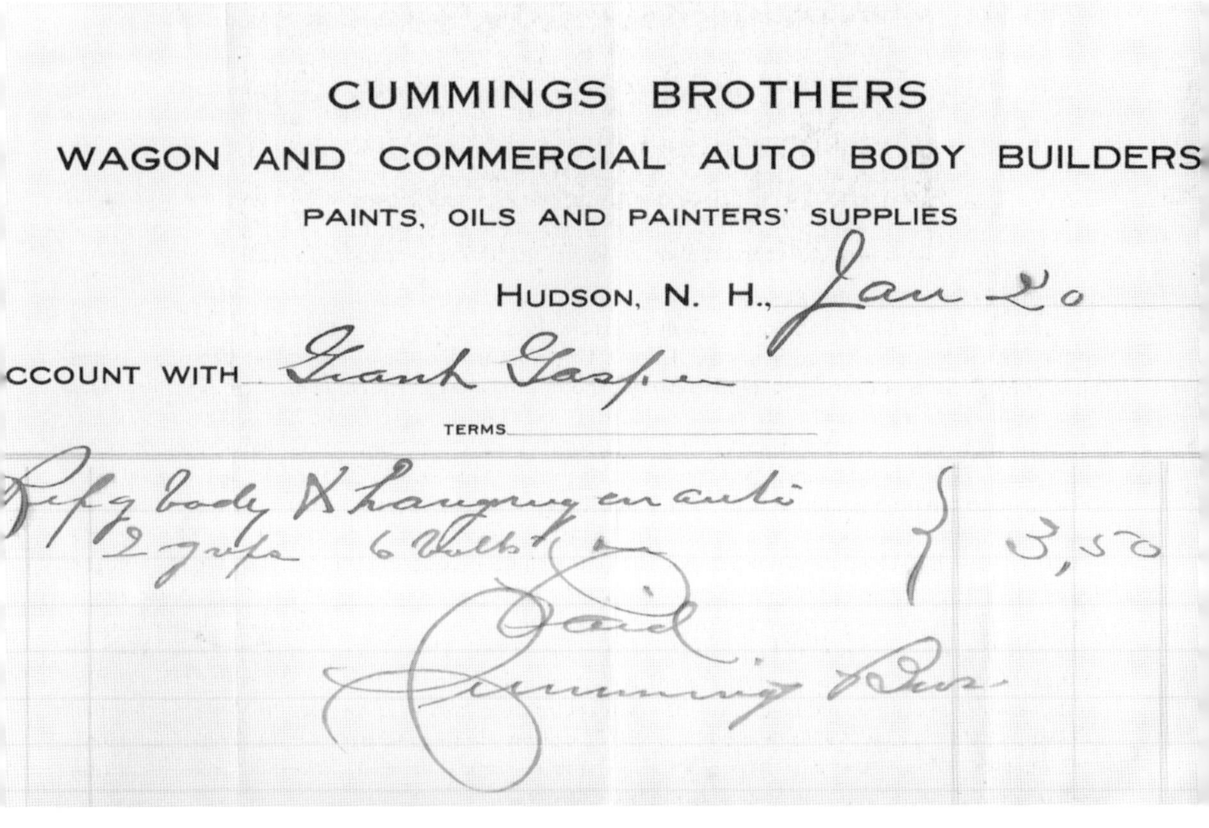

CUMMINGS BROTHERS

WAGON AND COMMERCIAL AUTO BODY BUILDERS

PAINTS, OILS AND PAINTERS' SUPPLIES

HUDSON, N. H., Jan 20

CCOUNT WITH Frank Gasper

TERMS

Repg body & hanging on auto } 3,50

Paid
Cumming Bros

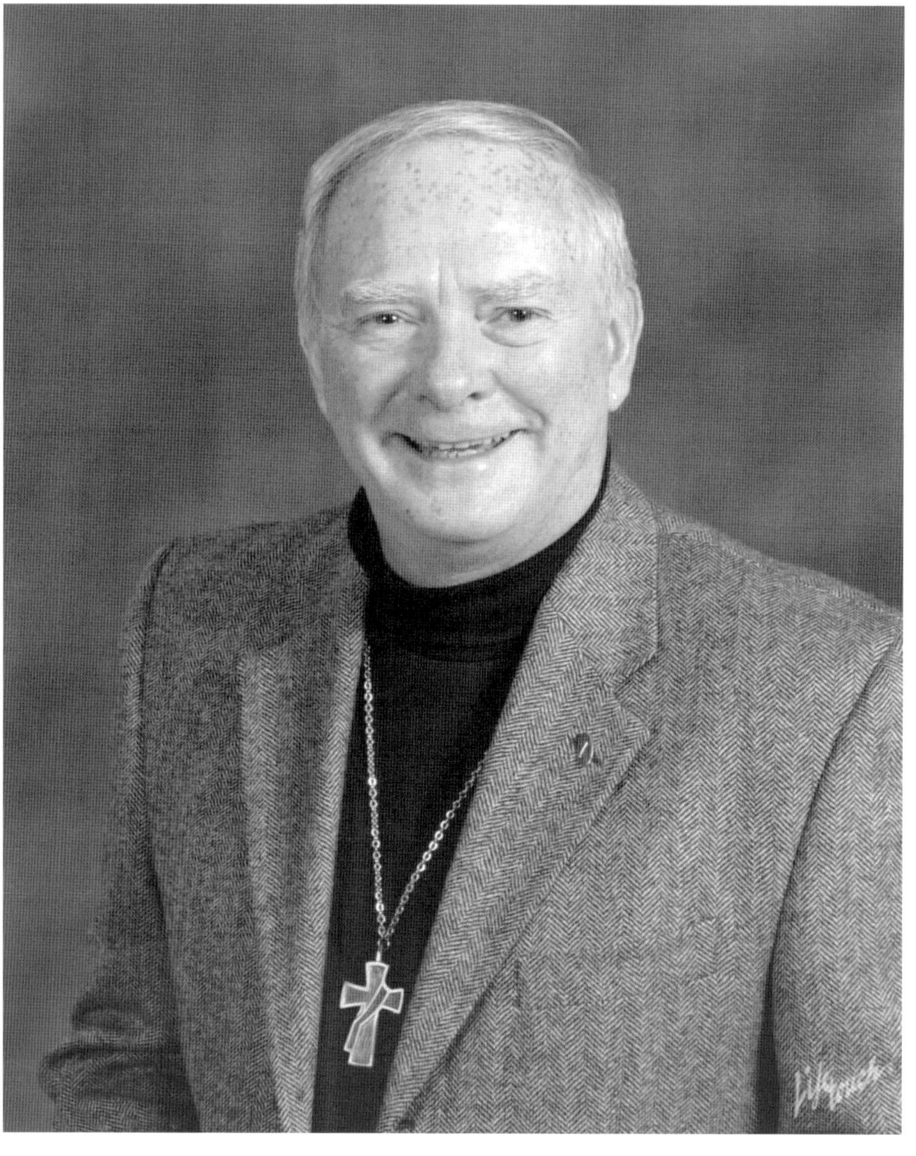

Deacon Robert Anderson

Deacon Robert Anderson, known as Deacon Bob, is a permanent deacon for the Roman Catholic Church. He arrived in Hudson with his wife, Geri, in September 1995. Upon attending St. Kathryn Church, he was so moved by the liturgy that he decided to introduce himself to the pastor. His words "I don't suppose you need a permanent deacon?" to Fr. Gary Belliveau were met with the immediate response, "Are you a deacon? I've been praying for a deacon!" Deacon Bob became the first permanent deacon to serve St. Kathryn Parish. He and Geri were deeply involved in many aspects of parish life, including the Coming Home to Catholicism program, the Lazarus Ministry, and numerous couples' retreats. Deacon Bob also ran the very successful parish golf tournament for 10 years. Additionally, he worked for the Diocese of Manchester for four years as director of the Respect Life Office, director of Institutional Ministries, and assistant director of Public Policy. Deacon Bob and Geri retired in 2005 and moved to Florida, where they continue to remain active in their church. They celebrated their 50th wedding anniversary in 2014 with their children and grandchildren. (Courtesy the Anderson family.)

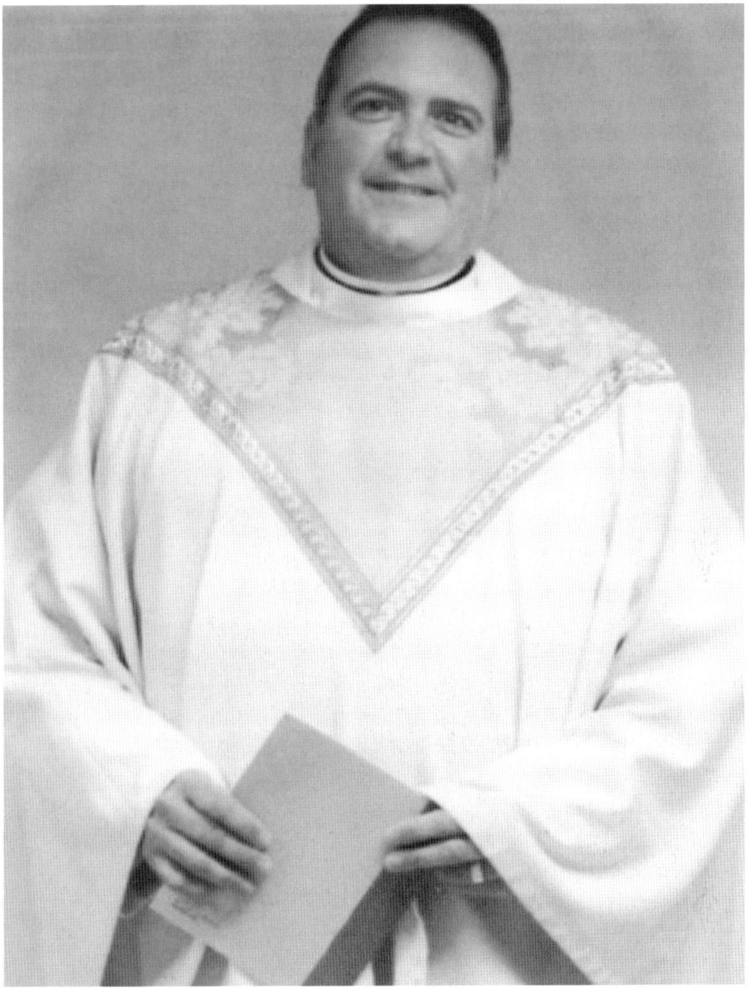

Rev. Gary J. Belliveau

Rev. Gary J. Belliveau served St. Kathryn Parish as pastor from December 9, 1993, to September 6, 2011, and enriched many lives during his time in Hudson. A native of Acushnet, Massachusetts, Father Gary graduated from Mount St. Mary Seminary in Emmitsburg, Maryland, and was ordained a priest for the Diocese of Manchester, New Hampshire, on May 18, 1985. When he arrived at the original St. Kathryn Church on the corner of Lowell and Wason Roads just before Christmas, it seemed almost certain that the future plans would be to close the struggling parish. However, under Father Gary's guidance, the parish began to thrive and outgrew the Wason Road location. During his tenure, the new St. Kathryn Church opened on August 12, 2000, on Dracut Road. Throughout his years with the parish, many programs expanded and new ones developed, as he encouraged everyone to share their gifts and built a thriving faith community. Father Gary's philosophy was to continue outreach to the youth and young families but also reconnect with traditions of the Church. He shared his deep spirituality, dedication to the liturgy, and gift as a homilist, along with his quick wit and sense of humor. He also encouraged and mentored numerous young people in their pursuit of religious vocations and continues to do so. The 40th anniversary of St. Kathryn Parish was celebrated in 2008, and Father Gary celebrated his 25th anniversary of priestly ordination in 2010. Father Gary was named pastor of Corpus Christi Parish in Portsmouth, New Hampshire, in 2011. Many of his former parishioners make the occasional trip to attend Mass in Portsmouth and visit.

Henry Brown

Henry C. Brown was the station agent for the Boston & Maine Railroad at Hudson Center, located at what is now Greeley Street and Route 111, starting in 1896. He was a member of the board of selectmen in 1887 and 1893 and a 10-year member of the board of education. Henry was appointed deputy sheriff of Hillsborough County in 1904 and also postmaster from 1896 until the office at Hudson Center was discontinued in 1910. Born in 1859, he and his wife, Clara, were married in 1883, and he died in 1940. Here, he is shown investigating the Baptist church parsonage fire. (Courtesy HHS.)

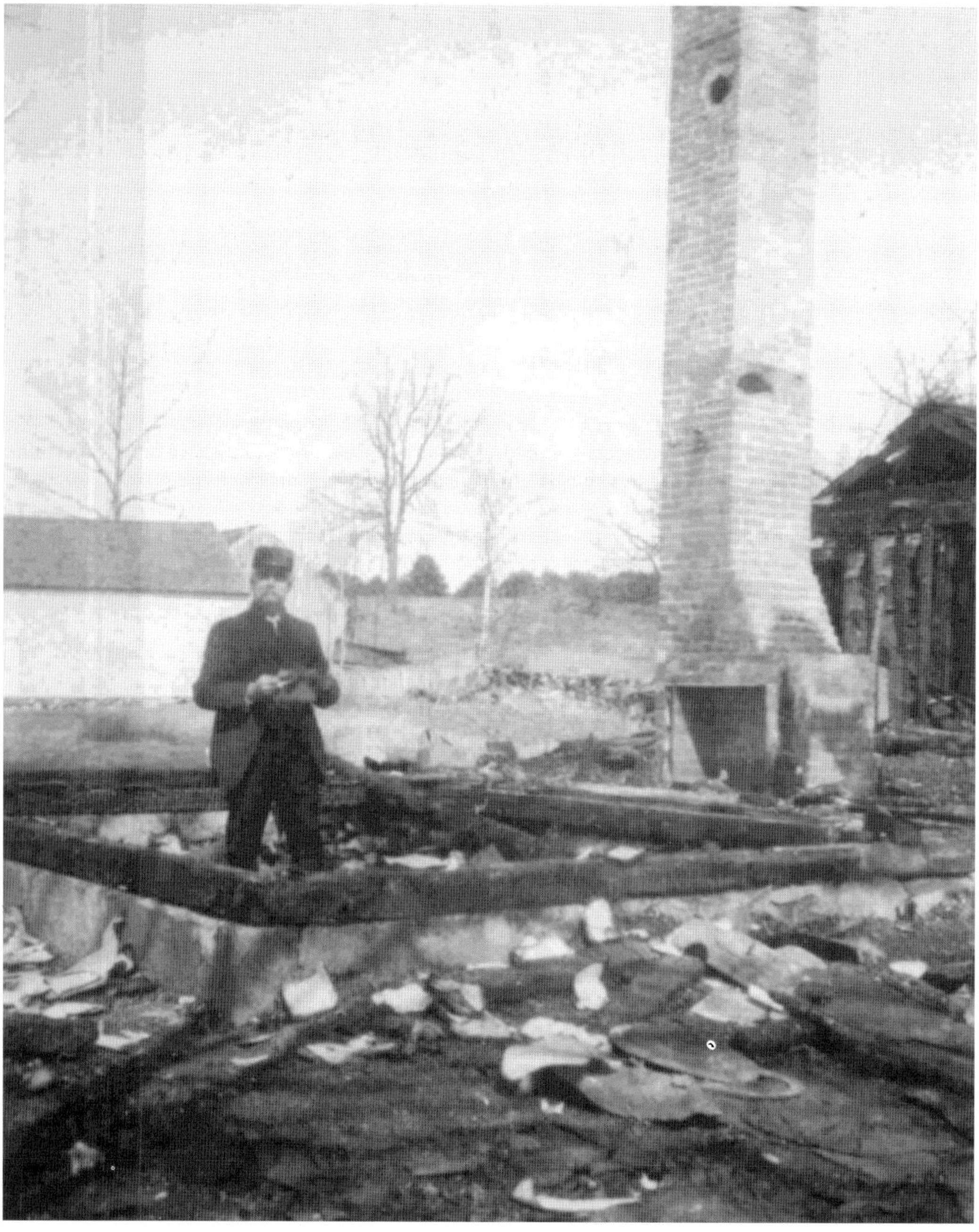

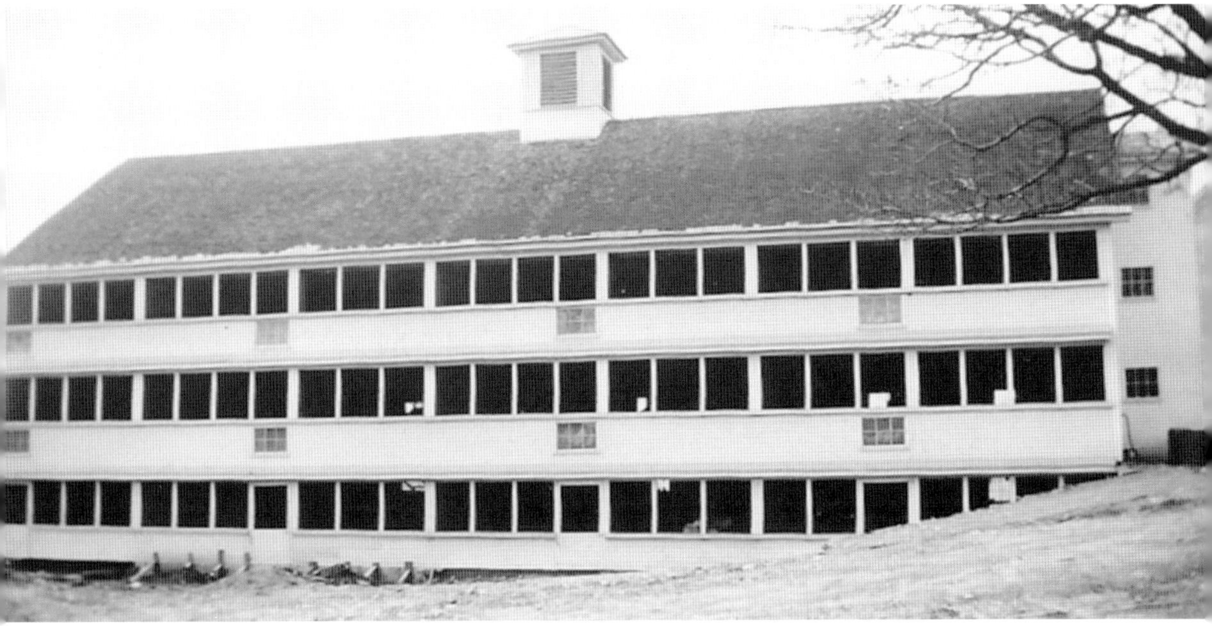

George Dooley

George Dooley owned the Stephen Greeley Farm, which was originally the Henry Hills Jr. Farm. He was a farmer, selectman, and state representative. In the years before electricity, he built a brick water tank on a hill across the street from the farm buildings. He placed a windmill on a well and pumped water up to the tank, giving him running water year round. He came from Londonderry, New Hampshire, and is buried there. The photographs show the Hills, Greeley, Dooley, Jasper Farm (in order of ownership). The first image shows the barn after its first remodeling as a hen house by Grant Jasper, but it retains its original roofline and size as when it was owned by Stephen Greeley. The windmill installed by George Dooley can be seen in front of the barn. The winter scene is from 1939 and was taken from Greeley Street. It shows the size of the barn after the addition. The cupola is the same one in both pictures. Stephen Greeley remodeled the original Colonial house in a Greek Revival style. Both the house and the barn are built with hand-hewn beams and are pegged together. (Both, courtesy the Jasper family.)

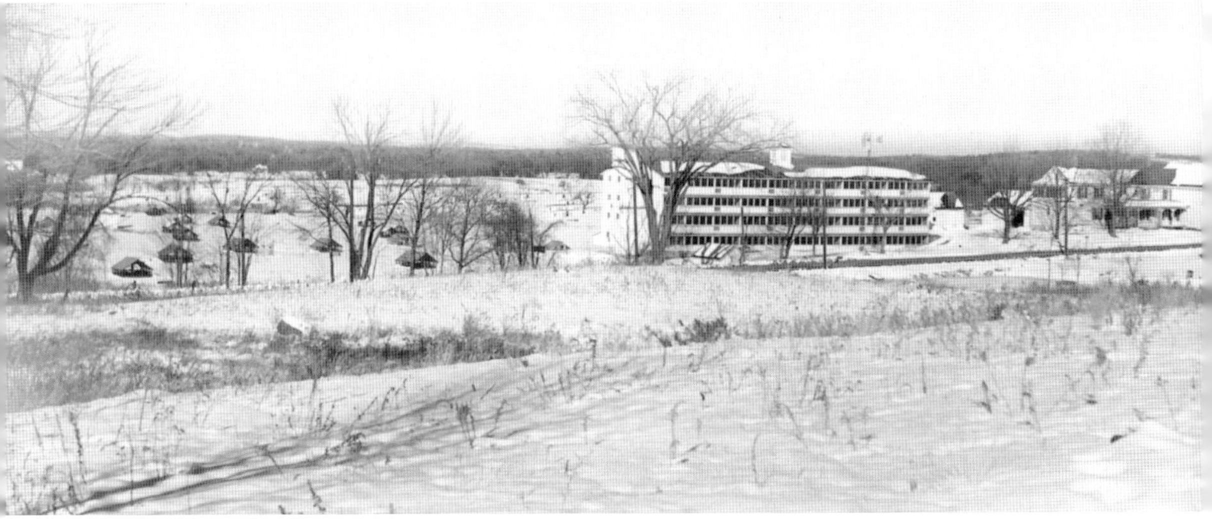

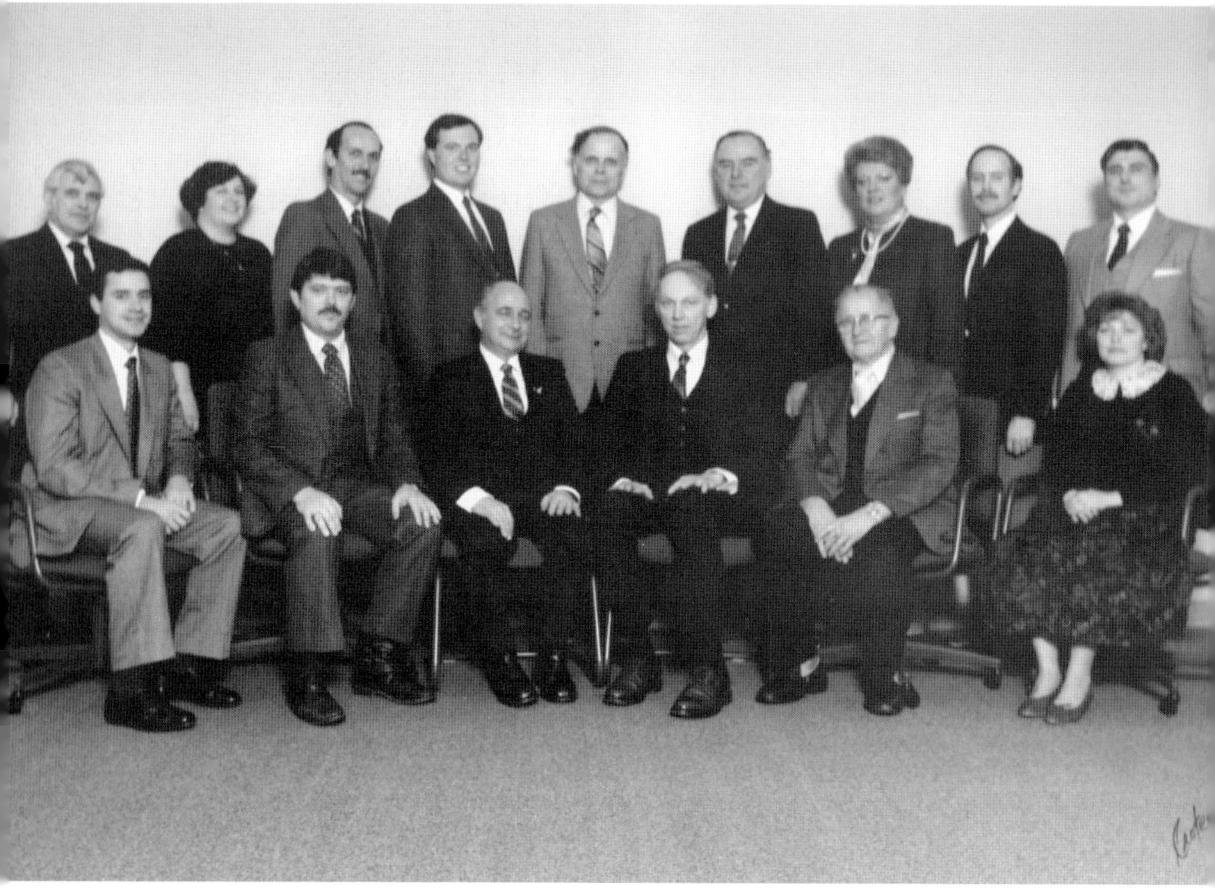

Town Council

From 1986 to 1992, Hudson changed its form of government from a board of selectmen to a town council, but the voters returned to the selectmen format. Pictured in this 1988 photograph are many prominent town residents who were members of the town council. Pictured from left to right are (first row) John Lavoie Jr., George Mouseau, William Arsenault, Joseph Wozniak, John Bednar, and Robin Andrews; (second row) Fidele Bernasconi, Nan Cote, Robert Landry, David Alukonis, Abbott Rice, Charles Coughlin, Hanna Blake, Paul Inderbitzen, and Edward Pallidino Jr. (Courtesy the Town of Hudson.)

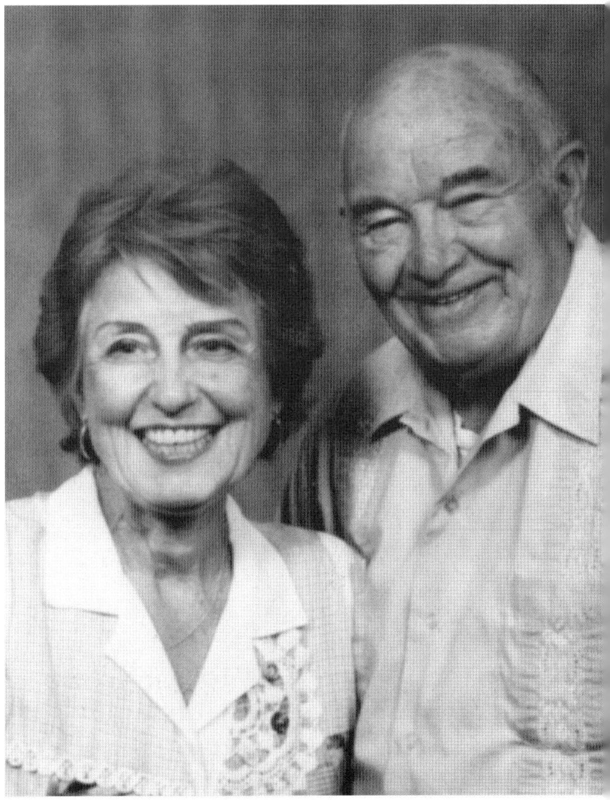

Stanley Searles

Stanley "Stan" N. Searles Sr. was born in Saugus, Massachusetts, in 1919, and his father died when he was seven years old. Stan went into the Army in 1944 and made it his career for the next 21 years. He met his wife, Maria, while stationed in Germany. The Searles family moved to Hudson when Stan retired from the service with the rank of major. Stan ran for elected office as early as 1967, when he ran for tax collector. He served on the budget committee in 1984, and he was elected to the school board in 1989 and served there for three terms. In 1990, Stan became a state representative where he served for the next five terms. Stan was well known for wearing flannel shirts and work pants to all his meetings. When he was elected to the statehouse, he was advised that he should wear a jacket, dress shirt, and tie. Searles said that was not him, and he was sworn into office in his flannel shirt, but never went back to Concord again without his shirt and tie. Stanley died at the Veterans' Home in Tilton, New Hampshire, in 2002 and is buried in the New Hampshire Veterans' Cemetery. (Both, courtesy Vicky Searles Vaccaro.)

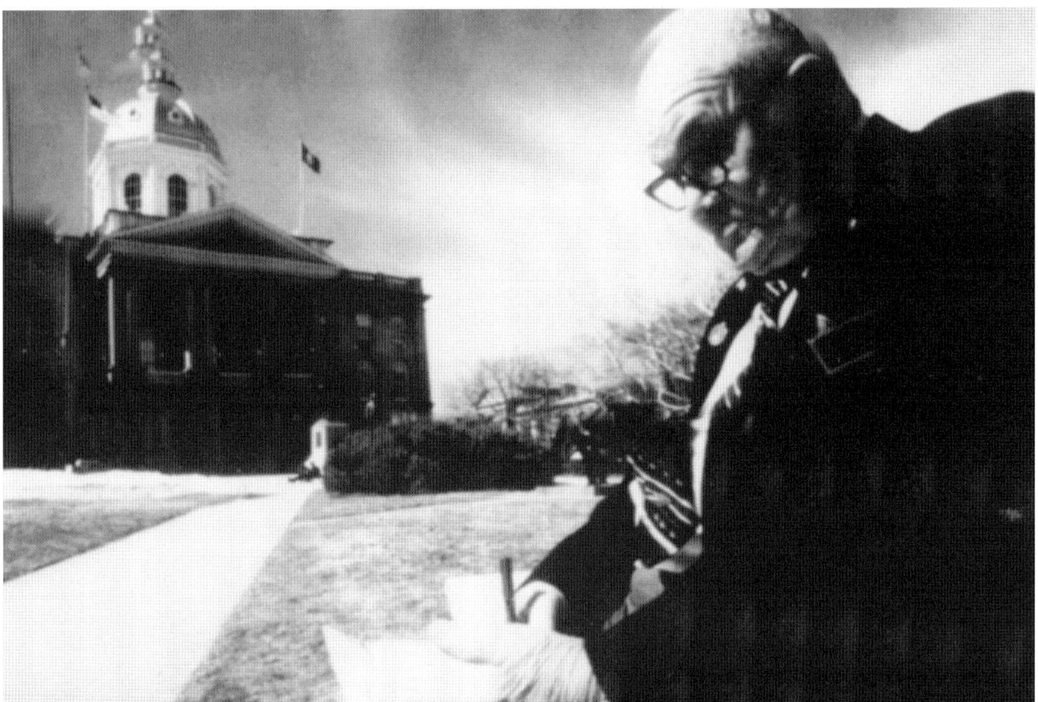

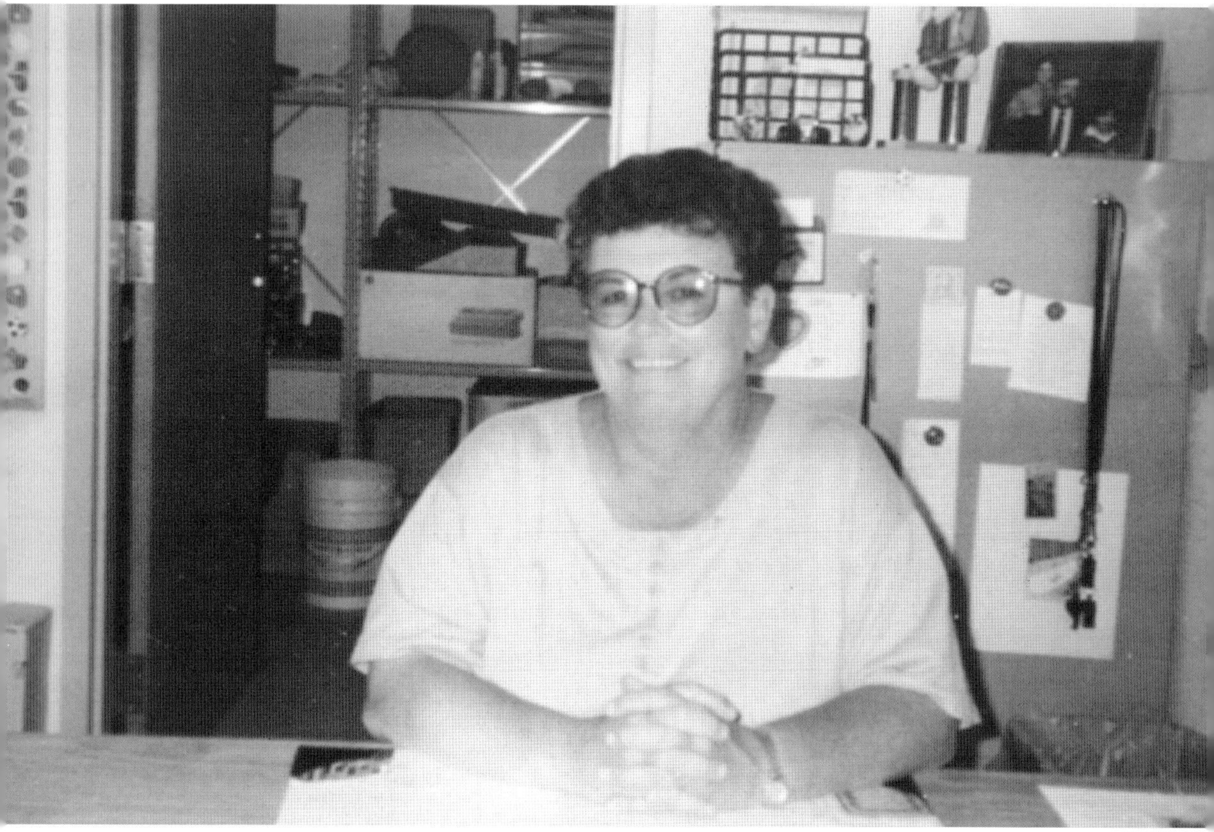

Barbara Hamilton

Barbara Hamilton taught physical education in Hudson for over 20 years. She was also the recreation director for many years, overseeing the summer program, soccer, and basketball for children, as well as the men's, women's, and seniors' programs. She enjoyed serving others, particularly the youth of Hudson. Barbara died in 1993, and Nottingham West Elementary School's gymnasium was dedicated in her memory in 1994. (Courtesy Sherri Lavoie.)

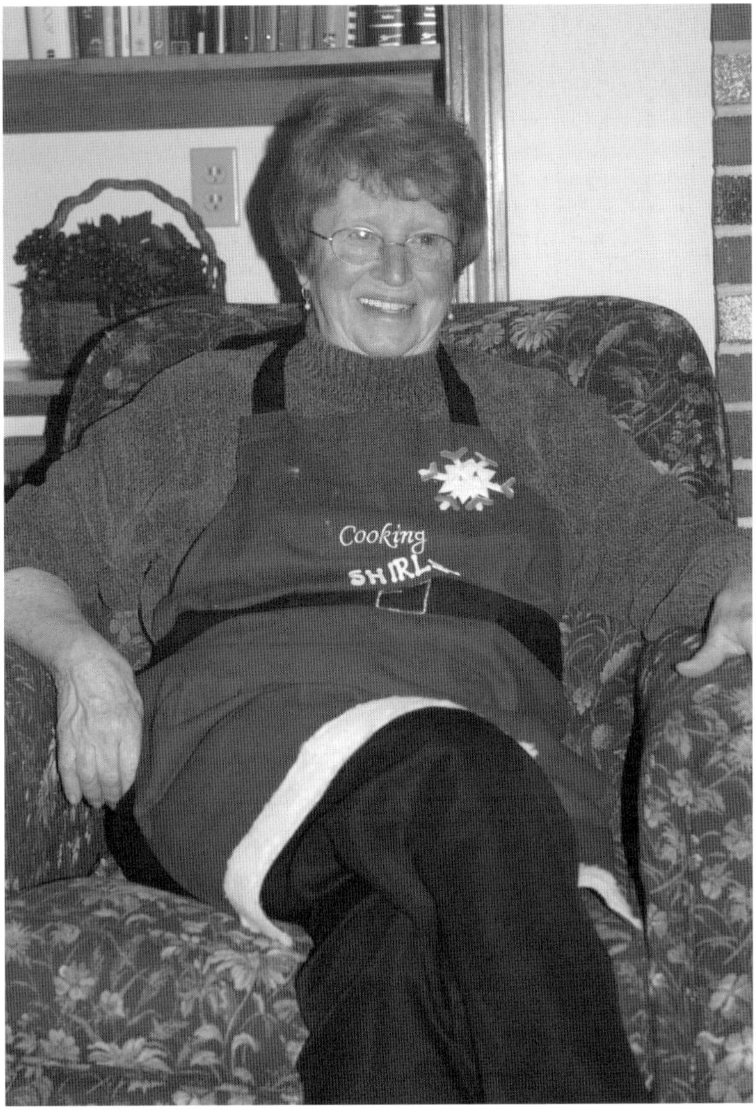

Shirley Nadeau
It seems everyone in Hudson knows Shirley. Shirley (Craig) Nadeau has lived in Hudson for over 50 years. Originally from Sturbridge, Massachusetts, she married Emery Nadeau in 1961 and moved to the Nadeau Farm on what was once called Derry Road. Emery's maternal grandfather, Joseph Lambert, had purchased the former Jackson E. Greeley Farm in 1902, and Emery's parents, Emery Henry and Marion (Lambert) Nadeau, bought the farm from her father in 1940. Shirley and her former husband, Emery, raised three children, Lori, Emery, and Elizabeth. Young Emery joined the family business after graduating from Alvirne High School in 1982. The farm was sold in 2000. Young Emery is now the manager of Alvirne High School's farm, and Shirley can be found on the farm every afternoon at milking time to assist with the cows or clean part of the barn. Shirley has always been active in town, whether as a member of the St. John's Women's Guild or helping out at the historical society's food tent on Old Home Days. Shirley has worked at Checkers Restaurant at Alvirne High School since 1995, and a new generation has gotten to know and love Shirley. She enjoys spending time with her children, grandchildren, family, and friends and keeping busy. (Courtesy the Nadeau family.)

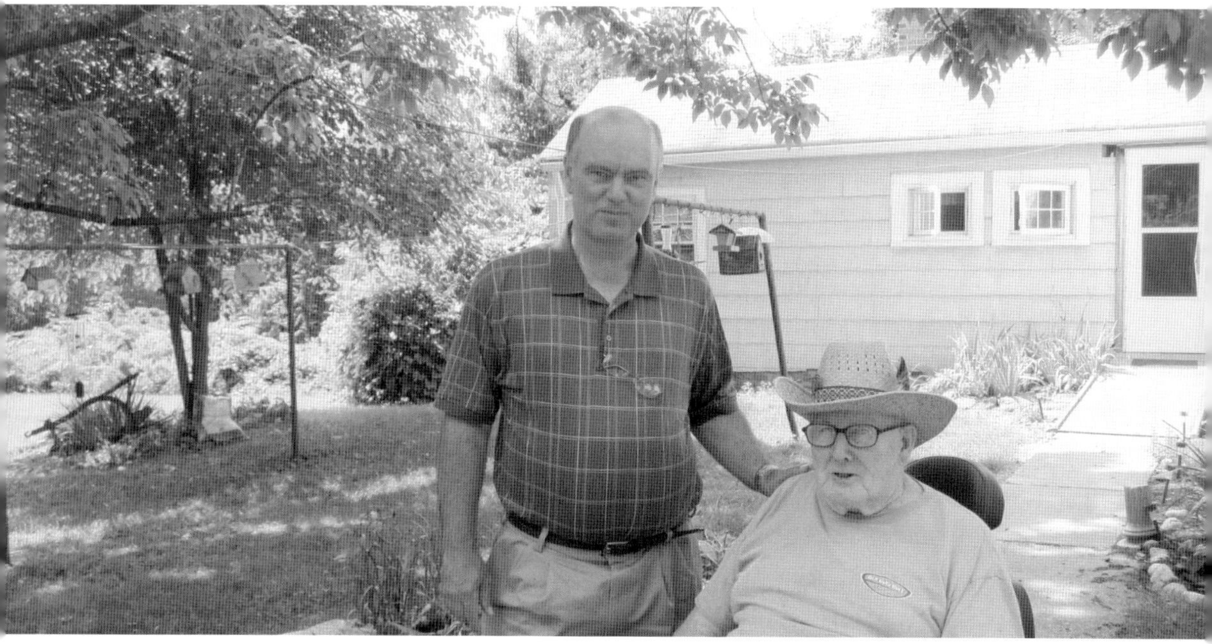

Paul Hills

Paul W. Hills (seated at right) is a direct descendant of James Hills in the seventh generation. He was not born in Hudson, as his father had moved away from the family farm on Barrett's Hill Road, which has been in the possession of the Hills family since Jeremiah purchased it. After the death of his aunt Sylvia Hills Fleming, Paul inherited the farm and moved into the family homestead. He, in turn, sold the farm's development rights to the town, which ensures that the land will not be developed but may continue to be used for agricultural purposes. Here, Paul Hills is shown with Ron Messner from Illinois, a descendant of the Hills family who visited the Hudson area in 2013. The Hills Farm is one of only two Bicentennial Farms in Hudson. This means the family farmed the same piece of land for at least 200 years.

Rhona Charbonneau

Rhona Charbonneau and her husband, Claude, brought up their family of five in Hudson. Rhona and her business partner, Alida Weergang, opened a successful chain of beauty parlors and decided to open a beauty school. Continental Academie of Hair Design has now been in business for 40 years, teaching the proper techniques of hair styling and customer service, and the next generation of Charbonneaus are now actively involved. Rhona began her involvement in politics in the early 1980s by serving as a state representative and a member of the town budget committee; she later represented Hudson as a state senator. She was a longtime Hudson selectman and Hillsborough County commissioner. Rhona also served as the New Hampshire Republican Party chairman. She was instrumental in Hudson's obtaining the former Benson's property from the state and has done many things for Hudson throughout the years. Sadly, in 2009, Rhona was driving in Nashua when an elderly driver hit her car. Amazingly, Rhona survived near-fatal injuries, but she lost most of her eyesight in the crash. She continues to follow Hudson news and events and is very involved with her children and grandchildren. Her can-do spirit has never waivered. Her sons Mark and Rick own and operate Continental Paving, Inc., one of the state's largest paving and road construction contractors. Continental was started by Rhona and Claude on Lowell Road in the 1970s as a trucking company. Pictured are, from left to right, (first row) Lorraine Madison and Ann Seabury; (second row) Rhona Charbonneau, Shawn Jasper, and Terry Stewart. (Courtesy Hudson Town Hall.)

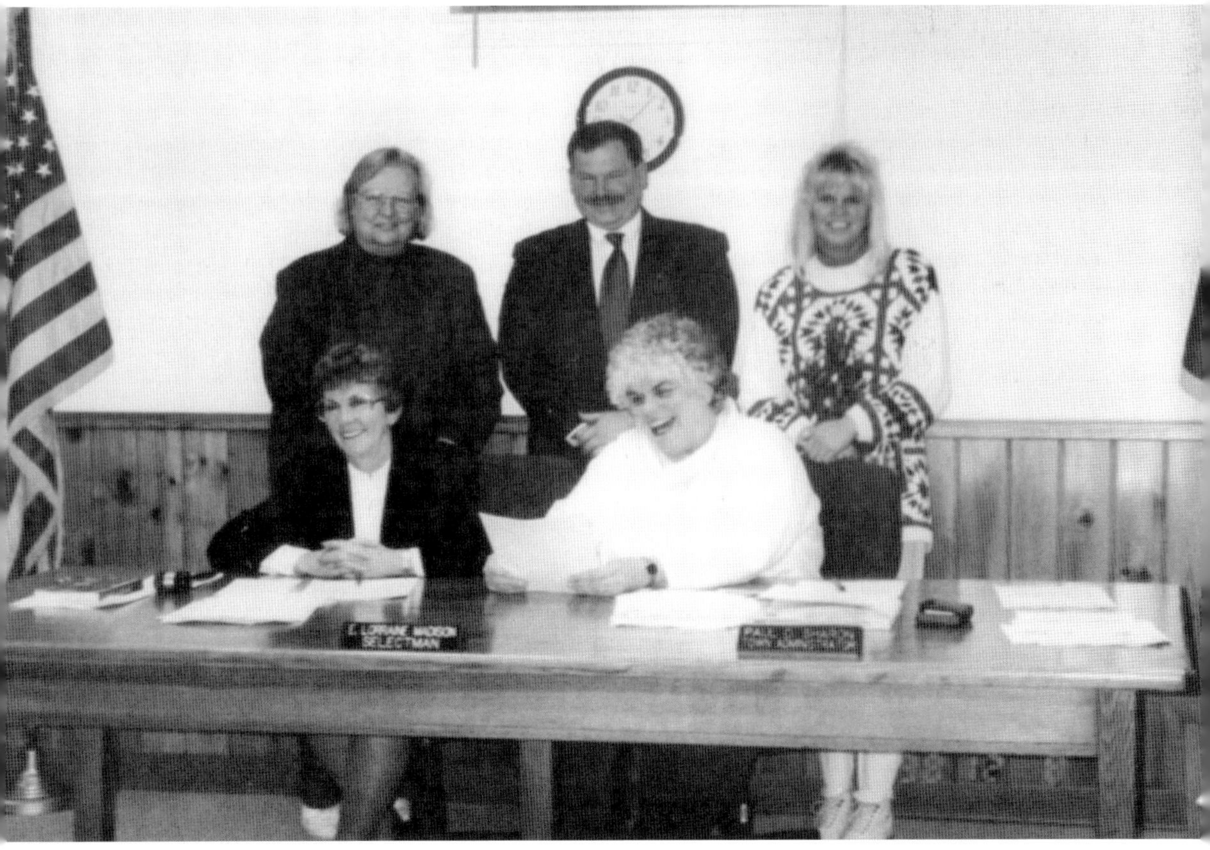

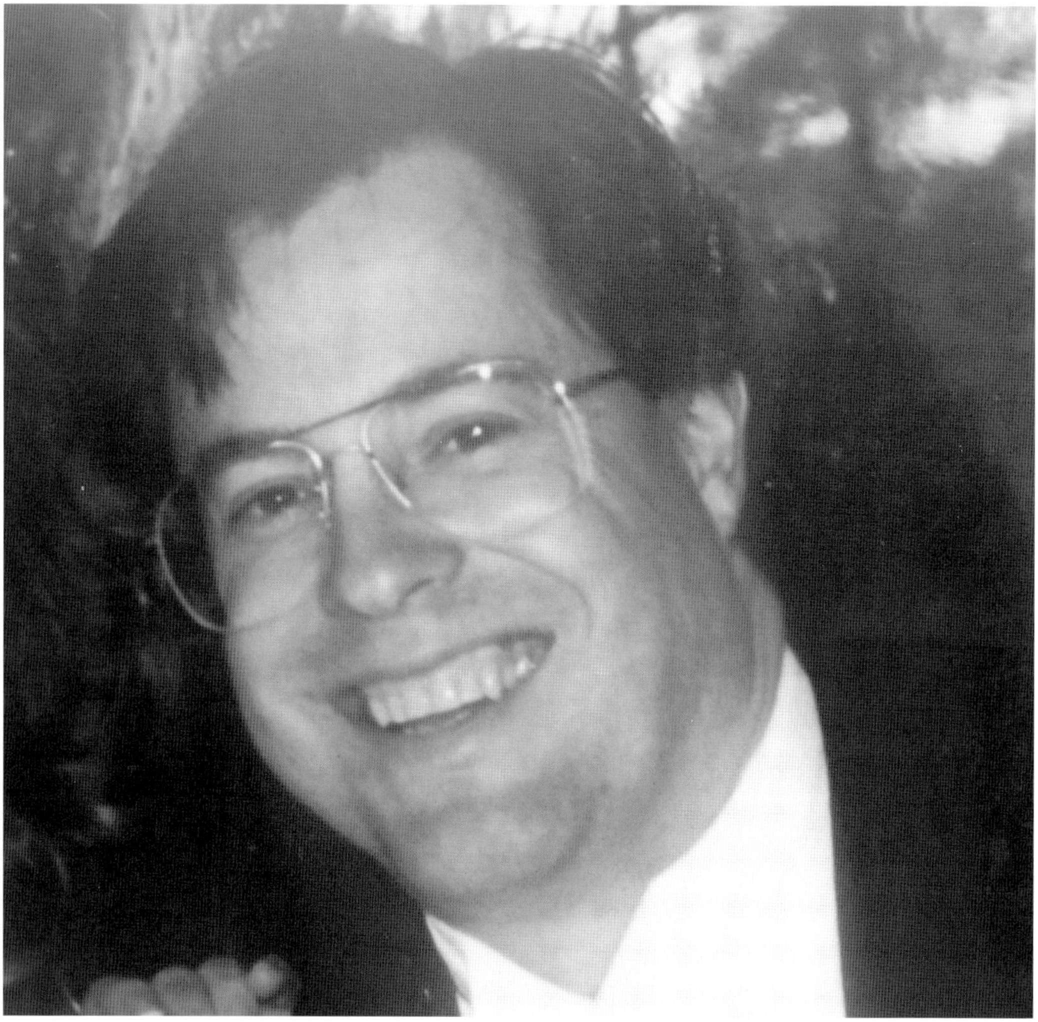

David Kovalcin

Hudson resident David Kovalcin, a senior mechanical engineer on a business trip for Raytheon, was a passenger on American Airlines Flight 11 on September 11, 2001, when his plane was hijacked by terrorists and flown into the World Trade Center in New York. He was 42 years old. The world changed for everyone that fateful day, especially for David's wife, Elizabeth, and daughters Rebecca, then four, and Marina, then one. One of his favorite Saturday morning things to do with his daughters was to visit the children's room of Hills Memorial Library. To honor him, his wife and daughters donated $25,000 to build the children's programming room in David's memory in the new Rodgers Memorial Library, which opened in 2009. His bright, beautiful daughters attend Hudson schools and his wife is an active volunteer for many school organizations and events, including Alvirne High School Friends of Music. (Courtesy Elizabeth Kovalcin.)

Alvirne Hills House

The Alvirne Hills House and grounds have been the center of community activities for many years, and it is the home of the Hudson Historical Society. Built in 1890 by Dr. Alfred K. Hills (see page 12), it was given to the Hudson School District in Dr. Hills's will. When Dr. Hills's wife Jessie died in 1963, it was boarded up and vandalized. The school board at the time wanted to tear it down to use the land for some other purpose. That is when the Hudson Historical Society was formed in 1966. Hudson is one of the few towns in New Hampshire to continue the tradition started by Gov. Frank Rollins called Old Home Days. Governor Rollins knew that New Hampshire was losing its population, and the state and many towns were in debt. In 1897, he wrote, "I wish that in the ear of every son and daughter of New Hampshire, in the summer days, might be heard whispered the persuasive words: Come back, come back. Do you not hear the call? What has become of the old home where you were born? Do you not remember it—the old farm back among the hills, with its rambling buildings, its well sweep casting its long shadows, the row of stiff poplar trees, the lilacs and the willows?" Old Home Week was implemented to bring former residents home, to spruce up the towns, and bring some much-needed economy back. While there have been years since 1897 when Hudson did not host an Old Home Days event, people have come to expect the celebration, held in the fields of Alvirne Hills House, each August. The Kiwanis Club ran the event for years, and the Hudson Historical Society has also been in charge. For the past several years, a group of volunteers has overseen the monumental task. Old Home Days continues to bring the people of Hudson, past and present, together. (Courtesy HHS.)

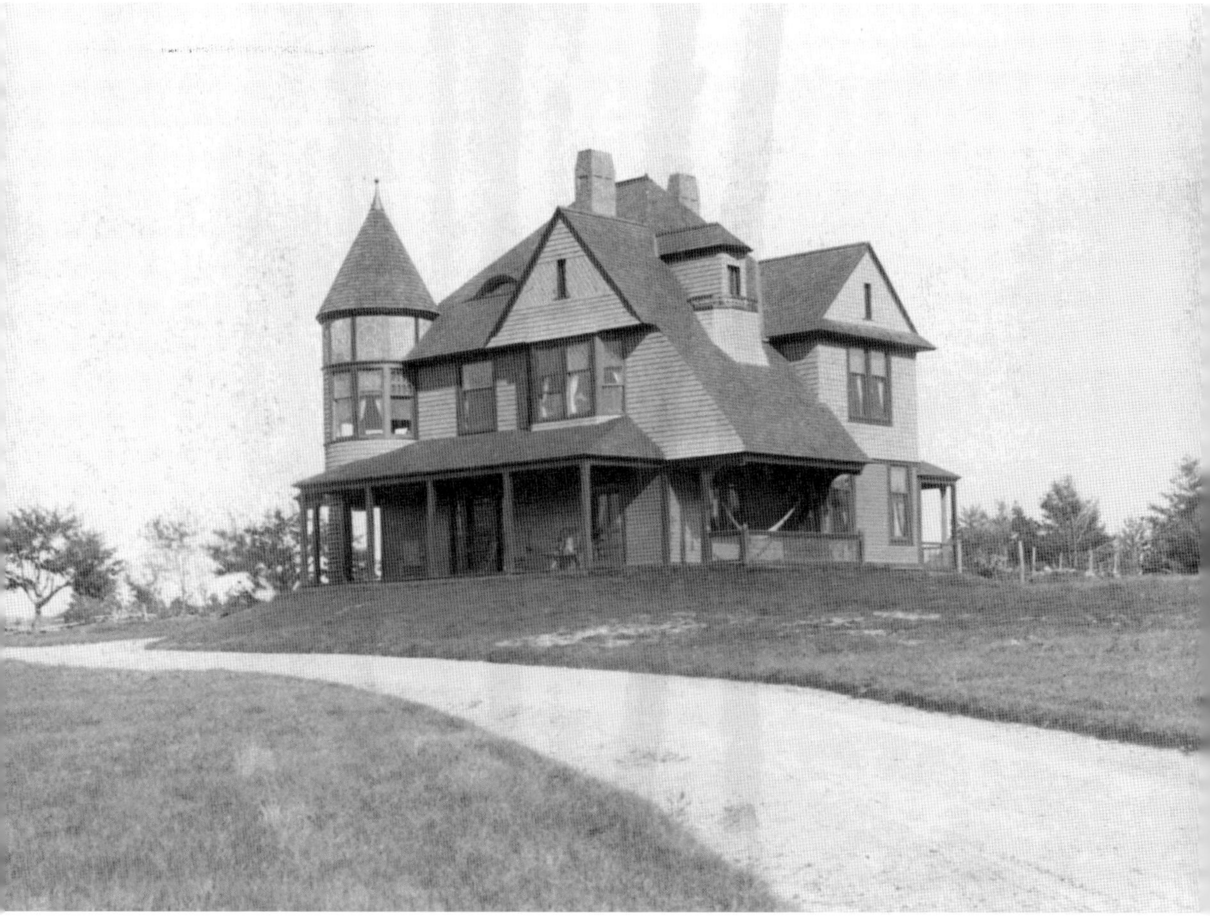

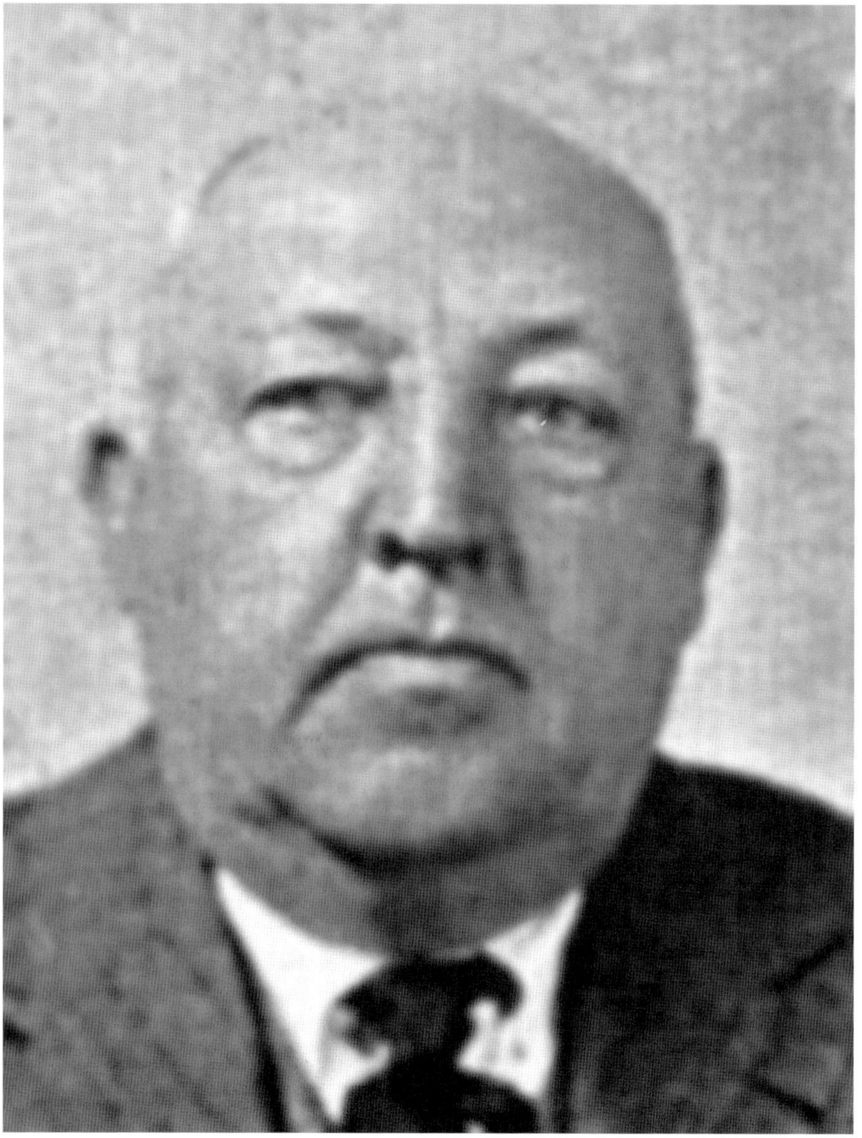

John T. Benson

John T Benson was born in England in 1879 and became a famous wild animal salesman and trainer. In 1924, he purchased land off of Route 111 and Kimball Hill Road to receive and train various animals he obtained from his travels all over the world for various circuses and even Hollywood films. Locals kept coming by to see the exotic animals. It is said that, to discourage this, Benson decided to charge people to see the animals. This idea backfired, so he decided to open his farm to the public and expanded it each year. It became Benson's Wild Animal Farm, the Strangest Farm on Earth. Many Hudson residents have fond memories of either working at or visiting Benson's Wild Animal Farm to see the animals and ride the rides. People traveled from all over New England to Benson's; there was even a special Jungle Train from Boston's North Station to Hudson on Sundays in the 1930s. Benson died in 1943. However, the Benson name lives on in Hudson with Benson Park, a beautiful town-owned passive recreation park created on Benson's former land. The Friends of Benson Park hope to complete a museum in the former elephant barn in the future. (Courtesy HHS.)

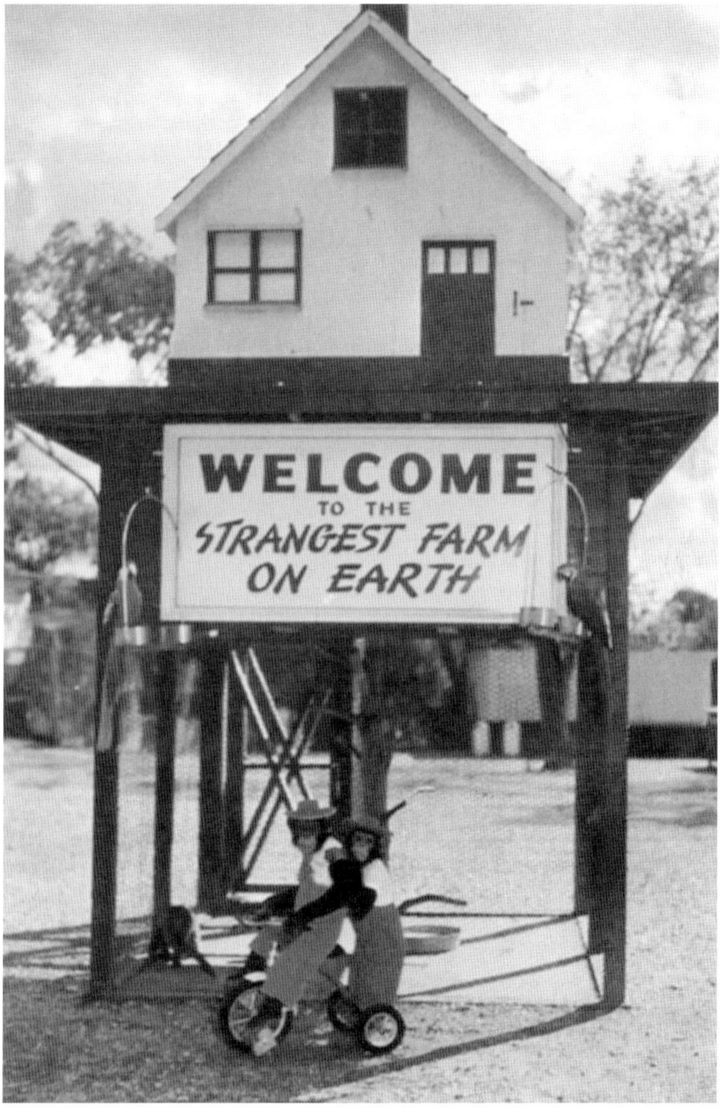

Strangest Farm on Earth

There have numerous newspaper articles, books, and even television shows devoted to Hudson's Benson's Wild Animal Farm, which put Hudson on the map. When it first opened, early advertising noted that Benson's was in Nashua, New Hampshire, apparently because no one knew Hudson. Benson's Wild Animal Farm changed all that. Even today, if people mention they live in Hudson, New Hampshire, they might hear in reply, "Oh, where Benson's was!"

Since the official purchase of the land from the State of New Hampshire on January 23, 2009, Benson Park has become another place of Hudson pride. The Hudson Highway Department, Friends of Benson Park, Benson Park Committee, and many volunteers have taken an active role in the cleanup, care, and maintenance of the recreation area. The recreation committee installed a beautiful playground, and many folks have adopted sections to take care of on their own. A poignant location in the park is the site of the 9/11 Memorial, which was dedicated on September 11, 2011, the 10th anniversary of the attack on the United States. The memorial includes a steel beam from one of New York's World Trade Center Towers.

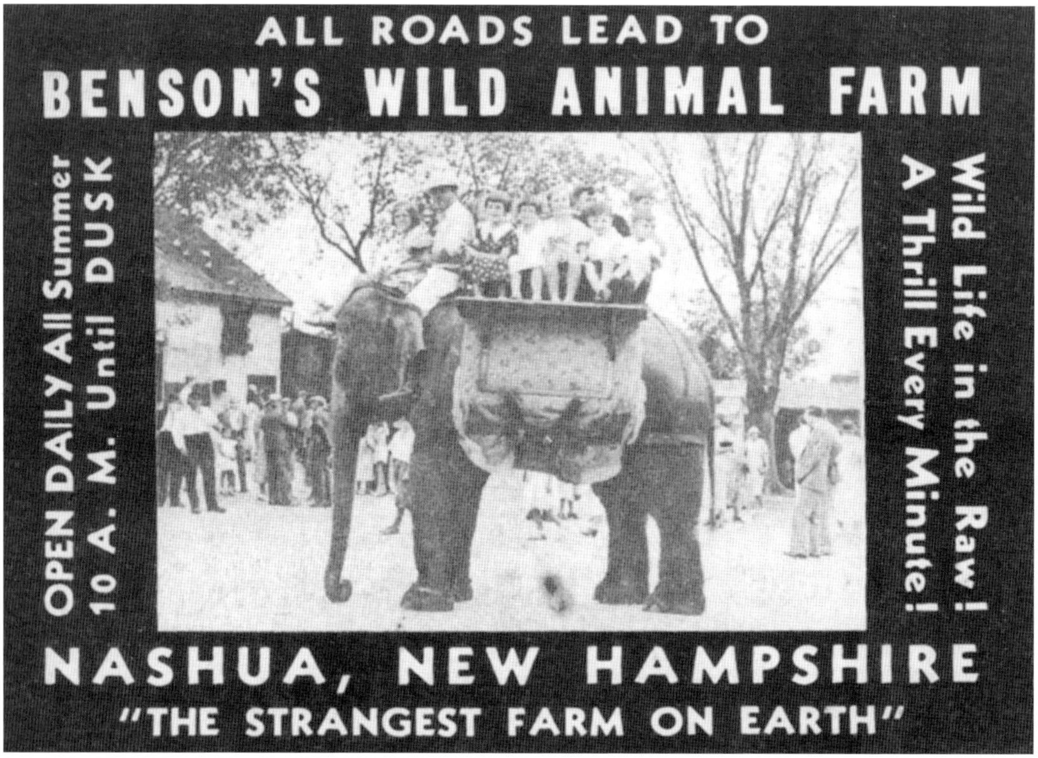

Betsy Ross the Elephant

Betsy the Elephant was one of the most beloved animals at Benson's Wild Animal Farm. An Indian elephant, she was trained by John T. Benson himself and lived at the park from the 1920s until her death in 1971. Benson officially named her Betsy Ross, and she was very popular with children and adults. A gentle soul, she was famous for giving rides on her back, slowly ambling through the crowds with her handler. In an article in the *Nashua Telegraph*, it was noted that on December 22, 1927, "Betsy Ross, the 3,800 pound elephant at Benson's Animal Farm in Hudson, managed to elude her keepers today and made a wild dash for an ice-covered pond on the farm. Surprisingly enough, the ice managed to hold her and she enjoyed her half-hour escapade as she slipped and slid over the ice before a large crowd of onlookers." Betsy was buried on the farm property.

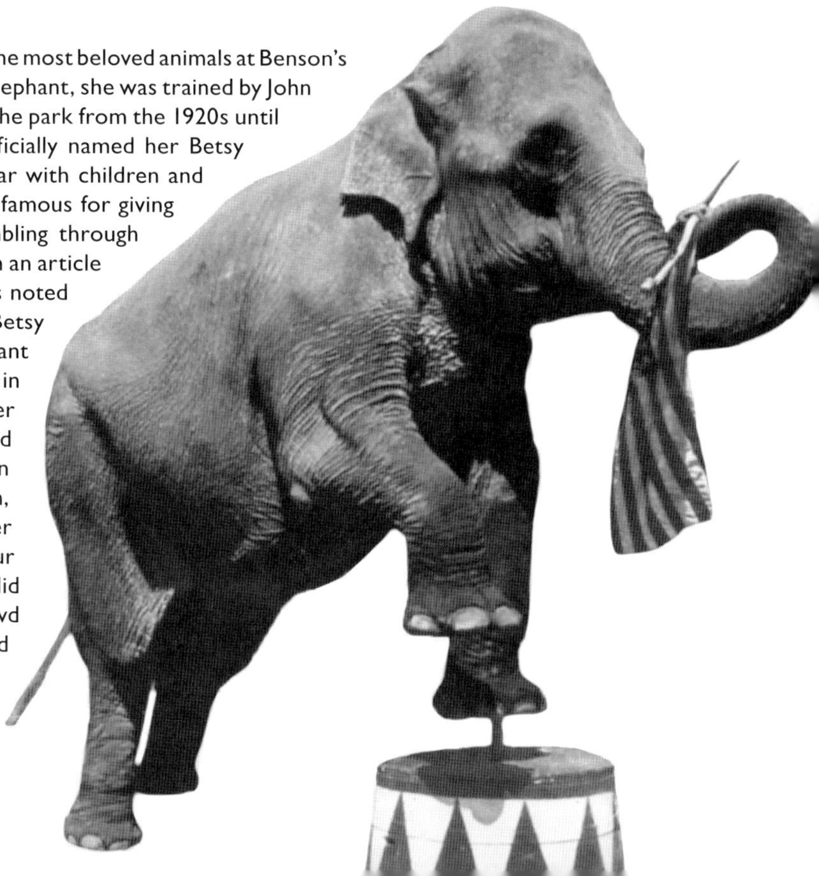

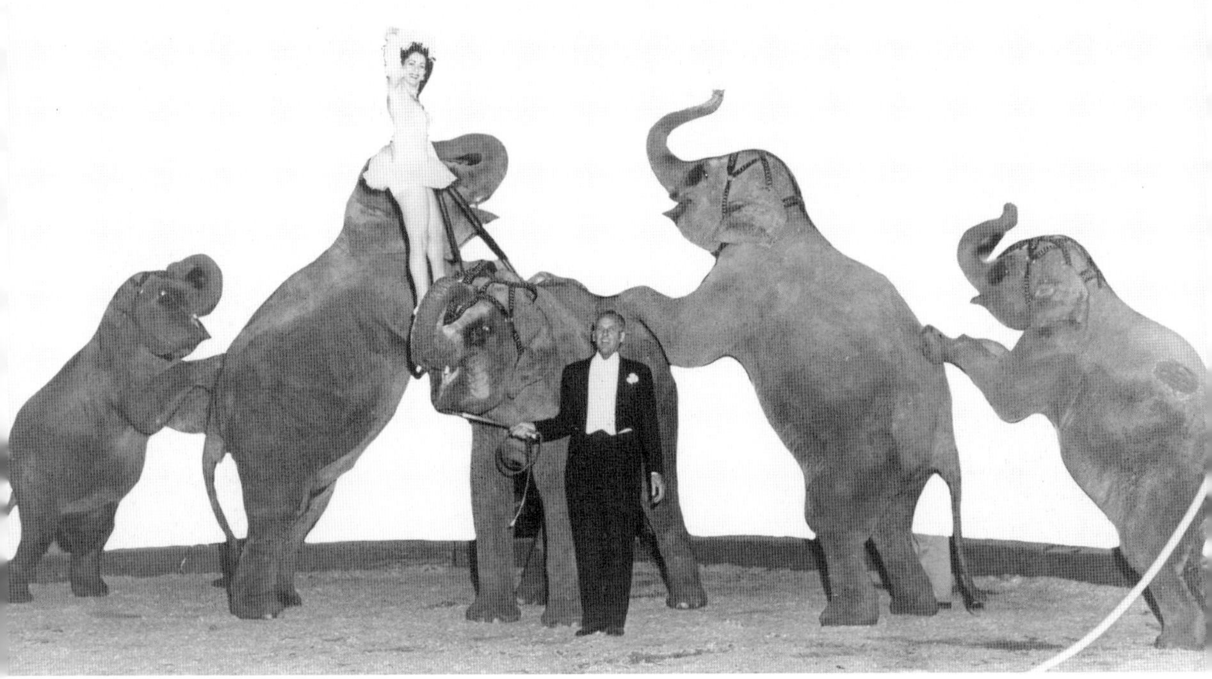

Pink Madison

The animals were always the stars of the show at Benson's Wild Animal Farm, and the elephants were always favorites of the crowds. Pink W. Madison and his brother C.J. "Slivers" Madison were elephant trainers and handlers who traveled with many shows and circuses. They both worked at Benson's Wild Animal Farm. Pink and his wife, June, worked at Benson's Wild Animal Farm for 10 years, retiring in 1973. Slivers died in 1975 in California, and Pink died in a car accident in Honolulu, Hawaii, in 1978. Pictured here are Pink and June performing and Pink with friends. (Both, courtesy HHS.)

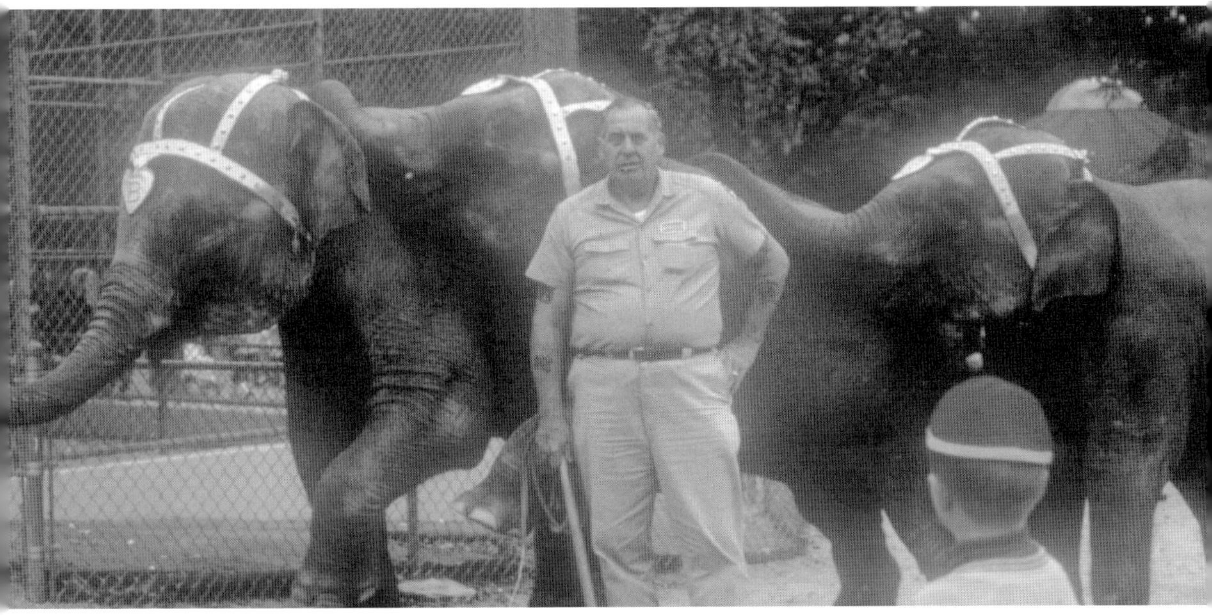

Tony "Colossus"

One of Benson's Wild Animal Farm's most famous residents was Tony, the silverback gorilla. Born in Africa in 1966, he arrived at Benson's as a youngster and lived there for over 20 years until the park closed. Tony's glassed-in, climate-controlled cage was a popular destination for park visitors. Tony enjoyed watching his television, and he had several favorite shows. As a publicity stunt, Benson's owner Arthur Provencher changed Tony's name to Colossus G. Benson and signed him up to run for president in the New Hampshire primary, promising, "A tire in every garage and a banana in every pot." Colossus died on April 11, 2006, at the age of 40 at the Cincinnati Zoo from anesthesia complications during dental work. (Courtesy *Hudson-Litchfield News.*)

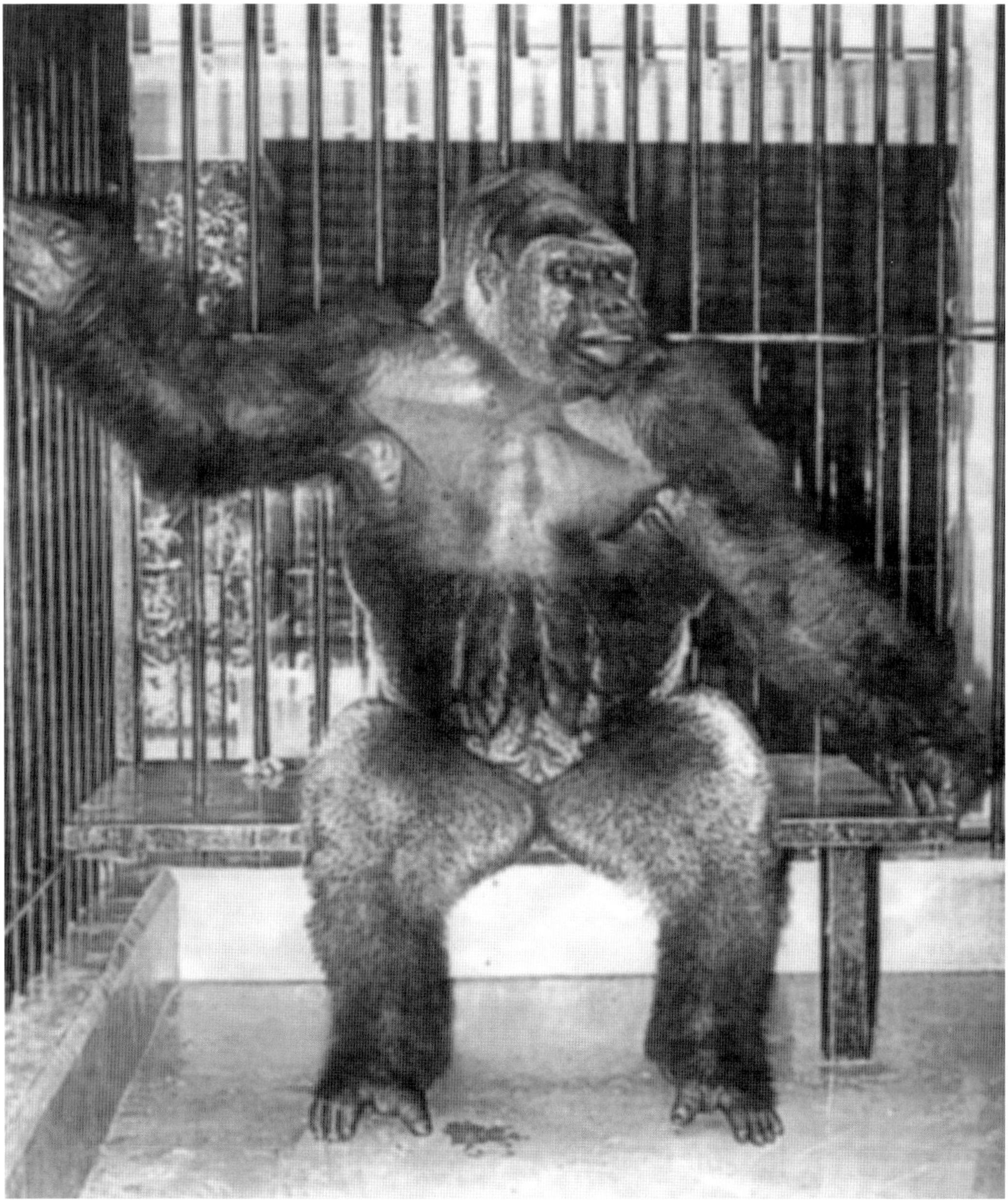

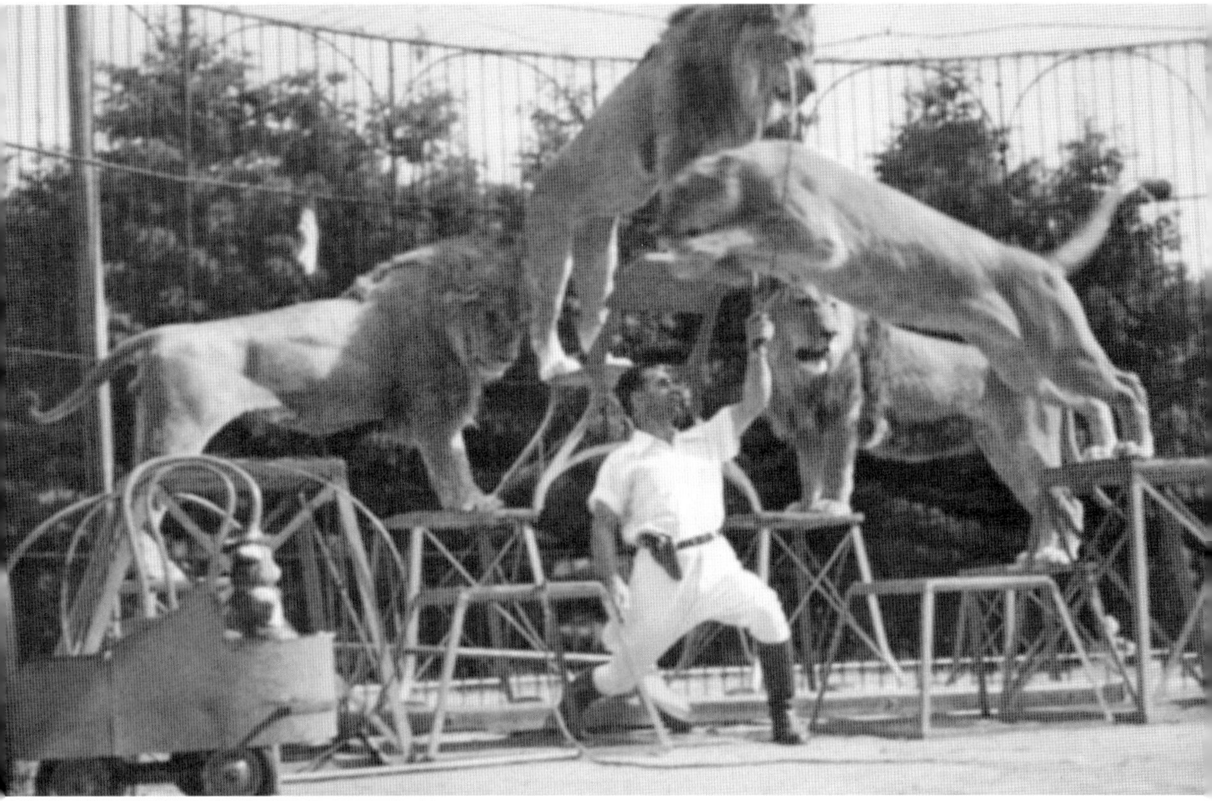

Joseph Arcaris

Joseph "Joe" Arcaris came to the United States from Scotland when he was 18 years old and found a job caring for animals. This slight, five-foot, three-inch man towered over his animals in the ring and commanded them with determination and great concentration. His first animal act was in Utah in 1934, where he trained two cougars. He worked in various places, including a zoo in Massachusetts, before coming to Benson's Wild Animal Farm. He worked at Benson's three different times, twice for four years, while in between working for other acts. He came back to Benson's in 1950 and retired in 1979. His acts were with the big cats—lions, tigers, leopards, and pumas—and were very popular with the crowds. Arcaris trained animals used in the movies out in California and even appeared in several movies himself, including a Tarzan film. For his efforts in saving a workman who was attacked in the ring in Florida, he received the Carnegie Hero Fund Commission Medal in 1940. Arcaris himself was not immune to injury; several times throughout his career he was attacked or injured, and he had the scars to prove it. Joe Arcaris died on August 15, 2002, at age 93 in Nashua, New Hampshire.

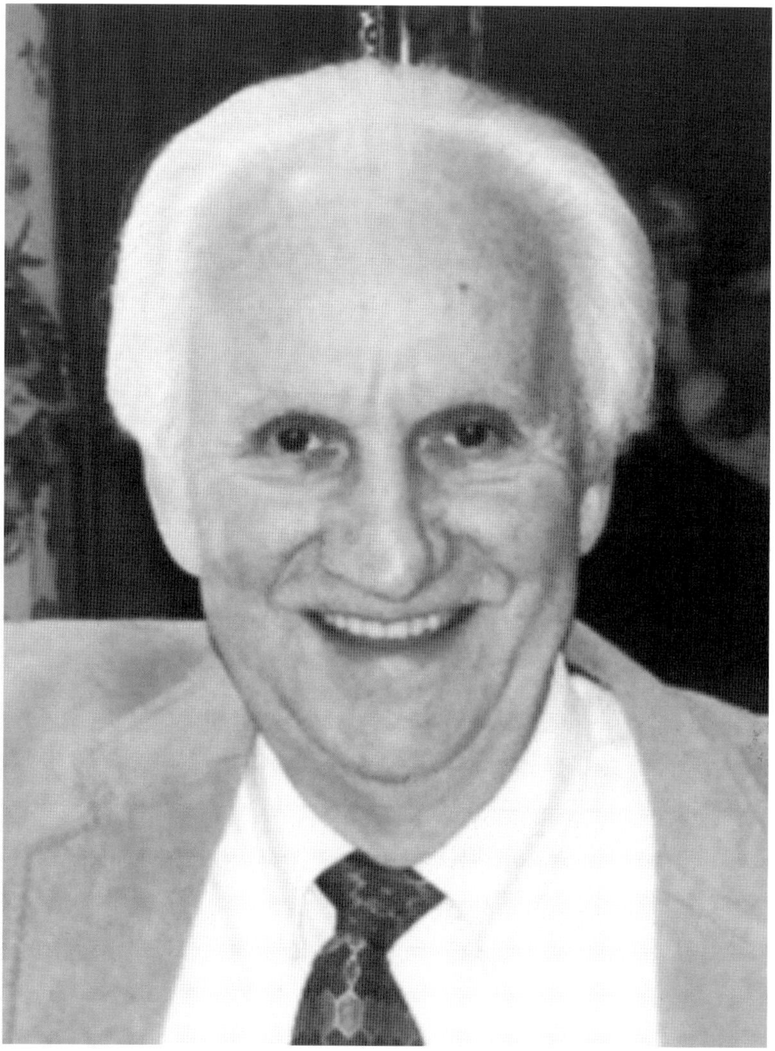

Arthur Provencher

Arthur Provencher was the third and final owner of Benson's Wild Animal Farm, purchasing the property in 1979. A native of Nashua, he was a successful businessman who had a small petting zoo on his industrial park land. Provencher always wanted to own an elephant, and he rescued an elephant from a traveling circus to add to his small menagerie. When he heard Benson's Wild Animal Farm was for sale, he decided to purchase it. He worked hard to keep the costs to the public down while trying to add new and innovative shows and rides. Unfortunately, the economy and other factors closed Benson's, which Provencher had renamed New England Playworld for the 1987 season, the park's last. The land was sold to the State of New Hampshire, which eventually sold it to the Town of Hudson in 2009, with many restrictions placed on the deed. The state had torn down many of the buildings. Hudson, with the help of many dedicated volunteers, has transformed the former wild animal farm into a beautiful passive recreation park, now called Benson Park. Arthur Provencher was very helpful to the Benson Park Committee and appreciated its work to beautify the long-neglected parcel of land, all the while keeping the history of the storied place. He sold a large portion of his Benson's collection to the committee for a future museum, which is still underway. Sadly, Arthur died on December 19, 2013, at the age of 83. (Courtesy the Provencher family.)

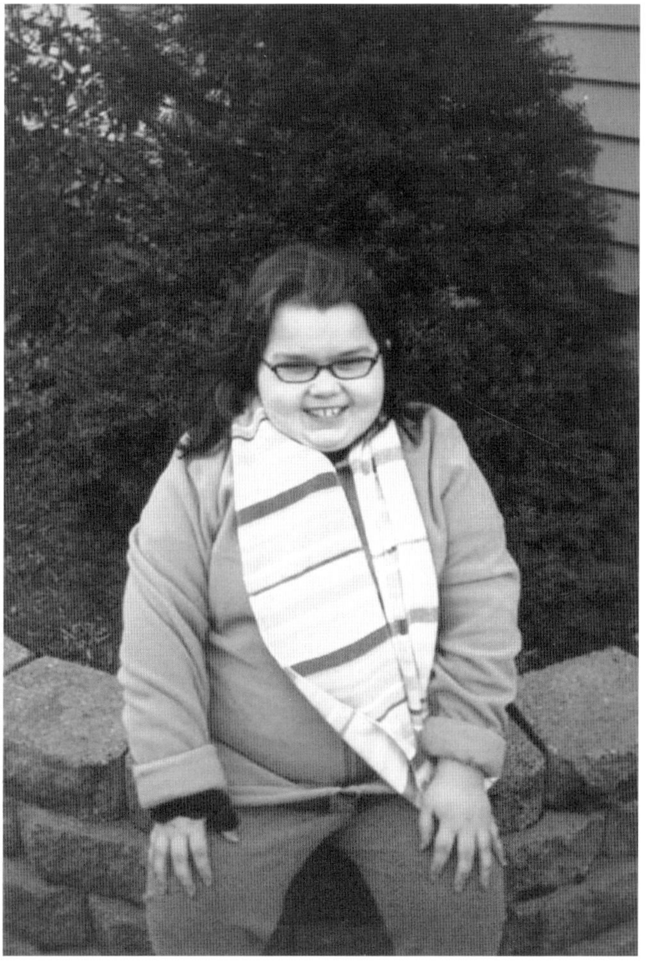

Mallory Gray

Mallory Gray was born in Lowell, Massachusetts, on February 1, 1996, a healthy little girl with a wonderful smile. Her family moved to Hudson in 1997. At age three, she was diagnosed with systemic juvenile rheumatoid arthritis, and for the 10-plus years that followed, she never once went into remission. Despite many hospitalizations, she remained a happy child and true "girlie girl" who loved jewelry, makeup, fashion, and the color purple. Mallory also loved cooking, arts and crafts, and animals, and she was a loyal friend. Her true passion was reading, and she received a special Super Reader Award and medal from Hudson's Hills Memorial Library, of which she was extremely proud. One of her favorite nonfiction books was Laurie Jasper's *Hudson, New Hampshire*, and she loved the third-grade Hudson History Tour field trip. Although Benson Park had not yet been restored to the beautiful passive recreation park it now is, Mallory loved the history of Benson's Wild Animal Farm. One of her favorite accessories was a bracelet from the former Benson's Wild Animal Farm that her mother had and gave to Mallory. Mallory was an honor roll student at Hudson Memorial School when she died on October 18, 2009, at Children's Hospital in Boston, Massachusetts, following a long and courageous battle with rheumatoid arthritis and then leukemia. Mallory was the beloved daughter of Christopher and Tracy Gray and the sister of Kenneth and Brandon. The future amphitheater at Benson Park will be built thanks to the fundraising efforts of the group Mal's Pals and will be named in Mallory's honor. Mallory always had a sweet smile for all and is deeply missed by her family and friends. (Courtesy the Gray family.)

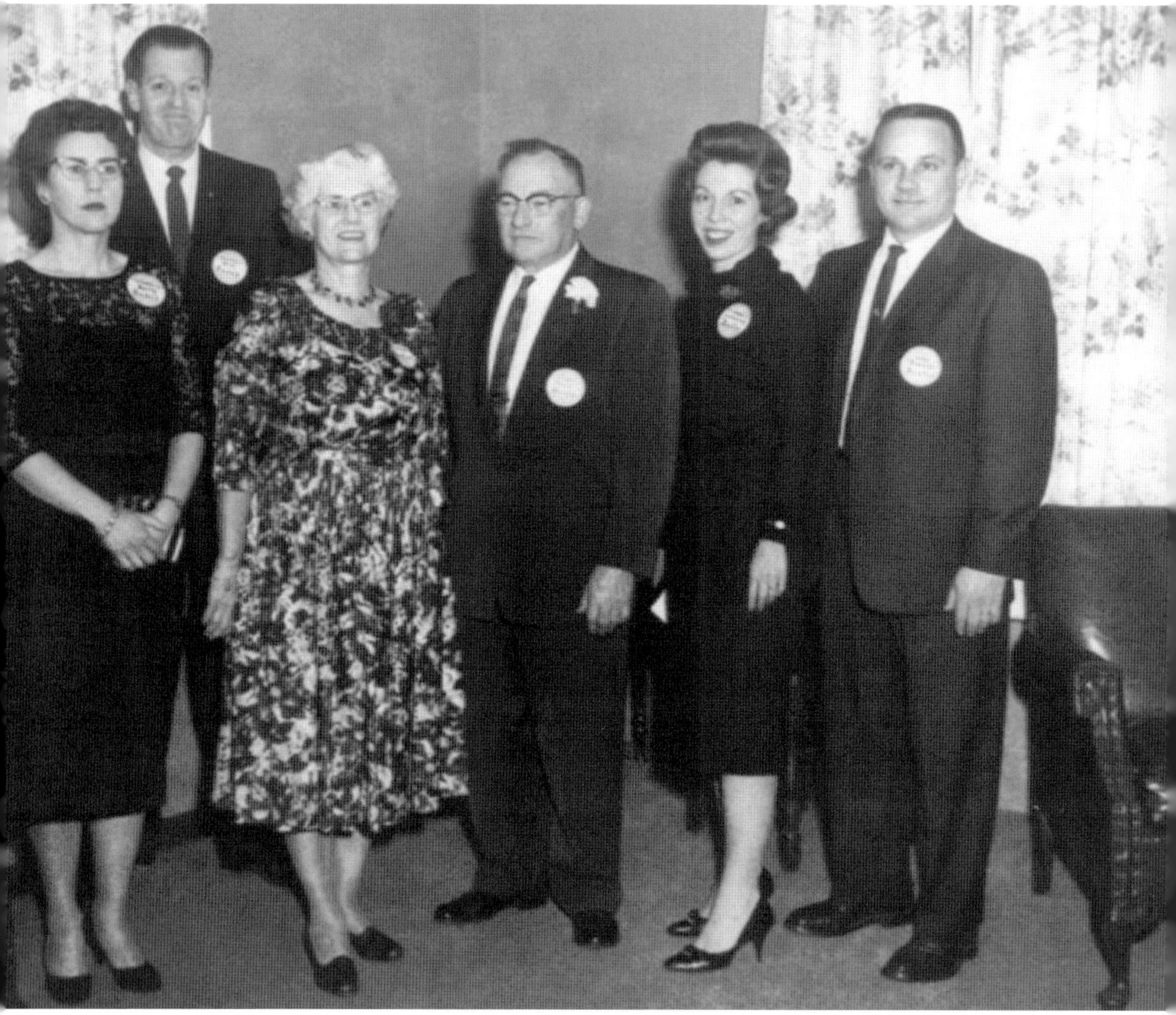

The Buxton Family

Paul Buxton was born in Nashua in 1897 and married Hazel Reynolds in 1918. By 1919, they were living in Hudson. Hazel served for several years beginning in 1926 as the librarian at the Hills Memorial Library. Paul became a member of the town's first planning board in 1940 and continued on that board until 1953. Paul joined the fire department in 1919 and served until 1965. In 1951, Paul also was appointed to the zoning board of adjustment, and his last year on the board was 1980. In 1981, he was serving on the building board of appeals, where he served until 1984. Both Hazel and Paul were active members of the historical society. If one visits the society's food booth at Old Home Days and see wooden napkin holders, Paul made them. Paul's grandson Timothy, who is the chef and teacher at Alvirne's Checkers Restaurant, lives in the house that Paul and Hazel built. Their son Robert was a member of the Hudson Fire Department from 1948 to 1976, serving for many years as a captain. Robert's son Michael was a member of the Nashua Fire Department, retiring from that department as chief. Michael's son Robert is the current chief of the Hudson Fire Department (see page 37). Hazel died in 1979, and Shawn Jasper was honored to serve as one of her pallbearers. Paul died in 1989 at age 92. Shown from left to right are Elizabeth Buxton Burns, Richard Burns, Hazel and Paul Buxton, and Lorraine and Robert Buxton. (Courtesy the Buxton family.)

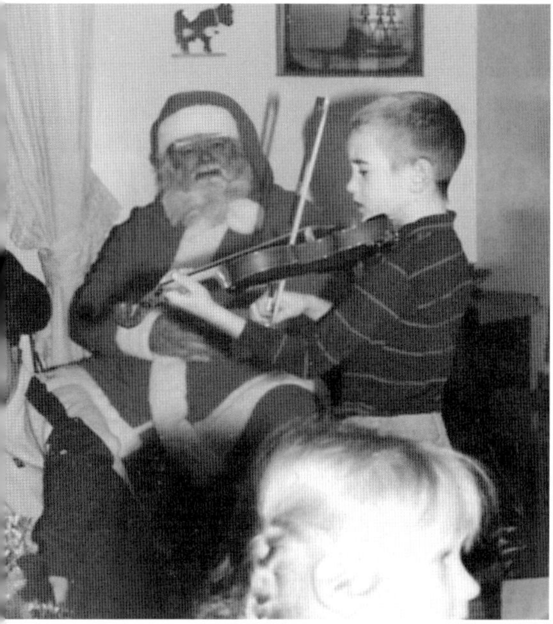

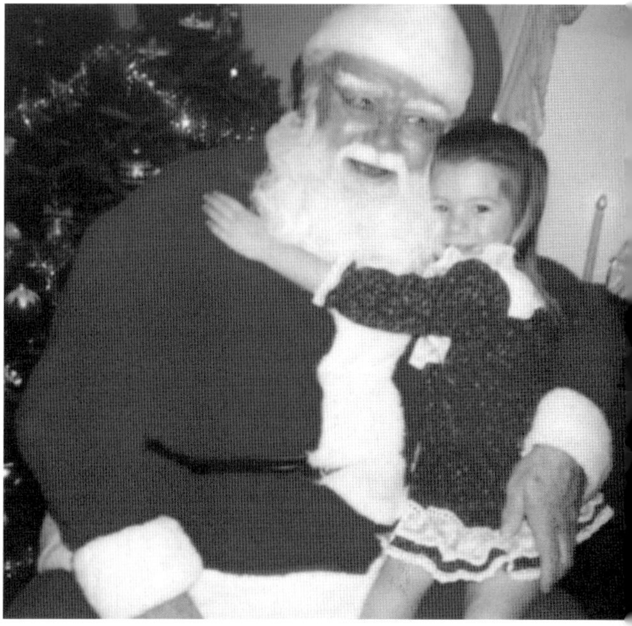

Paul "Moose" Anger

Paul "Moose" Anger was a longtime Hudson resident who was best known for his role as Santa Claus. Hudson children will long remember him for his arrival at Library Park in a fire engine for the annual Christmas tree lighting. He and his wife ran Santa's Quarters and Mad House Creations. Moose was a longtime employee of the Hudson Highway Department, and his son Joseph also works for the department. Two of his other sons are well known around town: Mark is the owner of M.L. Anger Trucking, and David is the owner of Anger Welding and Truck Equipment. Moose died in Arizona in 2009 at the age of 79. At right he is shown with Renee Boucher, granddaughter of Shirley Nadeau, and at left Moose is listening to a young Alan Marcotte, who wanted to play his violin for Santa. Alan is the son of Ray Marcotte, the longtime Alvirne School farm manager, and his wife, Gayle. Alan is now a police officer in Hudson. (Both, courtesy Shirley Nadeau.)

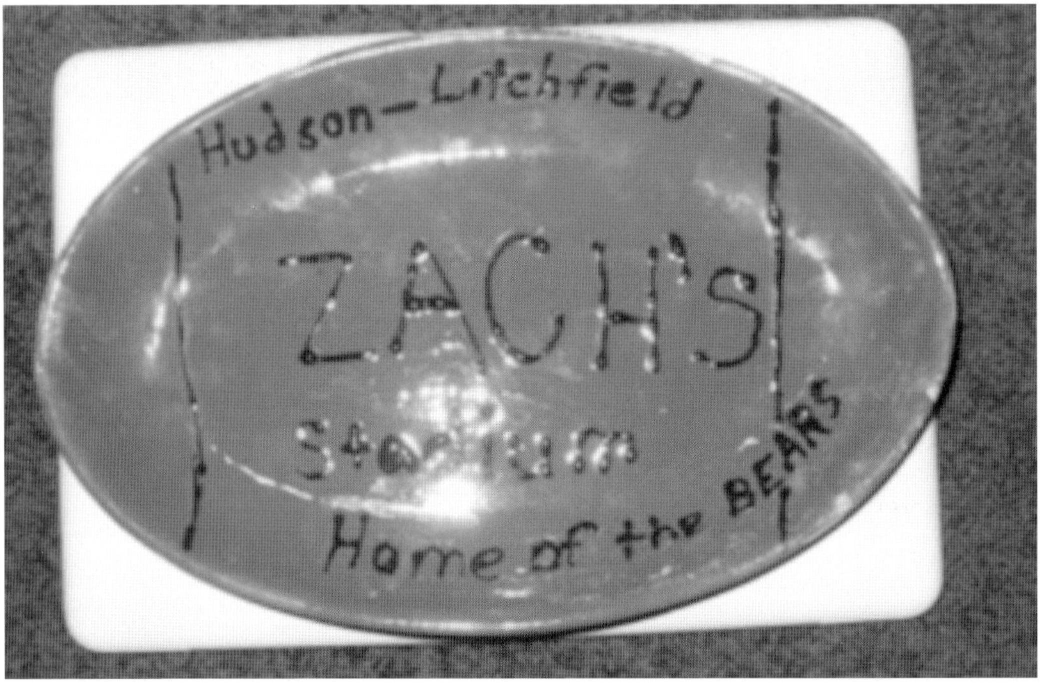

Zachary "Zach" Tompkins

Zachary Tompkins was a busy, active fifth-grade student at Hudson's Presentation of Mary Academy when he died unexpectedly in his sleep on March 8, 2010, of what was later determined to be an undetected genetic heart disease called Long QT (LQTS). Despite his family's grief, they wished to do something to honor Zach's memory. Zach, a football player with the Hudson Litchfield Bears, had told them he would love to build a stadium in Hudson for the Bears, and even made a ceramic plate with "Zach's Stadium" painted on it shortly before he died (seen in the photograph). The Zachary M. Tompkins Memorial Fund was established, the Town of Hudson generously donated the land for the stadium, and the ground breaking was held on October 26, 2012. Zach's dream will become a reality, and his legacy will live on in Hudson. (Above, courtesy the Tompkins family; right, courtesy *Hudson-Litchfield News*.)

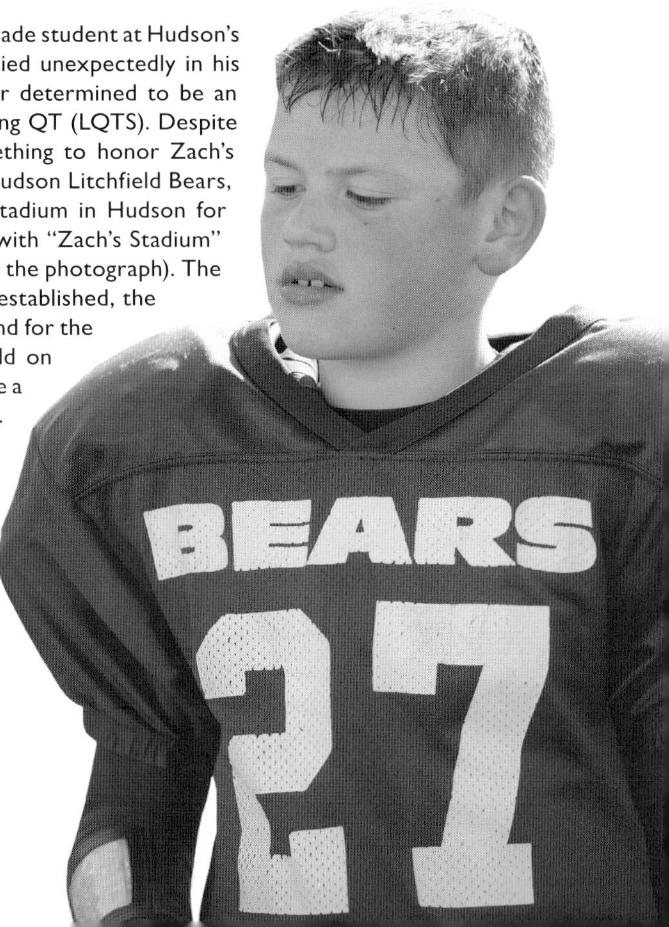

BIBLIOGRAPHY

Goldsack, Robert. Images of America: *Benson's Wild Animal Farm*. Charleston, SC: Arcadia Publishing, 2011.

Hudson Historical Society History Committee. *Town in Transition, Hudson, New Hampshire 1673–1977*. Canaan, NH: Phoenix Publishing, 1977.

Hudson-Litchfield News. Hudson, NH: Area News Group.

Jasper, Laurie A. Images of America: *Hudson, New Hampshire*. Charleston, SC: Arcadia Publishing, 1999.

Nashua Telegraph. Hudson, NH.

Webster, Kimball. *Webster's History of Hudson, New Hampshire, 1673 to 1913*. (Reprint). Manchester, NH: Granite State Publishing Company, 1977.

INDEX

INDEX

Consistent with our mission to preserve history on a local level, this book was printed in South Carolina on American-made paper and manufactured entirely in the United States. Products carrying the accredited Forest Stewardship Council (FSC) label are printed on 100 percent FSC-certified paper.

MADE IN THE USA